Understanding Market, Credit, and Operational Risk

LINDA ALLEN, JACOB BOUDOUKH, and ANTHONY SAUNDERS

UNDERSTANDING MARKET, CREDIT, AND OPERATIONAL RISK

THE VALUE AT RISK APPROACH

Blackwell
Publishing

350 Main Street, Malden, MA 02148-5020, USA
108 Cowley Road, Oxford OX4 1JF, UK
550 Swanston Street, Carlton, Victoria 3053, Australia

First published 2004 by Blackwell Publishing Ltd

Library of Congress Cataloging-in-Publication Data

Allen, Linda, 1954–
Understanding market, credit, and operational risk : the value at
risk approach / Linda Allen, Jacob Boudoukh, and Anthony Saunders.
p. cm.
Includes bibliographical references and index.
ISBN 0-631-22709-1
1. Financial futures. 2. Risk management. I. Boudoukh, Jacob.
II. Saunders, Anthony, 1949– III. Title.

HG6024.3.A45 2004
332.1′068′1–dc21   2003007540

A catalogue record for this title is available from the British Library.

Set in 10/12.5 pt Meridien
by Graphicraft Limited, Hong Kong
Printed and bound in the United Kingdom
by TJ International, Padstow, Cornwall

For further information on
Blackwell Publishing, visit our website:
http://www.blackwellpublishing.com

To my parents, Lillian and Myron Mazurek,
with love and gratitude

L.A.

To my beloved parents, Hela and Gabriel Boudoukh,
and in memory of the Strasberger family

J.B.

In memory of my parents

A.S.

SHORT CONTENTS

CONTENTS

LIST OF FIGURES

LIST OF TABLES

PREFACE

Since the publication of JP Morgan's RiskMetrics in 1994 there has been an explosion of research in the areas of value of risk and risk management in general. While the basic concepts surrounding Value at Risk are founded in the area of market risk measurement they have been extended, over the last decade, to other areas of risk management. In particular, Value at Risk models are now commonly used to measure both credit and operational risks.

Value at Risk models are used to predict risk exposure of an investor or financial institution in the next period (day, quarter, year) if a "bad period" occurs as defined by some statistical measure. For example, a financial institution may wish to know its exposure to credit risk if next year is the worst year in 100 years (i.e. the so-called 99th percentile worst case). With such a measure in hand, the financial institution can then assess its capital adequacy (i.e. the amount of capital reserves it has at hand to withstand such a large unexpected loss). Often, the total capital needs of a financial institution have been assessed by adding required capital in different areas of risk exposure (e.g. market, credit, and operational risks). However, with the emergence of other approaches to measuring these different risks, such as Value at Risk, the need for a more integrative approach becomes clear.

This book will be of use to both financial practitioners and undergraduate and MBA students interested in an introduction to the basic concept of Value at Risk and its application to different areas of risk measurement. As such, this book is essentially "introductory" in nature. We focus on the logic behind the mathematics and illustrate the concepts using real-world examples. Nevertheless, it is hoped that readers, after finishing the book, will have a sufficient foundation in the key concepts of modern risk measurement to explore the area and literature further. To aid that process, we offer an extensive list of references.

We would like to thank our editors Seth Ditchik and Elizabeth Wald for help in putting this book together. Helpful research work was provided by Victoria Ivashina.

L.A.

J.B.

A.S.

LIST OF ABBREVIATIONS

AMA	Advanced Measurement Approach
AR	autoregression
ATM	at-the-money
BIA	Basic Indicator Approach
BIS	Bank for International Settlements
BIS I	1988 Basel Capital Accord
BIS II	2003 Basel Capital Accord
bp	basis points
BRW	benchmark risk weight
CAPM	capital asset pricing model
CBOT	Chicago Board of Trade
CDD	cooling degree day
CMO	Collateralized mortgage obligation
CWI	creditworthiness index
DEAR	daily earnings at risk
DM	deutschmark
DM	default mode
DPG	derivatives policy group
EAD	exposure at default
ECU	European Currency Unit
EDF	expected default frequency
EL	expected loss
ERM	Exchange Rate Mechanism
EST	eastern standard time
EU	European Union
EVT	extreme value theory
FASB	Financial Accounting Standards Board
FoHF	fund of hedge funds
GAAP	generally accepted accounting principles

GARCH	General Autoregressive Conditional Heterskedasticity
GBP	British pound sterling
GNMA	Government National Mortgage Association
GPD	Generalized Pareto Distribution
HDD	heating degree day
HFLS	high frequency/low severity
HS	historical simulation
i.i.d.	independent and identically distributed
IMA	internal measurement approach
IRB	Internal Ratings-Based
ISDA	International Swaps and Derivatives Association
JGB	Japanese Government Bond
JPY	Japanese yen
LDA	loss distribution approach
LDC	less developed country
LFHS	low frequency/high severity
LGD	loss given default
LIED	loss in the event of default
LRM	long run mean
LTCM	Long Term Capital Management
MAE	mean absolute error
MBS	mortgage backed securities
MDE	multivariate density estimation
MSE	mean squared error
MtF	Mark-to-Future
MTM	mark-to-market
NAIC	National Association of Insurance Commissioners
OAEM	other assets especially mentioned
OBS	off-balance sheet
OCC	Office of the Comptroller of the Currency
OECD	Organisation for Economic Cooperation and Development
OTM	out-of-the-money
p.a.	per annum
PCS	Property and Claims Service
PD	probability of default
PWC	PricewaterhouseCoopers
QIS	Quantitative Impact Study
RAROC	risk-adjusted return on capital
RPI	retail price index
RW	risk weight

SMC   structured Monte Carlo
USAA   US Automobile Association
USD   US dollar
VaR   value at risk
VarCov   variance–covariance approach
WCS   worst case scenario

CHAPTER ONE

INTRODUCTION TO VALUE AT RISK (VaR)

Risk measurement has preoccupied financial market participants since the dawn of financial history. However, many past attempts have proven to be impractically complex. For example, upon its introduction, Harry Markowitz's Nobel prize-winning theory of portfolio risk measurement was not adopted in practice because of its onerous data requirements.[1] Indeed, it was Bill Sharpe who, along with others,[2] made portfolio theory the standard of financial risk measurement in real world applications through the adoption of the simplifying assumption that all risk could be decomposed into two parts: systematic, market risk and the residual, company-specific or idiosyncratic risk. The resulting Capital Asset Pricing Model theorized that since only undiversifiable market risk is relevant for securities pricing, only the market risk measurement β is necessary, thereby considerably reducing the required data inputs. This model yielded a readily measurable estimate of risk that could be practically applied in a real time market environment. The only problem was that β proved to have only a tenuous connection to actual security returns, thereby casting doubts on β's designation as the true risk measure.[3]

With β questioned, and with asset prcing in general being at a bit of a disarray with respect to whether the notion of "priced risk" is really relevant, market practitioners searched for a replacement risk measure that was both accurate and relatively inexpensive to estimate. Despite the consideration of many other measures and models, Value at Risk (VaR) has been widely adopted. Part of the reason leading to the widespread adoption of VaR was the decision of JP Morgan to create a transparent VaR measurement model, called RiskMetrics.™ RiskMetrics™ was supported by a publicly available database containing the critical inputs required to estimate the model.[4]

Another reason behind the widespread adoption of VaR was the introduction in 1998[5] by the Bank for International Settlements (BIS) of international bank capital requirements that allowed relatively sophisticated banks to calculate their capital requirements based on their own internal modes such as VaR. In this chapter, we introduce the basic concept of VaR as a measurement tool for market risk. In later chapters, we apply the VaR concept to the measurement of credit risk and operational risk exposures.

1.1   ECONOMICS UNDERLYING VaR MEASUREMENT

Financial institutions are specialists in risk management. Indeed, their primary expertise stems from their ability to both measure and manage risk exposure on their own behalf and on behalf of their clients – either through the evolution of financial market products to shift risks or through the absorption of their clients' risk onto their own balance sheets. Because financial institutions are risk intermediaries, they maintain an inventory of risk that must be measured carefully so as to ensure that the risk exposure does not threaten the intermediary's solvency. Thus, accurate measurement of risk is an essential first step for proper risk management, and financial intermediaries, because of the nature of their business, tend to be leading developers of new risk measurement techniques. In the past, many of these models were internal models, developed in-house by financial institutions. Internal models were used for risk management in its truest sense.

Indeed, the VaR tool is complementary to many other internal risk measures – such as RAROC developed by Bankers Trust in the 1970s.[6] However, market forces during the late 1990s created conditions that led to the evolution of VaR as a dominant risk measurement tool for financial firms.

The US financial environment during the 1990s was characterized by the de jure separation of commercial banking and investment banking that dated back to the Glass Steagall Act of 1933.[7] However, these restrictions were undermined in practice by Section 20 affiliates (that permitted commercial bank holding companies to engage in investment banking activities up to certain limits), mergers between investment and commercial banks, and commercial bank sales of some "insurance" products, especially annuities. Thus, commercial banks competed with investment banks and insurance companies to offer financial services to clients in an environment characterized by globalization, enhanced risk exposure, and rapidly evolving securities and market procedures. Concerned about the impact of the increasing risk environment on the safety and soundness of the banking system, bank regulators instituted (in 1992) risk-adjusted bank capital requirements that levied a capital charge for both on- and off-balance sheet credit risk exposures.[8]

Risk-adjusted capital requirements initially applied only to commercial banks, although insurance companies[9] and securities firms had to comply with their own reserve and haircut regulations as well as with market forces that demanded capital cushions against insolvency based on economic model-based measures of exposure – so called economic capital. Among other shortcomings of the BIS capital requirements were their neglect of diversification benefits, in measuring a bank's risk exposure. Thus, regulatory capital requirements tended to be higher than economically necessary, thereby undermining commercial banks' competitive position vis-à-vis largely unregulated investment banks. To compete with other financial institutions, commercial banks had the incentive to track economic capital requirements more closely notwithstanding their need to meet regulatory capital requirements. The more competitive the commercial bank was in providing investment banking activities, for example, the greater its incentive to increase its potential profitability by increasing leverage and reducing its capital reserves.

JP Morgan (now JP Morgan Chase) was one of a handful of globally diversified commercial banks that were in a special position relative to the commercial banking sector on the one hand and the investment banking sector on the other. These banks were caught in between, in a way. On the one hand, from an economic perspective, these banks could be thought of more as investment banks than as commercial banks, with large market risks due to trading activities, as well as advisory and other corporate finance activities. On the other hand this group of globally diversified commercial banks were holding a commercial banking license, and, hence, were subject to commercial bank capital adequacy requirements. This special position gave these banks, JP Morgan being a particular example, a strong incentive to come out with an initiative to remedy the capital adequacy problems that they faced. Specifically, the capital requirements for market risk in place were not representative of true economic risk, due to their limited account of the diversification effect. At the same time competing financial institutions, in particular, investment banks such as Merrill Lynch, Goldman Sachs, and Salomon Brothers, were not subject to bank capital adequacy requirements. As such, the capital they held for market risk was determined more by economic and investor considerations than by regulatory requirements. This allowed these institutions to bolster significantly more impressive ratios such as return on equity (ROE) and return on assets (ROA) compared with banks with a banking charter.

In response to the above pressures, JP Morgan took the initiative to develop an open architecture (rather than in-house) methodology, called RiskMetrics. RiskMetrics quickly became the industry benchmark in risk measurement. The publication of RiskMetrics was a pivotal step moving regulators toward adopting economic capital-based models in measuring a bank's capital adequacy. Indeed, bank regulators worldwide allowed (sophisticated) commercial banks to measure their market risk exposures using internal models that were often VaR-based. The market risk amendments to the Basel accord made in-house risk measurement models a mainstay in the financial sector. Financial institutions worldwide moved forward with this new approach and never looked back.

1.1.1   What is VaR?

It was Dennis Weatherstone, at the time the Chairman of JP Morgan, who clearly stated the basic question that is the basis for VaR as we know it today – "how much can we lose on our trading portfolio by tomorrow's close?" Note that this is a risk measurement, not a risk management question. Also, it is not concerned with obtaining a portfolio position to maximize the profitability of the bank's traded portfolio subject to a risk constraint, or any other optimization question. Instead, this is a pure question of risk measurement.

There are two approaches to answering Weatherstone's question. The first is a probabilistic/statistical approach that is the focus of the VaR measure. To put the VaR approach into perspective, we briefly consider the alternative approach – an event-driven, non-quantitative, subjective approach, which calculates the impact on the portfolio value of a scenario or a set of scenarios that reflect what is considered "adverse circumstances."[10]

As an example of the scenario approach, consider a specific example. Suppose you hold a $1 million portfolio of stocks tracking the S&P 500 index. For the purpose of our discussion we may assume that the tracking is perfect, i.e., there is no issue of tracking error. To address the question of how much this portfolio could lose on a "bad day," one could specify a particular bad day in history – say the October 1987 stock market crash during which the market declined 22 percent in one day. This would result in a $220,000 daily amount at risk for the portfolio if such an adverse scenario were to recur.

This risk measure raises as many questions as it answers. For instance, how likely is an October 1987-level risk event to recur? Is the October 1987 risk event the most appropriate risk scenario to use? Is it possible that other historical "bad days" should instead be used as the appropriate risk scenario? Moreover, have fundamental changes in global trading activity in the wake of October 1987 made the magnitude of a recurrence of the crash even larger, or, instead, has the installation of various circuit-breaker systems made the possibility of the recurrence of such a rare adverse event even smaller? In chapter 3, we discuss how these questions may be answered in implementing scenario analysis to perform stress testing of VaR-based risk measurement systems.

In contrast to the scenario approach, VaR takes a statistical or probabilistic approach to answering Mr. Weatherstone's question of how much could be lost on a "bad day." That is, we define a "bad day" in a statistical sense, such that there is only an x percent probability that daily losses will exceed this amount given a distribution of all possible daily returns over some recent past period. That is, we define a "bad day" so that there is only an x percent probability of an even worse day.

In order to more formally derive VaR, we must first define some notation. Since VaR is a probabilistic value the 1 percent VaR (or

VaR calculated on the basis of the worst day in 100 days) will yield a different answer than the 5 percent VaR (calculated on the basis of the worst day in 20 days). We denote a 1 percent VaR as $VaR_{1\%}$, a 5 percent VaR as $VaR_{5\%}$, etc. $VaR_{1\%}$ denotes a daily loss that will be equaled or exceeded only 1 percent of the time. Putting it slightly differently, there is a 99 percent chance that tomorrow's daily portfolio value will exceed today's value less the $VaR_{1\%}$. Similarly, $VaR_{5\%}$ denotes the minimum daily loss that will be equaled or exceeded only 5 percent of the time, such that tomorrow's daily losses will be less than $VaR_{5\%}$ with a 95 percent probability. The important practical question is how do we calculate these VaR measures?

1.1.2 Calculating VaR

Consider again the example used in the previous section of a $1 million equity portfolio that tracks the S&P 500 index. Suppose that daily returns on the S&P 500 index are normally distributed with a mean of 0 percent per day and a 100 basis point per day standard deviation. Weatherstone's question is how risky is this position, or, more specifically, how much can we lose on this position by tomorrow's market close?

To answer the question, recall first the basic properties of the normal distribution. The normal distribution is fully defined by two parameters: μ (the mean) and σ (the standard deviation). Figure 1.1 shows the shape of the normal probability density function. The cumulative distribution tells us the area under the standard normal density between various points on the X-axis. For example, there is

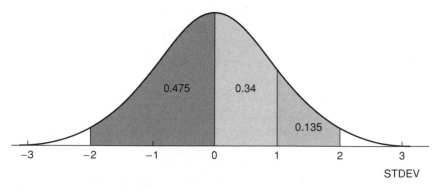

Figure 1.1 The normal probability distribution

Table 1.1 Normal distribution cumulative probabilities for commonly used VaR percentiles

Prob(X < z)	0.1%	0.5%	1.0%	2.5%	5.0%	10%
z	−3.090	−2.576	−2.326	−1.960	−1.645	−1.282
VaR	$30,900	$25,760	$23,260	$19,600	$16,450	$12,820

a 47.5 percent probability that an observation drawn from the normal distribution will lie between the mean and two standard deviations below the mean. Table 1.1 shows the probability cutoffs for the normal distribution using commonly used VaR percentiles.[11]

Reading table 1.1 is simple. Given that X is a standard normal random variable (with mean zero and standard deviation one) then, for example, Prob($X < -1.645$) = 5.0 percent. Stated more generally, for any normally distributed random variable, there is a 5 percent chance that an observation will be less than 1.645 standard deviations below the mean. Returning to our equity portfolio example, the daily fluctuations in the S&P 500 index are assumed to be normally distributed with a zero mean and a standard deviation of 100 bp. Using the properties of the normal distribution shown in table 1.1, there is a 5 percent chance that the S&P 500 will decline tomorrow by more than 1.645 × 100 bp = 1.645 percent. Based on the $1 million equity portfolio in the example, this represents a minimum daily loss of $16,450 (0.01645 × $1 million), which will be exceeded only 5 percent of the time. Thus, the equity portfolio's $VaR_{5\%}$ = $16,450. That is, there is a 5 percent chance that daily losses on the S&P 500-linked equity portfolio will equal or exceed $16,450. Alternatively, we could say that our portfolio has a 95 percent chance of being worth $983,550 or more ($1,000,000 − $16,450) tomorrow. Using table 1.1, we can compute other VaR measures. For example, $VaR_{1\%}$ = $23,260 (2.326 × 0.01 × $1 million), and so on, as shown in table 1.1. We can define VaR for whatever risk level (or confidence level) is deemed appropriate.

We have thus far considered only daily VaR measures. However, we might want to calculate the VaR over a period of time – say a week, a month or a year. This can be done using the daily VaR model and the "square root rule."[12] The rule states that the J-day VaR is $\sqrt{J} \times (daily\ VaR)$. Thus, the one week (5 business days) $VaR_{5\%}$ for the equity portfolio example is $\sqrt{5} \times$ $16,450 = $36,783. Similarly, the annual (using

250 days as the number of trading days in a year) $VaR_{5\%}$ for the equity portfolio example is $\sqrt{250} * \$16,450 = \$260,097$; that is, there is a 5 percent probability that the equity portfolio will lose $260,097 or more (or a 95 percent likelihood that the portfolio will be worth $739,903 or more) by the end of one year.

VaR can be calculated on either a dollar or a percentage basis. Up until this point, we have calculated the dollar VaR directly by examining the probability distribution of dollar losses. Alternatively, we could have calculated the percentage VaR by examining the probability distribution of percentage losses as represented by the distribution's standard deviation. For example, consider the weekly $VaR_{5\%}$ computed as $36,783 for the equity portfolio example. If instead of calculating the 5 day dollar $VaR_{5\%}$, the 5 day standard deviation of S&P 500 index returns were instead computed, we would obtain 100 bp $\times \sqrt{5} = 2.23607$ percent. Calculating the 5 day percentage $VaR_{5\%}$ we obtain $1.645 \times 2.23607 = 3.6783$ percent. This states that there is a 5 percent probability that the S&P 500-linked equity portfolio's value will decline by 3.6783 percent or more over the next week. Given a $1 million portfolio value, this translates into a $36,783 ($1m $\times 0.036783$) dollar $VaR_{5\%}$.

To be widely adopted as a risk measure, VaR certainly appears to satisfy the condition that it be easy to estimate. However, does it satisfy the other condition – that VaR is an accurate risk measure? The answer to that question hinges on the accuracy of the many assumptions that allow the easy calculation of VaR. Unfortunately, it is often the case that the simplicity of the VaR measures used to analyze the risk of the equity portfolio, for example, is in large part obtained with assumptions not supported by empirical evidence. The most important (and most problematic) of these assumptions is that daily equity returns are normally distributed. As we examine these (and other) assumptions in greater depth, we will find a tradeoff between the accuracy of assumptions and ease of calculation, such that greater accuracy is often accompanied by greater complexity.

1.1.3   The assumptions behind VaR calculations

There are several statistical assumptions that must be made in order to make VaR calculations tractable. First, we consider the *stationarity requirement*. That is, a 1 percent fluctuation in returns is equally likely to occur at any point in time. Stationarity is a common assumption in financial economics, because it simplifies computations considerably.

A related assumption is the *random walk* assumption of intertemporal unpredictability. That is, day-to-day fluctuations in returns are independent; thus, a decline in the S&P 500 index on one day of x percent has no predictive power regarding returns on the S&P 500 index on the next day. Equivalently, the random walk assumption can be represented as the assumption of an expected rate of return equal to zero, as in the equity portfolio example. That is, if the mean daily return is zero, then the best guess estimate of tomorrow's price level (e.g., the level of the S&P 500 index) is today's level. There is no relevant information available at time t that could help forecast prices at time $t + 1$.

Another straightforward assumption is the *non-negativity requirement*, which stipulates that financial assets with limited liability cannot attain negative values.[13] However, derivatives (e.g., forwards, futures, and swaps) can violate this assumption. The *time consistency requirement* states that all single period assumptions hold over the multiperiod time horizon.

The most important assumption is the *distributional assumption*. In the simple equity portfolio example, we assumed that daily return fluctuations in the S&P 500 index follow a normal distribution with a mean of zero and a standard deviation of 100 bp. We should examine the accuracy of each of these three assumptions. First, the assumption of a zero mean is clearly debatable, since at the very least we know that equity prices, in the particular case of the S&P 500, have a positive *expected* return – the risk free rate plus a market risk premium.[14] To calibrate the numbers for this non-zero mean return case, let us assume a mean risk free rate of 4 percent p.a. and a risk premium of 6 percent p.a. A total expected return, hence, of 10 percent p.a. translates into a mean return of approximately four basis points per day (i.e., 1000 bp/250 days = 4 bp/day). Hence, an alternative assumption could have been that asset returns are normally distributed with a mean return of four basis points per day rather than zero basis points per day. As we shall see later, this is not a critical assumption materially impacting overall VaR calculations.

Similarly, the assumption of a 100 bp daily standard deviation can be questioned. Linking daily volatility to annual volatility using the "square root rule" we can see that this is equivalent to assuming an annualized standard deviation of 15.8 percent p.a. for the S&P 500 index. The "square root rule" states that under standard assumptions,[15] the *J*-period volatility is equal to the one period volatility inflated by the square root of *J*. Here for example, the daily volatility is assumed to be 1 percent per day. Assuming 250 trading days in a year gives us an annual volatility of 1 percent/day $\times \sqrt{250}$ = 15.8 percent p.a. Historically, this is approximately the observed order of magnitude for the volatility of well-diversified equity portfolios or wide-coverage indices in well-developed countries.[16]

The most questionable assumption, however, is that of normality because evidence shows that most securities prices are not normally distributed.[17] Despite this, the assumption that continuously compounded returns are normally distributed is, in fact, a standard assumption in finance. Recall that the very basic assumption of the Black–Scholes option pricing model is that asset returns follow a log-normal diffusion. This assumption is the key to the elegance and simplicity of the Black–Scholes option pricing formula. The instantaneous volatility of asset returns is always multiplied by the square root of time in the Black–Scholes formula. Under the model's normality assumption, returns at any horizon are always independent and identically normally distributed; the scale is just the square root of the volatility. All that matters is the "volatility-to-maturity." Similarly, this is also the case (as shown earlier in section 1.1.2) for VaR at various horizons.

1.1.4   Inputs into VaR calculations

VaR calculations require assumptions about the possible future values of the portfolio some time in the future. There are at least three ways to calculate a rate of return from period t to $t + 1$:

- absolute change $\Delta S_{t,t+1} = s_{t+1} - s_t$ (1.1)
- simple return $R_{t,t+1} = (s_{t+1} - s_t)/s_t$ (1.2)
                                    (or $1 + R_{t,t+1} = s_{t+1}/s_t$)
- continuously compounded return $r_{t,t+1} = \ln(s_{t+1}/s_t)$.   (1.3)

Which computational method is the right one to choose? Let us examine which of these methods conforms to the assumptions discussed in section 1.1.3.

Calculating returns using the absolute change method violates the stationarity requirement. Consider, for example, using historical exchange rate data for the dollar–yen exchange rate through periods when this rate was as high as ¥200/$ or as low as ¥80/$. Do we believe that a change of ¥2 is as likely to occur at ¥200/$ as it is at ¥80/$?

Probably not. A more accurate description of exchange rate changes would be that a 1 percent change is about as likely at all times than a ¥1 change.[18]

The simple return as a measure of the change in the underlying factor, while satisfying the stationarity requirement, does not comply with the time consistency requirement. In contrast, however, using continuously compounded returns does satisfy the time consistency requirement. To see this, consider first the two period return defined as simple return, expressed as follows:

$$1 + R_{t,t+2} = (1 + R_{t,t+1})(1 + R_{t+1,t+2}).$$

Assume that the single period returns, $1 + R_{t,t+1}$ and $1 + R_{t+1,t+2}$, are normally distributed. What is the distribution of the two period return $1 + R_{t,t+2}$? There is little we can say analytically in closed form on the distribution of a product of two normal random variables.

The opposite is true for the case of the two period continuously compounded return. The two period return is just the sum of the two single period returns:

$$r_{t,t+2} = r_{t,t+1} + r_{t+1,t+2}.$$

Assume again that the single period returns, $r_{t,t+1}$ and $r_{t+1,t+2}$, are normally distributed. What is the distribution of the two period return? This distribution, the *sum* of two normals, does have a closed form solution. The sum of two random variables that are jointly normally distributed is itself normally distributed, and the mean and standard deviation of the sum can be derived easily. Thus, in general, throughout this book we will utilize the continuously compounded rate of return to represent financial market price fluctuations.

The mathematics of continuously compounded rates of return can be used to understand the "square root rule" utilized in section 1.1.2 to calculate multiperiod, long horizon VaR. Suppose that the compounded rate of return is normally distributed as follows:

$$r_{t,t+1}, r_{t+1,t+2} \sim N(\mu, \sigma^2).$$

For simplicity, assume a zero mean ($\mu = 0$) and constant volatility over time. In addition, assume that the two returns have zero correlation; that is, returns are not autocorrelated. The importance of these assumptions will be discussed in detail in chapter 2. The long horizon (here, for simplicity, two period) rate of return is $r_{t,t+2}$ (the sum of $r_{t,t+1}$ and $r_{t+1,t+2}$) is normally distributed with a mean of zero (the sum of the two zero mean returns) and a variance which is just the sum of the variances,[19] which is $2\sigma^2$. Hence, the two period continuously compunded return has a standard deviation which is $\sqrt{(2\sigma^2)} = \sigma\sqrt{2}$. More generally, the J-period return is normal, with zero mean, and a variance which is J times the single period variance:

$$r_{t,t+J} = r_{t,t+1} + r_{t+1,t+2} + \ldots + r_{t+J-1,t+J} \sim N(0, J\sigma^2). \qquad (1.4)$$

This provides us with a direct link between the single period distribution and the multiperiod distribution. If continuously compounded returns are assumed normal with zero mean and constant volatility, then the J-period return is also normal, with zero mean, and a standard deviation which is the square root of J times the single period standard deviation. To obtain the probability of long horizon tail events all we need to do is precisely what we did before – look up the percentiles of the standard normal distribution. Thus, using the above result, the VaR of the J-period return is just $\sqrt{J}$ times the single period VaR.

There is one exception to the generalization that we should use continuously compounded rates of return rather than absolute changes in the level of a given index to measure VaR. The exception is with all interest rate related variables, such as zero coupon rates, yields to maturity, swap spreads, Brady strip spreads, credit spreads, etc. When we measure the rate of change of various interest rates for VaR calculations, we measure the rate of absolute change in the underlying variable as follows:

$$\Delta i_{t,t+1} = i_{t+1} - i_t.$$

That is, we usually measure the change in terms of absolute basis point change. For example, if the spread between the yield on a portfolio of corporates of a certain grade and US Treasuries of similar maturity (or duration) widened from 200 to 210 basis points, we measure a 10 basis point change in what is called the "quality spread." A decline in three month zero rates from 5.25 percent annualized to 5.10 percent p.a., would be measured as a change of $\Delta i_{t,t+1} = -15$ bp.

Calculating VaR from unanticipated fluctuations in interest rates adds an additional complication to the analysis. Standard VaR calculations must be adjusted to account for the effect of duration (denoted D), i.e. the fact that a 1 percent move in the risk factor (interest rates) does not necessarily mean a 1 percent move in the position's value, but rather a $-D$ percent fluctuation in value. That is:

$$1 \text{ bp move in rates} \rightarrow -D \text{ bp move in bond value.} \qquad (1.5)$$

To illustrate this, consider a $1 million corporate bond portfolio with a duration (D) of 10 years and a daily standard deviation of returns equal to 9 basis points. This implies a $VaR_{5\%} = 1.645 \times .0009 \times 10 \times \$1$ million = $14,805. However, in general, simply incorporating duration into the VaR calculation as either a magnification or shrinkage factor raises some non-trivial issues. For example, VaR calculations must take into account the convexity effect – that is, duration is not constant at different interest rate levels. This and other issues will be discussed in Chapter 3 when we consider the VaR of nonlinear derivatives.

1.2   DIVERSIFICATION AND VaR

It is well known that risks can be reduced by diversifying across assets that are imperfectly correlated. Indeed, it was bank regulators' neglect of the benefits of diversification in setting capital requirements that motivated much of the innovation that led to the widespread adoption of VaR measurement techniques. We first illustrate the impact of diversification on VaR using a simple example and then proceed to the general specification.

Consider a position in two assets:

- long $100 million worth of British pound sterling (GBPs);
- short $100 million worth of Euros.

This position could be thought of as a "spread trade" or a "relative value" position[20] that represents a bet on a rise in the British pound (GBP) relative to the Euro. In order to determine the risk of this position, we must make some assumptions. First, assume that returns are normally distributed with a mean of zero and a daily standard deviation of 80 basis points for the Euro and 70 basis points for the GBP. The percentage $VaR_{5\%}$ of each position can be calculated easily. For the Euro position a 1.645 standard deviation move is equivalent to a move of $1.645 \times 80 = 132$ bp, and for the GBP a 1.645 standard devation move is equivalent to a move of $1.645 \times 70 = 115$ bp. Thus, the dollar $VaR_{5\%}$ of the positions are, $1.32 million for the Euro position ($100m × 0.0132) and $1.15 million for the GBP position ($100m × 0.0115).

What is the risk of the entire portfolio, however? Total risk, without accounting for the effect of diversification, could be thought of as the summation of each position's VaR: $1.32m + $1.15m = $2.41 million. However, this summation does not represent an economic measure because risks are not additive. Intuitively, the likelihood of losing money on both parts of this position are slim. This is because the correlation between the $/Euro rate and the $/GBP rate is likely to be fairly high and because the two opposite positions (one long and one short) act as a hedge for one another. With a relatively high correlation between the two risk factors, namely, the $/Euro rate and the $/GBP rate, the most statistically likely event is to see gains on one part of the trade being offset by losses on the other. If the long GBP position is making money, for example, then it is likely that the short position in the Euro is losing money. This is, in fact, precisely the nature of spread trades.

For the purpose of this example, we shall assume a correlation of 0.8 between the $/GBP and the $/Euro rates. This correlation is consistent with evidence obtained by examining historical correlations in the exchange rates over time. What is the $VaR_{5\%}$ for the entire foreign currency portfolio in this example?

To derive the formula for calculation of the VaR of a portfolio, we use results from standard portfolio theory. The continuous return on a two-asset portfolio can be written as follows:

$$r_p = wr_1 + (1 - w)r_2 \qquad (1.6)$$

where w represents the weight of the first asset and $(1 - w)$ is the fraction of the portfolio invested in the second asset.[21] The variance of the portfolio is:

$$\sigma_p^2 = w^2\sigma_1^2 + (1 - w)^2\sigma_2^2 + 2w(1 - w)\sigma_{1,2}, \qquad (1.7)$$

where σ_p^2, σ_1^2 and σ_2^2 are the variances on the portfolio, asset 1 and asset 2, respectively and $\sigma_{1,2}$ is the covariance between asset 1 and 2 returns. Restating equation (1.7) in terms of standard deviation (recall that $\sigma_{1,2} = \rho_{1,2}\sigma_1\sigma_2$) results in:

$$\sigma_p = \sqrt{\{w^2\sigma_1^2 + (1 - w)^2\sigma_2^2 + 2w(1 - w)\rho_{1,2}\sigma_1\sigma_2\}}, \qquad (1.8)$$

where $\rho_{1,2}$ is the correlation between assets 1 and 2. However, the percentage $VaR_{5\%}$ can be stated as $1.645\sigma_p$. Moreover, the 5 percent percentage VaR for asset 1 (asset 2) can be denoted as $\%VaR_1$ ($\%VaR_2$) and can be expressed as $1.645\sigma_1$ ($1.645\sigma_2$). Substituting the expressions for $\%VaR_p$, $\%VaR_1$ and $\%VaR_2$ into equation (1.8) and multiplying both sides by 1.645 yields the portfolio's percentage VaR as follows:

$$\%VaR_p = \sqrt{\{w^2\%VaR_1^2 + (1 - w)^2\%VaR_2^2}$$
$$+ 2w(1 - w)\rho_{1,2}\%VaR_1\%VaR_2\}. \qquad (1.9)$$

Equation (1.9) represents the formula for the percentage VaR for a portfolio consisting of two assets.[22] However, equation (1.9) is not directly applicable to our spread trade example because it is a zero invest-ment strategy and therefore the weights are undefined. Thus, we can restate equation (1.9) in terms of the dollar VaR. To do that, note that the dollar VaR is simply the percentage VaR multiplied by the size of the position. Thus, the weights drop out as follows:

$$\$VaR_p = \sqrt{\{\$VaR_1^2 + \$VaR_2^2 + 2\rho_{1,2}\$VaR_1\$VaR_2\}}. \qquad (1.10)$$

Note that in the equation (1.10) version of the VaR formula, the weights disappeared since they were already incorporated into the dollar VaR values.

Applying equation (1.10) to our spread trade example, we obtain the portfolio VaR as follows:

$$\$VaR_p = \sqrt{\{\$1.32^2 + (-\$1.15)^2 + 2 \times 0.80 \times \$1.32 \times (-\$1.15)\}}$$

$$= \$0.64MM.$$

In the example, the British pound position is long and therefore the $VaR = \$100m \times 0.0132 = \$1.35$ million. However, the Euro position is short and therefore the $VaR = -\$100m \times 0.0115 = -\$1.15$ million. These values are input into equation (1.10) to obtain the VaR esti-mate of $640,000, suggesting that there is a 5 percent probability that the portfolio will lose at least $640,000 in a trading day. This number is considerably lower than the sum of the two VaRs ($2.41 million). The risk reduction is entirely due to the diversification effect. The risk reduction is particularly strong here due to the negative value for the last term in the equation.[23]

There is a large economic difference between the undiversified risk measure, $2.41 million, and the diversified risk VaR measure $0.64 million. This difference is an extreme characterization of the economic impact of bank capital adequacy requirements prior to the enactment of the market risk amendment to the Basel Accord which recognized correlations among assets in internal models calculating capital requirements for market risk as part of overall capital requirements. Use of the undiversified risk measure in setting capital requirements (i.e. simply adding exposures) is tantamount to assuming perfect positive correlations between all exposures. This assumption is particularly inappropriate for well-diversified globalized financial instititutions.

1.2.1   Factors affecting portfolio diversification

Diversification may be viewed as one of the most important risk management measures undertaken by a financial institution. Just how risk sensitive the diversified portfolio is depends on the parameter values. To examine the factors impacting potential diversification benefits, we reproduce equation (1.8) representing the portfolio's standard deviation:

$$\sigma_p = \sqrt{\{w^2\sigma_1^2 + (1-w)^2\sigma_2^2 + 2w(1-w)\rho_{1,2}\sigma_1\sigma_2\}}.$$

Assuming $\sigma_1^2 = \sigma_2^2 \equiv \sigma^2$ the standard deviation can be rewritten as:

$$\sigma_p = \sigma\sqrt{\{1 - 2w(1-w)(1-\rho)\}}. \tag{1.11}$$

Minimizing risk could be viewed as minimizing the portfolio's standard deviation. Using equation (1.11), we can examine the parameter values that minimize σ_p.

Considering the impact of the position weights, w, we can solve for the value of that minimizes σ_p. For simplicity, assume that the position weights take on values between zero and 1 (i.e., there are no short positions allowed). The product of the weights, $w(1-w)$, rises as w rises from zero to 0.5, and then falls as w rises further to 1. Since $(1 - \rho)$ is always positive (or zero), maximizing $w(1-w)$ results in maximal risk reduction. Thus, the portfolio with $w = 0.50$ is the one with the lowest possible volatility. For $w = 0.50$, $w(1-w) = 0.25$. In contrast, if $w = 0.90$, the risk reduction potential is much lower, since $w(1-w) = 0.09$. This implies that risk diversification is reduced by asset concentration (i.e. 90 percent of the portfolio invested in a single position). This illustrates the diversification effect – risk is reduced when investments are evenly spread across several assets and not concentrated in a single asset.

Equation (1.11) also illustrates the power of correlations in obtaining risk diversification benefits. The correlation effect is maximized when the correlation coefficient (denoted ρ) achieves its lower bound of -1. If the correlation between the two porfolio components is perfectly negative and the portfolio is equally weighted (i.e., $w = 0.50$ and $\rho = -1$), then the portfolio's standard deviation is zero. This illustrates how two risky assets can be combined to create a riskless portfolio, such that for each movement in one of the assets there is a perfectly offsetting movement in the other asset – i.e., the portfolio is perfectly hedged.[24] Finally, equation (1.11) shows that the greater the asset volatility, σ, the greater the portfolio risk exposure – the so-called volatility effect.

1.2.2 Decomposing volatility into systematic and idiosyncratic risk

Total volatility can be decomposed into asset-specific (or idiosyncratic) volatility and systematic volatility. This is an important decomposition for large, well-diversified portfolios. The total volatility of an asset within the framework of a well-diversified portfolio is less important. The important component, in measuring an asset's marginal risk contribution, is that asset's systematic volatility since in a well-diversified portfolio asset-specific risk is diversified away.

To see the role of idiosyncratic and systematic risk, consider a large portfolio of N assets. As before, suppose that all assets have the same standard deviation σ and that the correlation across all assets is ρ. Assume further that the portfolio is equally weighted (i.e., all weights are equal to $1/N$). The portfolio variance is the sum of N terms of own-asset volatilities adjusted by the weight, and $N(N - 1)/2$ covariance terms:

$$\sigma_p = \sqrt{\{N(1/N)^2\sigma^2 + 2[N(N - 1)/2](1/N)(1/N)\rho\sigma^2\}}. \quad (1.12)$$

And, hence, we obtain:

$$\sigma_p = \sqrt{\{\sigma^2/N + [(N - 1)/N]\rho\sigma^2\}}, \quad (1.13)$$

or simplifying terms:

$$\sigma_p = \sigma\sqrt{\{1/N + \rho(N-1)/N\}}. \qquad (1.14)$$

As N gets larger, i.e., the portfolio becomes better diversified, the first term, $1/N$, approaches zero. That is, the role of the asset's own volatility diminishes. For a large portfolio of uncorrelated assets (i.e., $\rho = 0$) we obtain:

$$\lim_{N\to\infty}\sigma_p = \lim_{N\to\infty}\sqrt{\{\sigma^2/N\}} = 0. \qquad (1.15)$$

In words, the limit of the portfolio's standard deviation, as N goes to infinity, is zero – a riskfree portfolio. This results from the assumption of a portfolio with an infinite number of uncorrelated assets. Fluctuations in each asset in the portfolio would have a diminishingly small impact on the portfolio's overall volatility, to the point where the effect is zero so that all risk is essentially idiosyncratic. Of course, practically speaking, it would be impossible to find a large number of uncorrelated assets to construct this hypothetical portfolio. However, this is a limiting case for the more realistic case of a portfolio with both idiosyncratic and systematic risk exposures.

To summarise:

- High variance increases porfolio volatility.
- Asset concentration increases portfolio volatility.
- Well-balanced (equally weighted) portfolios benefit the most from the diversification effect.
- Lower correlation reduces portfolio volatility.
- Systematic risk is the most important determinant of the volatility of well-diversified portfolios.
- Assets' idiosyncratic volatility gets diversified away.

1.2.3   Diversification: Words of caution – the case of long-term capital management (LTCM)

Risk diversification is very powerful and motivates much financial activity. As an example, consider the economic rationale of what is known as a fund of hedge funds (FoHF). A FoHF invests in a number of different hedge funds. For example, suppose that a FoHF distributes a total of $900 million equally among nine hedge funds. Suppose the annualized standard deviation of each of these funds is 15 percent p.a. This is a fairly realistic assumption as such funds are in the habit of levering up their positions to the point that their total volatility is in the vicinity of overall market volatility. The undiversified standard deviation of this investment in the annual horizon is 15 percent p.a. or $135 million (0.15 × $900 million).

Suppose that the FoHF managers have two important selection criteria. First, they try to choose fund managers with excess performance ability as measured by their fund's Sharpe ratio – the ratio of expected excess return over and above the risk free rate to the volatility of the fund's assets. Suppose the standard that is applied is that managers are exected to provide a Sharpe ratio of at least 2 – that is, an expected excess return equal to twice the fund's volatility. Thus, the fund's target expected return is equal to the riskfree rate, say 5 percent, plus 2 × 15 percent, for a total expected return of 35 percent p.a.

The second criterion that the FoHF managers apply in choosing funds is to choose funds with low levels of cross correlation in order to better diversify across the investments. They pick one fund which is a macro fund (betting on macroeconomic events), another fund that is in the risk arbitrage business (betting on the results of mergers and acquisitions), another fund in the business of fixed income arbitrage, and so on. Suppose the FoHF managers are successful in obtaining a portfolio of nine such funds with distinct investment strategies such that they believe that a zero correlation across all strategies is a reasonable assumption.

As constructed above, the FoHF portfolio will achieve a strong diversification benefit. Using equation (1.15), the diversified portfolio's standard deviation is √9 × $15 million = $45 million, much lower than the undiversified standard deviation of $135 million. This represents a standard deviation for the entire FoHF equal to 5 percent ($45m/$900m), or about one-third of the single investment standard deviation of 15 percent. Moreover, since the expected excess return is still 35 percent per fund, the FoHF can achieve a much higher Sharpe ratio. The FoHF's expected excess return is 30 percent with a standard deviation of only 5 percent, thereby yielding a Sharpe ratio of 6 (= 30/5); far in excess of the target Sharpe ratio of 2.

This example describes the structure of Long Term Capital Management's (LTCM) hedge fund. The highly distinguished proprietors of the hedge fund based in Greenwich, Connecticut, thought that they were investing in a well-designed FoHF consisting of a number of trading strategies that were assumed to be independent. This independence assumption across all strategies allowed the firm to lever up significantly. The strategies that LTCM invested in included such trades as: (i) trading on-the-run vs. off-the-run US Treasuries; (ii) trading mortgage backed securities hedged by US Treasury futures; (iii) trading Japanese warrants hedged by related equities; (iv) trading Swedish vs. Italian government bonds betting on Euro convergence; (v) trading global swap spreads (over Treasuries); and (vi) trading long positions in corporates hedged by government bonds, betting on declines in spreads. Theoretically as well as empirically these trades had little in common and it was reasonable to expect that their correlations were close to zero.

Of course, that assumption proved to be fatally false. When Russia defaulted on its sovereign debt obligations in August 1998, all trades turned south together, thereby raising correlations and eliminating diversification benefits just at the moment when they were most needed. The stellar reputations of the managers of LTCM should serve as a reminder to us that any model is only as good as the quality of its assumptions about the model inputs and parameter estimates. As we evaluate different VaR models, we will return to this theme repeatedly, particularly when we attempt to measure operational risk and credit risk VaR using the "incomplete" data sets that are currently available.

CHAPTER TWO

QUANTIFYING VOLATILITY
IN VaR MODELS

2.1   THE STOCHASTIC BEHAVIOR OF RETURNS

2.1.1   Revisiting the assumptions

In the previous chapter we discussed the notion of VaR. Measuring VaR involves identifying the tail of the distribution of asset returns. One approach to the problem is to impose specific distributional assumptions on asset returns. This approach is commonly termed the *parametric approach*, requiring a specific set of distributional assumptions. As we saw in the previous chapter, if we are willing to make a specific parametric distributional assumption, for example, that asset returns are normally distributed, then all we need is to provide two parameters – the mean (denoted μ) and the standard deviation (denoted σ) of returns. Given those, we are able to fully characterize the distribution and comment on risk in any way required; in particular, quantifying VaR, percentiles (e.g., 50 percent, 98 percent, 99 percent, etc.) of a loss distribution.

The problem is that, in reality, asset returns tend to deviate from normality. While many other phenomena in nature are often well described by the Gaussian (normal) distribution, asset returns tend to deviate from normality in meaningful ways. As we shall see below in detail, asset returns tend to be:

- *Fat-tailed*: A fat-tailed distribution is characterized by having more probability weight (observations) in its tails relative to the normal distribution.
- *Skewed*: A skewed distribution in our case refers to the empirical fact that declines in asset prices are more severe than increases. This is in contrast to the symmetry that is built into the normal distribution.
- *Unstable*: Unstable parameter values are the result of varying market conditions, and their effect, for example, on volatility.

All of the above require a risk manager to be able to reassess distributional parameters that vary through time.

In what follows we elaborate and establish benchmarks for these effects, and then proceed to address the key issue of how to adjust our set of assumptions to be able to better model asset returns, and better predict extreme market events. To do this we use a specific dataset, allowing us to demonstrate the key points through the use of an example.

2.1.2 The distribution of interest rate changes

Consider a series of daily observations of interest rates. In the series described below we plot three-month US Treasury bill (T-bill) rates calculated by the Federal Reserve.[1] We use ten years of data and hence we have approximately 2,500 observations. For convenience let us assume we have 2,501 data points on interest rate levels, and hence 2,500 data points on daily interest rate changes. Figure 2.1 depicts the time series of the yield to maturity, fluctuating between 11 percent p.a. and 4 percent p.a. during the sample period (in this example, 1983–92).

The return on bonds is determined by interest rate *changes*, and hence this is the relevant variable for our discussion. We calculate daily interest changes, that is, the first difference series of observed yields. Figure 2.2 is a histogram of yield changes. The histogram is the result of 2,500 observations of daily interest rate changes from the above data set.

Using this series of 2,500 interest rate changes we can obtain the average interest rate change and the standard deviation of interest rate

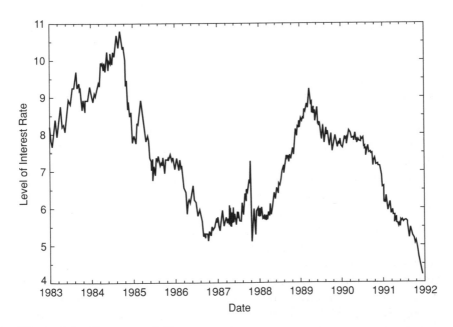

Figure 2.1 Three-month Treasury rates

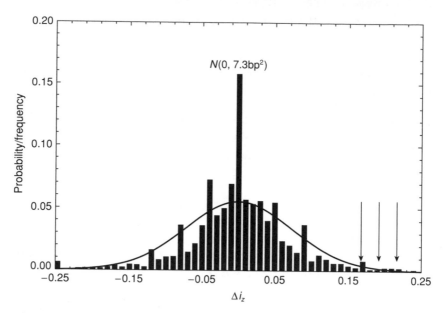

Figure 2.2   Three-month Treasury rate changes

changes over the period. The mean of the series is zero basis points per day. Note that the average daily change in this case is simply the last yield minus the first yield in the series, divided by the number of days in the series. The series in our case starts at 4 percent and ends at a level of 8 percent, hence we have a 400 basis point (bp) change over the course of 2,500 days, for an average change of approximately zero. Zero expected change as a forecast is, as we discussed in the previous chapter, consistent with the random walk assumption as well. The standard deviation of interest rate changes turns out to be 7.3bp/day.

Using these two parameters, figure 2.2 plots a normal distribution curve on the same scale of the histogram, with basis point changes on the X-axis and probability on the Y-axis. If our assumption of normality is correct, then the plot in figure 2.2 should resemble the theoretical normal distribution shown in figure 1.1. Observing figure 2.2 we find some important differences between the theoretical normal distribution using the mean and standard deviation from our data, and the empirical histogram plotted by actual interest rate changes. The difference is primarily the result of the "fat-tailed" nature of the distribution.

2.1.3   Fat tails

The term "fat tails" refers to the tails of one distribution *relative* to another reference distribution. The reference distribution here is the normal distribution. A distribution is said to have "fatter tails" than the normal distribution if it has a similar mean and variance, but different probability mass at the extreme tails of the probability distribution. The critical point is that the first two moments of the distribution, the mean and the variance, are the same.

This is precisely the case for the data in figure 2.2, where we observe the empirical distribution of interest rate changes. The plot includes a histogram of interest rate changes in different probability buckets. In addition to the histogram, and on the same plot, a normal distribution is also plotted, so as to compare the two distributions. The normal distribution has the same mean (zero) and the same volatility (7.3 basis points) as the empirical distribution.

We can observe "fat tail" effects by comparing the two distributions. There is extra probability mass in the empirical distribution relative to the normal distribution benchmark around zero, and there is a "missing" probability mass in the intermediate portions around the plus ten and minus ten basis point change region of the histogram. Although it is difficult to observe directly in figure 2.2, it is also the case that at the probability extremes (e.g., around 25bp and higher), there are more observations than the theoretical normal benchmark warrants. A more detailed figure focusing on the tails is presented later in this chapter.

This pattern, more probability mass around the mean and at the tails, and less around plus/minus one standard deviation, is precisely what we expect of a fat tailed distribution. Intuitively, a probability mass is taken from around the one standard deviation region, and distributed to the zero interest rate change and to the two extreme-change regions. This is done in such way so as to preserve the mean and standard deviation. In our case the mean of zero and the standard deviation of 7.3bp, are preserved by construction, because we plot the normal distribution benchmark given these two empirically determined parameters.

To illustrate the impact of fat tails, consider the following exercise. We take the vector of 2,500 observations of interest rate changes, and order this vector not by date but, instead, by the size of the interest rate change, in descending order. This ordered vector will have the larger interest rate increases at the top. The largest change may be, for example, an increase of 35 basis points. It will appear as entry number one of the ordered vector. The following entry will be the second largest change, say 33 basis points, and so on. Zero changes should be found around the middle of this vector, in the vicinity of the 1,250th entry, and large declines should appear towards the "bottom" of this vector, in entries 2,400 to 2,500.

If it were the case that, indeed, the distribution of interest rate changes were normal with a mean of zero and a standard deviation of 7.3 basis points, what would we expect of this vector, and, in particular, of the tails of the distribution of interest rate changes? In particular, what should be a one percentile (%) interest rate shock; i.e., an interest rate shock that occurs approximately once in every 100 days? For the standard normal distribution we know that the first percentile is delineated at 2.33 standard deviations from the mean. In our case, though, *losses* in asset values are related to *increases* in interest rates. Hence we examine the +2.33 standard deviation rather than the −2.33 standard deviation event (i.e., 2.33 standard deviations above the mean rather than 2.33 standard deviations below the mean). The +2.33 standard deviations event for the standard normal translates into an increase in interest rates of $\sigma \times 2.33$ or 7.3bp $\times$ 2.33 = 17bp. Under the assumption that interest rate changes are normal we should, therefore, see in 1 percent of the cases interest rate changes that are greater or equal to 17 basis points.

What do we get in reality? The empirical first percentile of the distribution of interest rate changes can be found as the 25th out of the 2,500 observations in the ordered vector of interest rate changes. Examining this entry in the vector we find an interest rate increase of 21 basis points. Thus, the empirical first percentile (21bp) does not conform to the theoretical 17 basis points implied by the normality assumption, providing a direct and intuitive example of the fat tailedness of the empirical distribution. That is, we find that the (empirical) tails of the actual distribution are fatter than the theoretical tails of the distribution.[2]

2.1.4 Explaining fat tails

The phenomenon of fat tails poses a severe problem for risk managers. Risk measurement, as we saw above, is focused on extreme events, trying to quantify the probability and magnitude of severe losses. The normal distribution, a common benchmark in many cases, seems to fail here. Moreover, it seems to fail precisely where we need it to work best – in the tails of the distributions. Since risk management is all about the tails, further investigation of the tail behavior of asset returns is required.

In order to address this issue, recall that the distribution we examine is the *unconditional distribution* of asset returns. By "unconditional" we mean that on any given day we assume the same distribution exists, regardless of market and economic conditions. This is in spite of the fact that there is information available to market participants about the distribution of asset returns at any given point in time which may be different than on other days. This information is relevant for an asset's *conditional distribution*, as measured by parameters, such as the conditional mean, conditional standard deviation (volatility), conditional skew and kurtosis. This implies two possible explanations for the fat tails: (i) conditional volatility is time-varying; and (ii) the conditional mean is time-varying. Time variations in either could, arguably, generate fat tails in the unconditional distribution, in spite of the fact that the conditional distribution is normal (albeit with different parameters at different points in time, e.g., in recessions and expansions).

Let us consider each of these possible explanations for fat tails. First, is it plausible that the fat tails observed in the unconditional distribution are due to time-varying conditional distributions? We will show that the answer is generally "no." The explanation is based on the implausible assumption that market participants know, or can predict in advance, future changes in asset prices. Suppose, for example, that interest rate changes are, in fact, normal, with a time-varying conditional mean. Assume further that the conditional mean of interest rate changes is known to market participants during the period under investigation, but is unknown to the econometrician. For simplicity, assume that the *conditional* mean can be +5bp/day on some days, and −5bp/day on other days. If the split between high mean and low mean days were 50–50, we would observe an unconditional mean change in interest rates of 0bp/day.

In this case when the econometrician or the risk manager approaches past data without the knowledge of the conditional means, he mistakes variations in interest rates to be due to volatility. Risk is overstated, and changes that are, in truth, distributed normally and are centered around plus or minus five basis points, are mistaken to be normal with a mean of zero. If this were the case we would have obtained a "mixture of normals" with varying means, that would appear to be, unconditionally, fat tailed.

Is this a likely explanation for the observed fat tails in the data? The answer is negative. The belief in efficient markets implies that asset prices reflect all commonly available information. If participants in the marketplace know that prices are due to rise over the next day, prices would have already risen today as traders would have traded on this information. Even detractors of market efficiency assumptions would agree that conditional means do not vary enough on a daily basis to make those variations a first order effect.

To verify this point consider the debate over the predictability of market returns. Recent evidence argues that the conditional risk premium, the expected return on the market over and above the risk free rate, varies through time in a predictable manner. Even if we assume this to be the case, predicted variations are commonly esti- mated to be between zero and 10 percent on an annualized basis. Moreover, variations in the expected premium are slow to change (the predictive variables that drive these variations vary slowly). If at a given point you believe the expected excess return on the market is 10 percent per annum rather than the unconditional value of, say, 5 per- cent, you predict, on a daily basis, a return which is 2bp different from the market's average premium (a 5 percent per annum difference equals approximately a return of 2bp/day). With the observed volatility of equity returns being around 100bp/day, we may view variations in the conditional mean as a second order effect.

The second possible explanation for the fat tail phenomenon is that volatility (standard deviation) is time-varying. Intuitively, one can make a compelling case against the assumption that asset return volatility is constant. For example, the days prior to important Federal announcements are commonly thought of as days with higher than usual uncertainty, during which interest rate volatility as well as equity return volatility surge. Important political events, such as the turmoil in the Gulf region, and significant economic events, such as the defaults of Russia and Argentina on their debts, are also associ- ated with a spike in global volatility. Time-varying volatility may also be generated by regular, predictable events. For example, volatility in the Federal funds market increases dramatically on the last days of the reserve maintenance period for banks as well as at quarter-end in response to balance sheet window dressing.[3] Stochastic volatility is clearly a candidate explanation for fat tails, especially if the econometrician fails to use relevant information that generates excess volatility.[4]

2.1.5   Effects of volatility changes

How does time-varying volatility affect our distributional assumptions, the validity of the normal distribution model and our ability to provide a useful risk measurement system? To illustrate the problem and its potential solution, consider an illustrative example. Suppose interest rate changes do not fit the normal distribution model with a mean of zero and a standard deviation of 7.3 basis points per day. Instead, the true conditional distribution of interest rate changes is normal with a mean of zero but with a time-varying volatility that during some periods is 5bp/day and during other periods is 15bp/day.

This type of distribution is often called a "regime-switching volatility model." The regime switches from low volatility to high volatility, but is never in between. Assume further that market participants are aware of the state of the economy, i.e., whether volatility is high or low. The econometrician, on the other hand, does not have this knowledge. When he examines the data, oblivious to the true regime-switching distribution, he estimates an unconditional volatility of 7.3bp/day that is the result of the mixture of the high volatility and low volatility regimes. Fat tails appear only in the unconditional distribution. The conditional distribution is always normal, albeit with a varying volatility.[5]

Figure 2.3 provides a schematic of the path of interest rate volatility in our regime-switching example. The solid line depicts the true volatility, switching between 5bp/day and 15bp/day. The econometrician observes periods where interest rates change by as much as, say, 30 basis points. A change in interest rates of 30bp corresponds to a change of more than four standard deviations given that the estimated standard deviation is 7.3bp. According to the normal

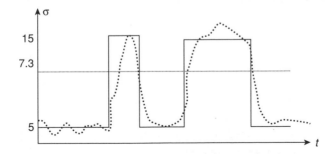

Figure 2.3   A schematic of actual and estimated volatility

Table 2.1 Tail event probability and odds under normality

No. of deviations Z	Prob($X < z$) (in %)	Odds (one in . . . days)
−1.50	6.68072	15
−2.00	2.27501	44
−2.50	0.62097	161
−3.00	0.13500	741
−3.50	0.02327	4,298
−4.00	0.00317	31,560
−4.50	0.00034	294,048
−5.00	0.00003	3,483,046

distribution benchmark, a change of four standard deviations or more should be observed very infrequently. More precisely, the probability that a truly random normal variable will deviate from the mean by four standard deviations or more is 0.003 percent. Putting it differently, the odds of seeing such a change are one in 31,560, or once in 121 years. Table 2.1 provides the number of standard deviations, the probability of seeing a random normal being less than or equal to this number of standard deviations, in percentage terms, and the odds of seeing such an event.

The risk manager may be puzzled by the empirical observation of a relatively high frequency of four or more standard deviation moves. His risk model, one could argue, based on an unconditional normal distribution with a standard deviation of 7.3bp, is of little use, since it under-predicts the odds of a 30bp move. In reality (in the reality of our illustrative example), the change of 30bp occurred, most likely, on a high volatility day. On a high volatility day a 30bp move is only a two standard deviation move, since interest rate changes are drawn from a normal distribution with a standard deviation of 15bp/day. The probability of a change in interest rates of two standard deviations or more, equivalent to a change of 30bp or more on high volatility days, is still low, but is economically meaningful. In particular, the probability of a 30bp move conditional on a high volatility day is 2.27 percent, and the odds are one in 44.

The dotted line in figure 2.3 depicts the estimated volatility using a volatility estimation model based on historical data. This is the typical picture for common risk measurement engines – the estimated volatility trails true volatility. Estimated volatility rises after having observed an increase, and declines having observed a decrease. The estimation error and estimation lag is a central issue in risk measurement, as we shall see in this chapter.

This last example illustrates the challenge of modern dynamic risk measurement. The most important task of the risk manager is to raise a "red flag," a warning signal that volatility is expected to be high in the near future. The resulting action given this information may vary from one firm to another, as a function of strategy, culture, appetite for risk, and so on, and could be a matter of great debate. The importance of the risk estimate as an input to the decision making process is, however, not a matter of any debate. The effort to improve risk measurement engines' dynamic prediction of risk based on market conditions is our focus throughout the rest of the chapter.

This last illustrative example is an extreme case of stochastic volatility, where volatility jumps from high to low and back periodically. This model is in fact quite popular in the macroeconomics literature, and more recently in finance as well. It is commonly known as regime switching.[6]

2.1.6   Can (conditional) normality be salvaged?

In the last example, we shifted our concept of normality. Instead of assuming asset returns are normally distributed, we now assume that asset returns are *conditionally normally distributed*. Conditional normality, with a time-varying volatility, is an economically reasonable description of the nature of asset return distributions, and may resolve the issue of fat tails observed in unconditional distributions.

This is the focus of the remainder of this chapter. To preview the discussion that follows, however, it is worthwhile to forewarn the reader that the effort is going to be, to an extent, incomplete. Asset returns are generally non-normal, both unconditionally as well as conditionally; i.e., fat tails are exhibited in asset returns regardless of the estimation method we apply. While the use of dynamic risk measurement models capable of adapting model parameters as a function of changing market conditions is important, these models do not eliminate all deviations from the normal distribution benchmark. Asset returns keep exhibiting asymmetries and unexpectedly large movements regardless of the sophistication of estimation models. Putting it more simply – large moves will always occur "out of the blue" (e.g., in relatively low volatility periods).

One way to examine conditional fat tails is by normalizing asset returns. The process of normalizations of a random normal variable is simple. Consider X, a random normal variable, with a mean of μ and a standard deviation σ,

$$X \sim N(\mu, \sigma^2).$$

A standardized version of X is

$$(X - \mu)/\sigma \sim N(0, 1).$$

That is, given the mean and the standard deviation, the random variable X less its mean, divided by its standard deviation, is distributed according to the standard normal distribution.

Consider now a series of interest rate changes, where the mean is assumed, for simplicity, to be always zero, and the volatility is re-estimated every period. Denote this volatility estimate by σ_t. This is the forecast for next period's volatility based on some volatility estimation model (see the detailed discussion in the next section). Under the normality assumption, interest rate changes are now conditionally normal

$$\Delta i_{t,t+1} \sim N(0, \sigma_t^2).$$

We can standardize the distribution of interest rate changes dynamically using our estimated conditional volatility σ_t, and the actual change in interest rate that followed $\Delta i_{t,t+1}$. We create a series of standardized variables.

$$\Delta i_{t,t+1}/\sigma_t \sim N(0, 1).$$

This series should be distributed according to the standard normal distribution. To check this, we can go back through the data, and with the benefit of hindsight put all pieces of data, drawn under the null assumption of conditional normality from a normal distribution with time-varying volatilities, on equal footing. If interest rate changes are, indeed, conditionally normal with a time-varying volatility, then the unconditional distribution of interest rate changes can be fat tailed. However, the distribution of interest rate changes standardized by their respective conditional volatilities should be distributed as a standard normal variable.

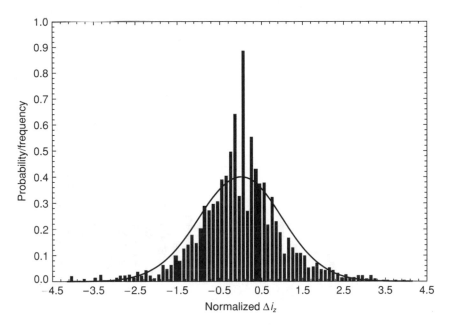

Figure 2.4 Standardized interest rate changes – empirical distribution relative to the $N(0, 1)$ benchmark

Figure 2.4 does precisely this. Using historical data we estimate conditional volatility.[7] We plot a histogram similar to the one in figure 2.2, with one exception. The X-axis here is not in terms of interest rate changes, but, instead, in terms of *standardized interest rate changes*. All periods are now adjusted to be comparable, and we may expect to see a "well-behaved" standard normal. Standardized interest rate changes are going to be well behaved on two conditions: (i) that interest rate changes are, indeed, conditionally normal; and (ii) that we accurately estimated conditional volatility, i.e., that we were able to devise a "good" dynamic volatility estimation mechanism. This joint condition can be formalized into a statistical hypothesis that can be tested.

Normalized interest rate changes, plotted in figure 2.4, provide an informal test. First note that we are not interested in testing for normality *per se*, since we are not interested in the entire distribution. We only care about our ability to capture tail behavior in asset returns – the key to dynamic risk measurement. Casual examination of figure 2.5, where the picture focuses on the tails of the conditional distribution, vividly shows the failure of the conditional normality model to describe the data. Extreme movements of *standardized* interest rate

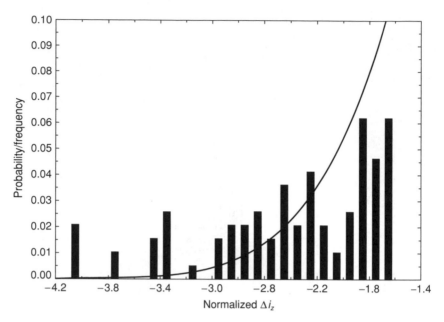

Figure 2.5   Tail standardized interest rate changes

movements – deviating from the conditional normality model – are still present in the data. Recall, though, that this is a failure of the joint model – conditional normality and the method for dynamic estimation of the conditional volatility.[8] In principle it is still possible that an alternative model of volatility dynamics will be able to capture the conditional distribution of asset returns better and that the conditional returns based on the alternative model will indeed be normal.

2.1.7   Normality cannot be salvaged

The result apparent in figure 2.5 holds true, however, to a varying degree, for most financial data series. Sharp movements in asset returns, even on a normalized basis, occur in financial data series no matter how we manipulate the data to estimate volatility. Conditional asset returns exhibit sharp movements, asymmetries, and other difficult-to-model effects in the distribution. This is, in a nutshell, the problem with all extant risk measurement engines. All VaR-based systems tend to encounter difficulty where we need them to perform best – at the tails. Similar effects are also present for the multivariate distribution of portfolios of assets – correlations as well tend to be unstable – hence making VaR engines often too conservative at the worst possible times.

This is a striking result with critical implications for the practice of risk management. The relative prevalence of extreme moves, even after adjusting for current market conditions, is the reason we need additional tools, over and above the standard VaR risk measurement tool. Specifically, the need for *stress testing* and *scenario analysis* is related directly to the failure of VaR-based systems.

Nevertheless, the study of conditional distributions is important. There is still important information in current market conditions, e.g., conditional volatility, that can be exploited in the process of risk assessment. In this chapter we elaborate on risk measurement and VaR methods. In the next chapter we augment our set of tools discussing stress testing and scenario analysis.

2.2   VaR ESTIMATION APPROACHES

There are numerous ways to approach the modeling of asset return distribution in general, and of tail behavior (e.g., risk measurement) in particular. The approaches to estimating VaR can be broadly divided as follows

- *Historical-based approaches.* The common attribute to all the approaches within this class is their use of historical time series data in order to determine the shape of the conditional distribution.

    - *Parametric approach.* The parametric approach imposes a specific distributional assumption on conditional asset returns. A representative member of this class of models is the conditional (log) normal case with time-varying volatility, where volatility is estimated from recent past data.
    - *Nonparametric approach.* This approach uses historical data directly, without imposing a specific set of distributional assumptions. Historical simulation is the simplest and most prominent representative of this class of models.
    - *Hybrid approach.* A combined approach.

- *Implied volatility based approach.* This approach uses derivative pricing models and current derivative prices in order to impute an implied volatility without having to resort to historical data. The use of implied volatility obtained from the Black–Scholes option pricing model as a predictor of future volatility is the most prominent representative of this class of models.

2.2.1   Cyclical volatility

Volatility in financial markets is not only time-varying, but also sticky, or predictable. As far back as 1963, Mandelbrot wrote

> large changes tend to be followed by large changes – of either sign – and small changes by small changes.   (Mandelbrot 1963)

This is a very useful guide to modeling asset return volatility, and hence risk. It turns out to be a salient feature of most extant models that use historical data. The implication is simple – since the magnitude (but not the sign) of recent changes is informative, the most recent history of returns on a financial asset should be most informative with respect to its volatility in the near future. This intuition is implemented in many simple models by placing more weight on recent historical data, and little or no weight on data that is in the more distant past.

2.2.2   Historical standard deviation

Historical standard deviation is the simplest and most common way to estimate or predict future volatility. Given a history of an asset's continuously compounded rate of returns we take a specific window of the K most recent returns. The data in hand are, hence, limited by choice to be $r_{t-1,t}, r_{t-2,t-1}, \ldots, r_{t-K,t-K+1}$. This return series is used in order to calculate the current/conditional standard deviation σ_t, defined as the square root of the conditional variance

$$\sigma_t^2 = (r_{t-K,t-K+1}^2 + \ldots + r_{t-2,t-1}^2 + r_{t-1,t}^2)/K.$$

This is the most familiar formula for calculating the variance of a random variable – simply calculating its "mean squared deviation." Note that we make an explicit assumption here, that the conditional mean is zero. This is consistent with the random walk assumption.

The standard formula for standard deviation[9] uses a slightly different formula, first demeaning the range of data given to it for calculation. The estimation is, hence, instead

$$\mu_t = (r_{t-K,t-K+1} + \ldots + r_{t-2,t-1} + r_{t-1,t})/K,$$

$$\sigma_t^2 = ((r_{t-K,t-K+1} - \mu_t)^2 + \ldots + (r_{t-2,t-1} - \mu_t)^2 + (r_{t-1,t} - \mu_t)^2)/(K - 1).$$

Note here that the standard deviation is the mean of the squared deviation, but the mean is taken by dividing by $(K - 1)$ rather than K. This is a result of a statistical consideration related to the loss of one degree of freedom because the conditional mean, μ_t, has been estimated in a prior stage. The use of $K - 1$ in the denominator guarantees that the estimator σ_t^2 is unbiased.

This is a minor variation that makes very little practical difference in most instances. However, it is worthwhile discussing the pros and cons of each of these two methods. Estimating the conditional mean μ_t from the most recent K days of data is risky. Suppose, for example, that we need to estimate the volatility of the stock market, and we decide to use a window of the most recent 100 trading days. Suppose further that over the past 100 days the market has declined by 25 percent. This can be represented as an average decline of 25bp/day ($-2,500$bp/100days $= -25$bp/day). Recall that the econometrician is trying to estimate the conditional mean and volatility that were known to market participants during the period. Using -25bp/day as μ_t, the conditional mean, and then estimating σ_t^2, implicitly assumes that market participants knew of the decline, and that their conditional distribution was centered around minus 25bp/day.

Since we believe that the decline was entirely unpredictable, imposing our priors by using $\mu_t = 0$ is a logical alternative. Another approach is to use the unconditional mean, or an expected change based on some other theory as the conditional mean parameter. In the case of equities, for instance, we may want to use the unconditional average return on equities using a longer period – for example 12 percent per annum, which is the sum of the average risk free rate (approximately 6 percent) plus the average equity risk premium (6 percent). This translates into an average daily increase in equity prices of approximately 4.5bp/day. This is a relatively small number that tends to make little difference in application, but has a sound economic rationale underlying its use.

For other assets we may want to use the forward rate as the estimate for the expected average change. Currencies, for instance, are expected to drift to equal their forward rate according to the expectations hypothesis. If the USD is traded at a forward premium of 2.5 percent p.a. relative to the Euro, a reasonable candidate for the mean parameter would be μ_t = 1bp/day. The difference here between 0bp and 1bp seems to be immaterial, but when VaR is estimated for longer horizons this will become a relevant consideration, as we discuss later.

2.2.3 Implementation considerations

The empirical performance of historical standard deviation as a predictor of future volatility is affected by statistical error. With respect to statistical error, it is always the case in statistics that "more is better". Hence, the more data available to us, the more precise our estimator will be to the true return volatility. On the other hand, we estimate standard deviation in an environment where we believe, a priori, that volatility itself is unstable. The stickiness of time variations in volatility are important, since it gives us an intuitive guide that recent history is more relevant for the near future than distant history.

In figure 2.6 we use the series of 2,500 interest rate changes in order to come up with a series of rolling estimates of conditional volatility. We use an estimation window K of different lengths in order to demonstrate the tradeoff involved. Specifically, three different

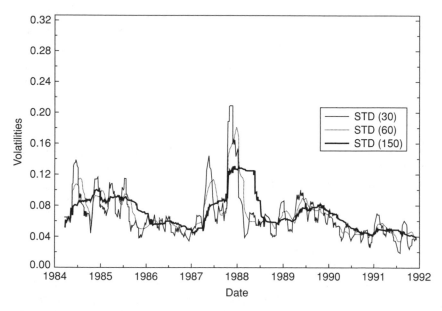

Figure 2.6 Time-varying volatility using historical standard deviation with various window lengths

window-lengths are used: $K = 30$, $K = 60$, and $K = 150$. On any given day we compare these three lookback windows. That is, on any given day (starting with the 151st day), we look back 30, 60, or 150 days and calculate the standard deviation by averaging the squared interest rate changes (and then taking a square root). The figure demonstrates the issues involved in the choice of K. First note that the forecasts for series using shorter windows are more volatile. This could be the result of a statistical error – 30 observations, for example, may provide only a noisy estimate of volatility. On the other hand, variations could be the result of true changes in volatility. The longer window length, $K = 150$ days, provides a relatively smoother series of estimators/forecasts, varying within a tighter range of 4–12 basis points per day. Recall that the unconditional volatility is 7.3bp/day. Shorter window lengths provide extreme estimators, as high as 22bp/day. Such estimators are three times larger than the unconditional volatility.

The effect of the statistical estimation error is particularly acute for small samples, e.g., $K = 30$. The STDEV estimator is particularly sensitive to extreme observations. To see why this is the case, recall that the calculation of STDEV involves an equally weighted average of *squared* deviations from the mean (here zero). Any extreme, perhaps non-normal, observation becomes larger in magnitude by taking it to the power of two. Moreover, with small window sizes each observation receives higher weight by definition. When a large positive or negative return is observed, therefore, a sharp increase in the volatility forecast is observed.

In this context it is worthwhile mentioning that an alternative procedure of calculating the volatility involves averaging absolute values of returns, rather than squared returns. This method is considered more robust when the distribution is non-normal. In fact it is possible to show that while under the normality assumption STDEV is optimal, when returns are non-normal, and, in particular, fat tailed, then the absolute squared deviation method may provide a superior forecast.

This discussion seems to present an argument that longer observation windows reduce statistical error. However, the other side of the coin is that small window lengths provide an estimator that is more adaptable to changing market conditions. In the extreme case where volatility does not vary at all, the longer the window length is, the more accurate our estimates. However, in a time varying volatility environment we face a tradeoff – short window lengths are less precise, due to estimation error, but more adaptable to innovations in volatility. Later in this chapter (in Section 2.2.4.2) we discuss the issue of benchmarking various volatility estimation models and describe simple optimization procedures that allow us to choose the most appropriate window length. Intuitively, for volatility series that are in and of themselves more volatile, we will tend to shorten the window length, and vice versa.

Finally, yet another important shortcoming of the STDEV method for estimating conditional volatility is the periodic appearance of large decreases in conditional volatility. These sharp declines are the result of extreme observations disappearing from the rolling estimation window. The STDEV methodology is such that when a large move occurs we use this piece of data for K days. Then, on day $K + 1$ it falls off the estimation window. The extreme return carries the same weight of $(100/K)$ percent from day $t - 1$ to day $t - K$, and then disappears. From an economic perspective this is a counterintuitive way to describe memory in financial markets. A more intuitive description would be to incorporate a gradual decline in memory such that when a crisis occurs it is very relevant for the first week, affecting volatility in financial markets to a great extent, and then as time goes by it becomes gradually less important. Using STDEV with equal weights on observations from the most recent K days, and zero thereafter (further into the past) is counterintuitive. This shortcoming of STDEV is precisely the one addressed by the exponential smoothing approach, adopted by RiskMetrics™ in estimating volatility.

2.2.4   Exponential smoothing – RiskMetrics™ volatility

Suppose we want to use historical data, specifically, squared returns, in order to calculate conditional volatility. How can we improve upon our first estimate, STDEV? We focus on the issue of information decay and on giving more weight to more recent information and less weight to distant information. The simplest, most popular, approach is exponential smoothing. Exponential smoothing places exponentially declining weights on historical data, starting with an initial weight, and then declining to zero as we go further into the past.

The smoothness is achieved by setting a parameter λ, which is equal to a number greater than zero, but smaller than one, raised to a power (i.e., $0 < \lambda < 1$). Any such smoothing parameter λ, when raised to a high enough power, can get arbitrarily small. The sequence of numbers $\lambda^0, \lambda^1, \lambda^2, \ldots \lambda^i, \ldots$ has the desirable property that it starts with a finite number, namely λ^0 ($= 1$), and ends with a number that could become arbitrarily small (λ^i where i is large). The only problem with this sequence is that we need it to sum to 1 in order for it to be a weighting scheme.

In order to rectify the problem, note that the sequence is geometric, summing up to $1/(1 - \lambda)$. For a smoothing parameter of 0.9 for example, the sum of 0.9^0, 0.9^1, 0.9^2, ... 0.9^i, ... is $1/(1 - 0.9) = 10$. All we need is to define a new sequence which is the old sequence divided by the sum of the sequence and the new sequence will then sum to 1. In the previous example we would divide the sequence by 10. More generally we divide each of the weights by $1/(1 - \lambda)$, the sum of the geometric sequence. Note that dividing by $1/(1 - \lambda)$ is equivalent to multiplying by $(1 - \lambda)$. Hence, the old sequence λ^0, λ^1, λ^2, ... λ^i, ... is replaced by the new sequence

$$(1 - \lambda)\lambda^0, \ (1 - \lambda)\lambda^1, \ (1 - \lambda)\lambda^2, \ \ldots, \ (1 - \lambda)\lambda^i, \ \ldots$$

This is a "legitimate" weighting scheme, since by construction it sums to one. This is the approach known as the RiskMetrics™ exponential weighting approach to volatility estimation.

The estimator we obtain for conditional variance is:

$$\sigma_t^2 = (1 - \lambda)*(\lambda^0 r_{t-1,t}^2 + \lambda^1 r_{t-2,t-1}^2 + \lambda^2 r_{t-3,t-2}^2 + \ldots + \lambda^N r_{t-N-1,t-N}^2),$$

where N is some finite number which is the truncation point. Since we truncate after a finite number (N) of observations the sum of the series is not 1. It is, in fact, λ^N. That is, the sequence of the weights we drop, from the "$N + 1$"th observation and thereafter, sum up to $\lambda^N/(1 - \lambda)$. For example, take $\lambda = 0.94$:

Weight 1	$(1 - \lambda)\lambda^0$	$= (1 - 0.94)$	$= 6.00\%$
Weight 2	$(1 - \lambda)\lambda^1$	$= (1 - 0.94)*0.94$	$= 5.64\%$
Weight 3	$(1 - \lambda)\lambda^2$	$= (1 - 0.94)*0.94^2$	$= 5.30\%$
Weight 4	$(1 - \lambda)\lambda^3$	$= (1 - 0.94)*0.94^3$	$= 4.98\%$
. . .			
Weight 100	$(1 - \lambda)\lambda^{99}$	$= (1 - 0.94)*0.94^{99}$	$= 0.012\%$

The residual sum of truncated weights is $0.94^{100}/(1 - 0.94) = 0.034$.
We have two choices with respect to this residual weight

1   We can increase N so that the sum of residual weight is small (e.g., $0.94^{200}/(1 - 0.94) = 0.00007$);

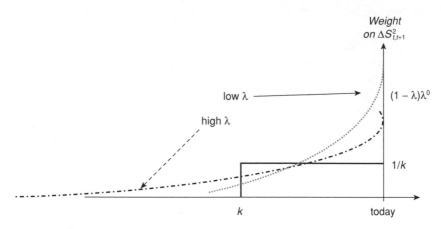

Figure 2.7 STDEV and exponential smoothing weighting schemes

2 or divide by the truncated sum of weights $(1 - \lambda^N)/(1 - \lambda)$ rather than the infinite sum $1/(1 - \lambda)$. In our previous example this would mean dividing by 16.63 instead of 16.66 after 100 observations.

This is a purely technical issue. Either is technically fine, and of little real consequence to the estimated volatility.

In figure 2.7 we compare RiskMetrics™ to STDEV. Recall the important commonalities of these methods

- both methods are parametric;
- both methods attempt to estimate conditional volatility;
- both methods use recent historical data;
- both methods apply a set of weights to past squared returns.

The methods differ only as far as the weighting scheme is concerned. RiskMetrics™ poses a choice with respect to the smoothing parameter λ, (in the example above, equal to 0.94) similar to the choice with respect to K in the context of the STDEV estimator. The tradeoff in the case of STDEV was between the desire for a higher precision, consistent with higher K's, and quick adaptability to changes in conditional volatility, consistent with lower K's. Here, similarly, a λ parameter closer to unity exhibits a slower decay in information's relevance with less weight on recent observations (see the dashed-dotted line in figure 2.7), while lower λ parameters provide a weighting scheme with more weight on recent observations, but effectively a smaller sample (see the dashed line in figure 2.7).

2.2.4.1   The optimal smoother lambda

Is there a way to determine an optimal value to the estimation parameter, whether it is the window size K or the smoothing parameter λ? As it turns out, one can optimize on the parameters λ or K. To outline the procedure, first we must define the mean squared error (MSE) measure, which measures the statistical error of a series of estimates for each specific value of a parameter. We can then search for a minimum value for this MSE error, thereby identifying an optimal parameter value (corresponding with the minimal error).

First, it is important to note that true realized volatility is unobservable. Therefore, it is impossible to directly compare predicted volatility to true realized volatility. It is therefore not immediately clear how to go about choosing between various λ or K parameters. We can only "approximate" realized volatility. Specifically, the closest we can get is to take the observed value of $r_{t,t+1}{}^2$ as an approximate measure of realized volatility. There is no obvious way around the measurement error in measuring true volatility. The MSE measures the deviation between predicted and realized (not true) volatility. We take the squared error between predicted volatility (a function of the smoothing parameter we choose) $\sigma(\lambda)_t^2$, and realized volatility $r_{t,t+1}{}^2$ such that:

$$MSE(\lambda) = AVERAGE_{t=1,2,\ldots T}\{(\sigma(\lambda)_t^2 - r_{t,t+1}{}^2)^2\}.$$

We then minimize the MSE(λ) over different choices of λ,

$$Min_{\lambda<1}\{MSE(\lambda)\},$$

subject to the constraint that λ is less than one.

This procedure is similar in spirit, although not identical, to the *Maximum Likelihood Method* in statistics. This method attempts to choose the set of parameters given a certain model that will make the observed data the most likely to have been observed. The optimal λ can be chosen for every series independently. The optimal parameter may depend on sample size – for example, how far back in history we choose to extend our data. It also depends critically on the true nature of underlying volatility. As we discussed above, financial time series such as oil prices are driven by a volatility that may exhibit rapid and sharp turns. Since adaptability becomes important in such extremely volatile cases, a low λ will tend to be optimal (minimize MSE). The reverse would hold true for "well-behaved" series.

Variations in optimal λ are wide. The RiskMetrics™ technical document provides optimal λ for some of the 480 series covered. Money market optimal λ are as high as 0.99, and as low as 0.92 for some currencies. The globally optimal λ is derived so as to minimize the weighted average of MSEs with one optimal λ. The weights are determined according to individual forecast accuracy. The optimal overall parameter used by RiskMetrics™ has been $\lambda^{RM} = 0.94$.

2.2.4.2   Adaptive volatility estimation

Exponential smoothing can be interpreted intuitively using a restatement of the formula for generating volatility estimates. Instead of writing the volatility forecast σ_t^2 as a function of a sequence of past returns, it can be written as the sum of last period's forecast σ_{t-1}^2 weighted by λ, and the news between last period and today, $r_{t-1,t}^2$, *weighted by the residual weight* $1 - \lambda$:

$$\sigma_t^2 = \lambda\sigma_{t-1}^2 + (1 - \lambda)r_{t-1,t}^2.$$

This is a recursive formula. It is equivalent to the previous formulation since the last period's forecast can be now restated as a function of the volatility of the period prior to that and of the news in between $- \sigma_{t-1}^2 = \lambda\sigma_{t-2}^2 + (1 - \lambda)r_{t-2,t-1}^2$. Plugging in σ_{t-1}^2 into the original formula, and doing so repeatedly will generate the standard RiskMetrics™ estimator, i.e., current volatility σ_t^2 is an exponentially declining function of past squared returns.

This model is commonly termed an "adaptive expectations" model. It gives the risk manager a rule that can be used to adapt prior beliefs about volatility in the face of news. If last period's estimator of volatility was low, and extreme news (i.e., returns) occurred, how should the risk manager update his or her information? The answer is to use this formula – place a weight of λ on what you believed yesterday, and a weight of $(1 - \lambda)$ on the news between yesterday and today. For example, suppose we estimated a conditional volatility of 100bp/day for a portfolio of equities. Assume we use the optimal λ – that is, $\lambda^{RM} = 0.94$. The return on the market today was –300bp. What is the new volatility forecast?

$$\sigma_t = \sqrt{(0.94*100^2 + (1 - 0.94)*(-300)^2)} = 121.65.$$

The sharp move in the market caused an increase in the volatility forecast of 21 percent. The change would have been much lower for a

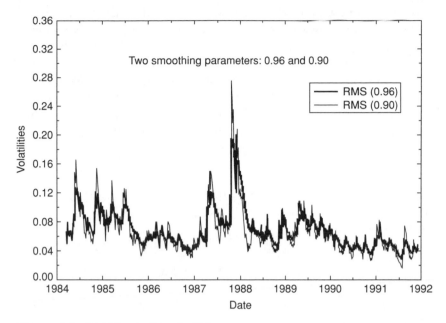

Figure 2.8 RiskMetrics™ volatilities

higher λ. A higher λ not only means more weight on recent observations, it also means that our current beliefs have not changed dramatically from what we believed to be true yesterday.

2.2.4.3   The empirical performance of RiskMetrics™

The intuitive appeal of exponential smoothing is validated in empirical tests. For a relatively large portion of the reasonable range for lambdas (most of the estimators fall above 0.90), we observe little visible difference between various volatility estimators. In figure 2.8 we see a series of rolling volatilities with two different smoothing parameters, 0.90 and 0.96. The two series are close to being superimposed on one another. There are extreme spikes using the lower lambda parameter, 0.9, but the choppiness of the forecasts in the back end that we observed with STDEV is now completely gone.[10]

2.2.4.4   GARCH

The exponential smoothing method recently gained an important extension in the form of a new time series model for volatility. In a sequence of recent academic papers Robert Engel and Tim Bollereslev introduced a new estimation methodology called GARCH, standing for General Autoregressive Conditional Heteroskedasticity. This sequence of relatively sophisticated-sounding technical terms essentially means that GARCH is a statistical time series model that enables the econometrician to model volatility as time varying and predictable. The model is similar in spirit to RiskMetrics™. In a GARCH(1,1) model the period t conditional volatility is a function of period $t - 1$ conditional volatility and the return from $t - 1$ to t squared,

$$\sigma_t^2 = a + br_{t-1,t}^2 + c\sigma_{t-1}^2,$$

where a, b, and c are parameters that need to be estimated empirically. The general version of GARCH, called GARCH(p,q), is

$$\sigma_t^2 = a + b_1 r_{t-1,t}^2 + b_2 r_{t-2,t-1}^2 + \ldots + b_p r_{t-p+1,t-p}^2$$
$$+ c_1 \sigma_{t-1}^2 + c_2 \sigma_{t-2}^2 + \ldots + c_q \sigma_{t-q}^2,$$

allowing for p lagged terms on past returns squared, and q lagged terms on past volatility.

With the growing popularity of GARCH it is worth pointing out the similarities between GARCH and other methods, as well as the possible pitfalls in using GARCH. First note that GARCH(1,1) is a generalized case of RiskMetrics™. Put differently, RiskMetrics™ is a restricted case of GARCH. To see this, consider the following two constraints on the parameters of the GARCH(1,1) process:

$$a = 0, \quad b + c = 1.$$

Substituting these two restrictions into the general form of GARCH(1,1) we can rewrite the GARCH model as follows

$$\sigma_t^2 = (1 - c)r_{t-1,t}^2 + c\sigma_{t-1}^2.$$

This is identical to the recursive version of RiskMetrics™.

The two parameter restrictions or constraints that we need to impose on GARCH(1,1) in order to get the RiskMetrics™ exponential smoothing parameter imply that GARCH is more general or less restrictive. Thus, for a given dataset, GARCH should have better explanatory power than the RiskMetrics™ approach. Since GARCH offers more degrees of freedom, it will have lower error or better describe a given set of data. The problem is that this may not constitute a real advantage in practical applications of GARCH to risk management-related situations.

In reality, we do not have the full benefit of hindsight. The challenge in reality is to predict volatility out-of-sample, not in-sample. Within sample there is no question that GARCH would perform better, simply because it is more flexible and general. The application of GARCH to risk management requires, however, forecasting ability.

The danger in using GARCH is that estimation error would generate noise that would harm the out-of-sample forecasting power. To see this consider what the econometrician interested in volatility forecasting needs to do as time progresses. As new information arrives the econometrician updates the parameters of the model to fit the new data. Estimating parameters repeatedly creates variations in the model itself, some of which are true to the change in the economic environment, and some simply due to sampling variation. The econometrician runs the risk of providing less accurate estimates using GARCH relative to the simpler RiskMetrics™ model in spite of the fact that RiskMetrics™ is a constrained version of GARCH. This is because while the RiskMetrics™ methodology has just one fixed model – a lambda parameter that is a constant (say 0.94) – GARCH is chasing a moving target. As the GARCH parameters change, forecasts change with it, partly due to true variations in the model and the state variables, and partly due to changes in the model due to estimation error. This can create model risk.

Figure 2.9 illustrates this risk empirically. In this figure we see a rolling series of GARCH forecasts, re-estimated daily using a moving window

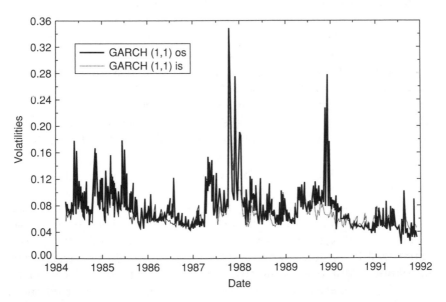

Figure 2.9   GARCH in- and out-of-sample

of 150 observations. The extreme variations in this series relative to a relatively smooth RiskMetrics™ volatility forecast series, that appears on the same graph, demonstrates the risk in using GARCH for forecasting volatility, using a short rolling window.[11]

2.2.5   Nonparametric volatility forecasting

2.2.5.1   *Historical simulation*

So far we have confined our attention to parametric volatility estimation methods. With parametric models we use all available data, weighted one way or another, in order to estimate parameters of a given distribution. Given a set of relevant parameters we can then determine percentiles of the distribution easily, and hence estimate the VaR of the return on an asset or a set of assets. Nonparametric methods estimate VaR, i.e., percentile of return distribution, directly from the data, without making assumptions about the entire distribution of returns. This is a potentially promising avenue given the phenomena we encountered so far – fat tails, skewness and so forth.

The most prominent and easiest to implement methodology within the class of nonparametric methods is historical simulation (HS). HS uses the data directly. The only thing we need to determine up front is the lookback window. Once the window length is determined, we order returns in descending order, and go directly to the tail of this ordered vector. For an estimation window of 100 observations, for example, the fifth lowest return in a rolling window of the most recent 100 returns is the fifth percentile. The lowest observation is the first percentile. If we wanted, instead, to use a 250 observations window, the fifth percentile would be somewhere between the 12th and the 13th lowest observations (a detailed discussion follows), and the first percentile would be somewhere between the second and third lowest returns.

This is obviously a very simple and convenient method, requiring the estimation of *zero* parameters (window size aside). HS can, in theory, accommodate fat tails skewness and many other peculiar properties of return series. If the "true" return distribution is fat tailed, this will come through in the HS estimate since the fifth observation will be more extreme than what is warranted by the normal distribution. Moreover, if the "true" distribution of asset returns is left skewed since market falls are more extreme than market rises, this will surface through the fact that the 5th and the 95th ordered observations will not be symmetric around zero.

This is all true in theory. With an infinite amount of data we have no difficulty estimating percentiles of the distribution directly. Suppose, for example, that asset returns are truly non-normal, and the correct model involves skewness. If we assume normality we also assume symmetry, and in spite of the fact that we have an infinite amount of data we suffer from model specification error – a problem which is insurmountable. With the HS method we could take, say, the 5,000th of 100,000 observations, a very precise estimate of the fifth percentile.

In reality, however, we do not have an infinite amount of data. What is the result of having to use a relatively small sample in practice? Quantifying the precision of percentile estimates using HS in finite samples is a rather complicated technical issue. The intuition is, however, straightforward. Percentiles around the median (the 50th percentile) are easy to estimate relatively accurately even in small samples. This is because every observation contributes to the estimation by the very fact that it is under or over the median.

Estimating extreme percentiles, such as the first or the fifth percentile, is much less precise in small samples. Consider, for example, estimating the fifth percentile in a window of 100 observations. The fifth percentile is the fifth smallest observation. Suppose that a crisis occurs and during the following ten trading days five new extreme declines were observed. The VaR using the HS method grows sharply. Suppose now that in the following few months no new extreme declines occurred. From an economic standpoint this is news – "no news is good news" is a good description here. The HS estimator of the VaR, on the other hand, reflects the same extreme tail for the following few months, until the observations fall out of the 100 day observation window. There is no updating for 90 days, starting from the ten extreme days (where the five extremes were experienced) until the ten extreme days start dropping out of the sample. This problem can become even more acute with a window of one year (250 observations) and a 1 percent VaR, that requires only the second and third lowest observations.

This problem arises because HS uses data very inefficiently. That is, out of a very small initial sample, focus on the tails requires throwing away a lot of useful information. Recall that the opposite holds true for the parametric family of methods. When the standard deviation is estimated, every data point contributes to the estimation. When

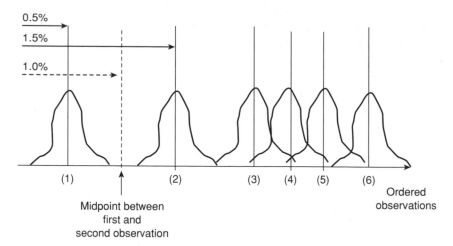

Figure 2.10 Historical simulation method

extremes are observed we update the estimator upwards, and when calm periods bring into the sample relatively small returns (in absolute value), we reduce the volatility forecast. This is an important advantage of the parametric method(s) over nonparametric methods – data are used more efficiently. Nonparametric methods' precision hinges on large samples, and falls apart in small samples.

A minor technical point related to HS is in place here. With 100 observations the first percentile could be thought of as the first observation. However, the observation itself can be thought of as a random event with a probability mass centered where the observation is actually observed, but with 50 percent of the weight to its left and 50 percent to its right. As such, the probability mass we accumulate going from minus infinity to the lowest of 100 observations is only ½ percent and not the full 1 percent. According to this argument the first percentile is somewhere in between the lowest and second lowest observation. Figure 2.10 clarifies the point.

Finally, it might be argued that we can increase the precision of HS estimates by using more data; say, 10,000 past daily observations. The issue here is one of regime relevance. Consider, for example, foreign exchange rates going back 10,000 trading days – approximately 40 years. Over the last 40 years, there have been a number of different exchange rate regimes in place, such as fixed exchange rates under Bretton Woods. Data on returns during periods of fixed exchange rates would have no relevance in forecasting volatility under floating exchange rate regimes. As a result, the risk manager using conventional HS is often forced to rely on the relatively short time period relevant to current market conditions, thereby reducing the usable number of observations for HS estimation.

2.2.5.2   Multivariate density estimation

Multivariate density estimation (MDE) is a methodology used to estimate the joint probability density function of a set of variables. For example, one could choose to estimate the joint density of returns and a set of predetermined factors such as the slope of the term structure, the inflation level, the state of the economy, and so forth. From this distribution, the conditional moments, such as the mean and volatility of returns, conditional on the economic state, can be calculated.

The MDE volatility estimate provides an intuitive alternative to the standard set of approaches to weighting past (squared) changes in determining volatility forecasts. The key feature of MDE is that the weights are no longer a constant function of time as in RiskMetrics™ or STDEV. Instead, the weights in MDE depend on how the current state of the world compares to past states of the world. If the current state of the world, as measured by the state vector x_t, is similar to a particular point in the past, then this past squared return is given a lot of weight in forming the volatility forecast, *regardless of how far back in time it is.*

For example, suppose that the econometrician attempts to estimate the volatility of interest rates. Suppose further that according to his model the volatility of interest rates is determined by the level of rates – higher rates imply higher volatility. If today's rate is, say 6 percent, then the relevant history is any point in the past when interest rates were around 6 percent. A statistical estimate of current volatility that uses past data should place high weight on the magnitude of interest rate changes during such times. Less important, although relevant, are times when interest rates were around 5.5 percent or 6.5 percent, even less important although not totally irrelevant are times when interest rates were 5 percent or 7 percent, and so on. MDE devises a weighting scheme that helps the econometrician decide how far the relevant state variable was at any point in the past from its value today. Note that to the extent that relevant state variables are going to be autocorrelated, MDE weights may look, to an extent, similar to RiskMetrics™ weights.

The critical difficulty is to select the relevant (economic) state variables for volatility. These variables should be useful in describing the economic environment in general, and be related to volatility specifically. For example, suppose that the level of inflation is related to the level of return volatility, then inflation will be a good conditioning variable. The advantages of the MDE estimate are that it can be interpreted in the context of weighted lagged returns, and that the functional form of the weights depends on the true (albeit estimated) distribution of the relevant variables.

Using the MDE method, the estimate of conditional volatility is

$$\sigma_t^2 = \sum_{i=1,2,\ldots,K} \omega(x_{t-i}) r_{t-i}^2.$$

Here, x_{t-i} is the vector of variables describing the economic state at time $t - i$ (e.g., the term structure), determining the appropriate weight $\omega(x_{t-i})$ to be placed on observation $t - i$, as a function of the "distance" of the state x_{t-i} from the current state x_t. The relative weight of "near" relative to "distant" observations from the current state is measured via the kernel function.[12]

MDE is extremely flexible in allowing us to introduce dependence on state variables. For example, we may choose to include past squared returns as conditioning variables. In doing so the volatility forecasts will depend nonlinearly on these past changes. For example, the exponentially smoothed volatility estimate can be added to an array of relevant conditioning variables. This may be an important extension to the GARCH class of models. Of particular note, the estimated volatility is still based directly on past squared returns and thus falls into the class of models that places weights on past squared returns.

The added flexibility becomes crucial when one considers cases in which there are other relevant state variables that can be added to the current state. For example, it is possible to capture: (i) the dependence of interest rate volatility on the level of interest rates; (ii) the dependence of equity volatility on current implied volatilities; and (iii) the dependence of exchange rate volatility on interest rate spreads, proximity to intervention bands, etc.

There are potential costs in using MDE. We must choose a weighting scheme (a kernel function), a set of conditioning variables, and the number of observations to be used in estimating volatility. For our purposes, the bandwidth and kernel function are chosen objectively (using standard criteria). Though they may not be optimal choices, it is important to avoid problems associated with data snooping and overfitting. While the choice of conditioning variables is at our discretion and subject to abuse, the methodology does provide a considerable

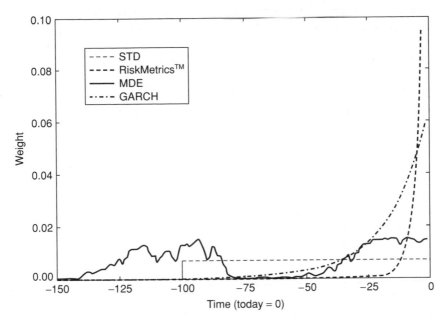

Figure 2.11   MDE weights on past returns squared

advantage. Theoretical models and existing empirical evidence may suggest relevant determinants for volatility estimation, which MDE can incorporate directly. These variables can be introduced in a straightforward way for the class of stochastic volatility models we discuss.

The most serious problem with MDE is that it is data intensive. Many data are required in order to estimate the appropriate weights that capture the joint density function of the variables. The quantity of data that is needed increases rapidly with the number of conditioning variables used in estimation. On the other hand, for many of the relevant markets this concern is somewhat alleviated since the relevant state can be adequately described by a relatively low dimensional system of factors.[13]

As an illustration of the four methodologies put together, figure 2.11 shows the weights on past squared interest rate changes as of a specific date estimated by each model. The weights for STDEV and RiskMetrics™ are the same in every period, and will vary only with the window length and the smoothing parameter. The GARCH(1,1) weighting scheme varies with the parameters, which are re-estimated every period, given each day's previous 150-day history. The date was selected at random. For that particular day, the GARCH parameter selected is $b = 0.74$. Given that this parameter is relatively low, it is not surprising that the weights decay relatively quickly. Figure 2.11 is particularly illuminating with respect to MDE. As with GARCH, the weights change over time. The weights are high for dates t through $t - 25$ (25 days prior) and then start to decay. The state variables chosen here for volatility are the level and the slope of the term structure, together providing information about the state of interest rate volatility (according to *our* choice). The weights decrease because the economic environment, as described by the interest rate level and spread, is moving further away from the conditions observed at date t. However, we observe an increase in the weights for dates $t - 80$ to $t - 120$. Economic conditions in this period (the level and spread) are similar to those at date t. MDE puts high weight on relevant information, regardless of how far in the past this information is.[14]

2.2.6   A comparison of methods

Table 2.2 compares, on a period-by-period basis, the extent to which the forecasts from the various models line up with realized future volatility. We define realized daily volatility as the average squared daily changes during the following (trading) week, from day $t + 1$ to day $t + 5$. Recall our discussion of the mean squared error. In order to benchmark various methods we need to test their accuracy vis-à-vis realized volatility – an unknown before and after the fact. If we used the realized squared return during the day following each volatility forecast we run into estimation error problems. On the other hand

Table 2.2   A comparison of methods

	STDEV	RiskMetrics™	MDE	GARCH
Mean	0.070	0.067	0.067	0.073
Std. Dev	0.022	0.029	0.024	0.030
Autocorr.	0.999	0.989	0.964	0.818
MSE	0.999	0.930	0.887	1.115
		Linear regression		
Beta	0.577	0.666	0.786	0.559
(s.e.)	(0.022)	(0.029)	(0.024)	(0.030)
R^2	0.100	0.223	0.214	0.172

if we measure realized volatility as standard deviation during the following month, we run the risk of inaccuracy due to over aggregation because volatility may shift over a month's time period. The tradeoff between longer and shorter horizons going forward is similar to the tradeoff discussed in section 2.2.3 regarding the length of the lookback window in calculating STDEV. We will use the realized volatility, as measured by mean squared deviation during the five trading days following each forecast. Interest rate changes are mean-adjusted using the sample mean of the previous 150-day estimation period.

The comparison between realized and forecasted volatility is done in two ways. First, we compare the out-of-sample performance over the entire period using the mean-squared error of the forecasts. That is, we take the difference between each model's volatility forecast and the realized volatility, square this difference, and average through time. This is the standard MSE formulation. We also regress realized volatility on the forecasts and document the regression coefficients and R^2s.

The first part of table 2.2 documents some summary statistics that are quite illuminating. First, while all the means of the volatility forecasts are of a similar order of magnitude (approximately seven basis points per day), the standard deviations are quite different, with the most volatile forecast provided by GARCH(1,1). This result is somewhat surprising because GARCH(1,1) is supposed to provide a relatively smooth volatility estimate (due to the moving average term). However, for rolling, out-of-sample forecasting, the variability of the parameter estimates from sample to sample induces variability in the forecasts. These results are, however, upwardly biased, since GARCH would commonly require much more data to yield stable parameter estimates. Here we re-estimate GARCH every day using a 150-day lookback period. From a practical perspective, this finding of unstable forecasts for volatility is a model disadvantage. In particular, to the extent that such numbers serve as inputs in setting time-varying rules in a risk management system (for example, by setting trading limits), smoothness of these rules is necessary to avoid large swings in positions.

Regarding the forecasting performance of the various volatility models, table 2.2 provides the mean squared error measure (denoted MSE). For this particular sample and window length, MDE minimizes the MSE, with the lowest MSE of 0.887. RiskMetrics™ (using $\lambda = 0.94$ as the smoothing parameter) also performs well, with an MSE of 0.930.

Note that this comparison involves just one particular GARCH model (i.e., GARCH(1,1)), over a short estimation window, and does not necessarily imply anything about other specifications and window lengths. One should investigate other window lengths and specifications, as well as other data series, to reach general conclusions regarding model comparisons. It is interesting to note, however, that, nonstationarity aside, exponentially smoothed volatility is a special case of GARCH(1,1) in sample, as discussed earlier. The results here suggest, however, the potential cost of the error in estimation of the GARCH smoothing parameters on an out-of-sample basis.

An alternative approach to benchmarking the various volatility-forecasting methods is via linear regression of realized volatility on the forecast. If the conditional volatility is measured without error, then the slope coefficient (or beta) should equal one. However, if the forecast is unbiased but contains estimation error, then the coefficient will be biased downwards. Deviations from one reflect a combination of this estimation error plus any systematic over- or underestimation. The ordering in this "horse race" is quite similar to the previous one. In particular, MDE exhibits the beta coefficient closest to one (0.786), and exponentially smoothed volatility comes in second, with a beta parameter of 0.666. The goodness of fit measure, the R^2 of each of the regressions, is similar for both methods.

2.2.7   The hybrid approach

The hybrid approach combines the two simplest approaches (for our sample), HS and RiskMetrics™, by estimating the percentiles of the return directly (similar to HS), and using exponentially declining weights on past data (similar to RiskMetrics™). The approach starts with ordering the returns over the observation period just like the HS approach. While the HS approach attributes equal weights to each observation in building the conditional empirical distribution, the hybrid approach attributes exponentially declining weights to historical returns. Hence, while obtaining the 1 percent VaR using 250 daily returns involves identifying the third lowest observation in the HS approach, it may involve more or less observations in the hybrid approach. The exact number of observations will depend on whether the extreme low returns were observed recently or further in the past. The weighting scheme is similar to the one applied in the exponential smoothing (EXP hence) approach.

The hybrid approach is implemented in three steps:

Step 1: Denote by $r_{t-1,1}$ the realized return from $t - 1$ to t. To each of the most recent K returns: $r_{t-1,t},\ r_{t-2,t-1},\ \ldots,\ r_{t-K,t-k-1}$ assign a weight $[(1 - \lambda)/(1 - \lambda^K)]$, $[(1 - \lambda)/(1 - \lambda^K)]\lambda,\ \ldots,$ $[(1 - \lambda)/(1 - \lambda^K)]\lambda^{K-1}$, respectively. Note that the constant $[(1 - \lambda)/(1 - \lambda^K)]$ simply ensures that the weights sum to one.

Step 2: Order the returns in ascending order.

Step 3: In order to obtain the x percent VaR of the portfolio, start from the lowest return and keep accumulating the weights until x percent is reached. Linear interpolation is used between adjacent points to achieve exactly x percent of the distribution.

Consider the following example, we examine the VaR of a given series at a given point in time, and a month later, assuming that no extreme observations were realized during the month. The parameters are $\lambda = 0.98$, $K = 100$.

The top half of table 2.3 shows the ordered returns at the initial date. Since we assume that over the course of a month no extreme

Table 2.3 The hybrid approach – an example

Order	Return	Periods ago	Hybrid weight	Hybrid cumul. weight	HS weight	HS cumul. weight
Initial date:						
1	−3.30%	3	0.0221	0.0221	0.01	0.01
2	−2.90%	2	0.0226	0.0447	0.01	0.02
3	−2.70%	65	0.0063	0.0511	0.01	0.03
4	−2.50%	45	0.0095	0.0605	0.01	0.04
5	−2.40%	5	0.0213	0.0818	0.01	0.05
6	−2.30%	30	0.0128	0.0947	0.01	0.06
25 days later:						
1	−3.30%	28	0.0134	0.0134	0.01	0.01
2	−2.90%	27	0.0136	0.0270	0.01	0.02
3	−2.70%	90	0.0038	0.0308	0.01	0.03
4	−2.50%	70	0.0057	0.0365	0.01	0.04
5	−2.40%	30	0.0128	0.0494	0.01	0.05
6	−2.30%	55	0.0077	0.0571	0.01	0.06

returns are observed, the ordered returns 25 days later are the same. These returns are, however, further in the past. The last two columns show the equally weighted probabilities under the HS approach. Assuming an observation window of 100 days, the HS approach estimates the 5 percent *VaR* to be 2.35 percent for both cases (note that VaR is the negative of the actual return). This is obtained using interpolation on the actual historical returns. That is, recall that we assume that half of a given return's weight is to the right and half to the left of the actual observation (see figure 2.10). For example, the −2.40 percent return represents 1 percent of the distribution in the HS approach, and we assume that this weight is split evenly between the intervals from the actual observation to points halfway to the next highest and lowest observations. As a result, under the HS approach, −2.40 percent represents the 4.5th percentile, and the distribution of weight leads to the 2.35 percent VaR (halfway between 2.40 percent and 2.30 percent).

In contrast, the hybrid approach departs from the equally weighted HS approach. Examining first the initial period, table 2.3 shows that the cumulative weight of the −2.90 percent return is 4.47 percent and 5.11 percent for the −2.70 percent return. To obtain the 5 percent VaR for the initial period, we must interpolate as shown in figure 2.10. We obtain a cumulative weight of 4.79 percent for the −2.80 percent return. Thus, the 5th percentile VaR under the hybrid approach for the initial period lies somewhere between 2.70 percent and 2.80 percent. We define the required VaR level as a linearly interpolated return, where the distance to the two adjacent cumulative weights determines the return. In this case, for the initial period the 5 percent VaR under the hybrid approach is:

$$2.80\% - (2.80\% - 2.70\%)*[(0.05 - 0.0479)/(0.0511 - 0.0479)]$$

$$= 2.73\%.$$

Similarly, the hybrid approach estimate of the 5 percent VaR 25 days later can be found by interpolating between the −2.40 percent return (with a cumulative weight of 4.94 percent) and −2.35 percent (with a cumulative weight of 5.33 percent, interpolated from the values on table 2.3). Solving for the 5 percent VaR:

$$2.35\% - (2.35\% - 2.30\%)*[(0.05 - 0.0494)/(0.0533 - 0.0494)]$$

$$= 2.34\%.$$

Thus, the hybrid approach initially estimates the 5 percent VaR as 2.73 percent. As time goes by and no large returns are observed, the VaR estimate smoothly declines to 2.34 percent. In contrast, the HS approach yields a constant 5 percent VaR over both periods of 2.35 percent, thereby failing to incorporate the information that returns were stable over the two month period. Determining which methodology is appropriate requires backtesting (see Appendix 2.1).

2.3   RETURN AGGREGATION AND VaR

Our discussion of the HS and hybrid methods missed one key point so far. How do we aggregate a number of positions into a single VaR number for a portfolio comprised of a number of positions? The answer to this question in the RiskMetrics™ and STDEV approaches is simple – under the assumption that asset returns are jointly normal, the return on a portfolio is also normally distributed. Using the variance–covariance matrix of asset returns we can calculate portfolio volatility and VaR. This is the reason for the fact that the RiskMetrics™ approach is commonly termed the Variance–Covariance approach (VarCov).

The HS approach needs one more step – missing so far from our discussion – before we can determine the VaR of a portfolio of positions. This is the aggregation step. The idea is simply to aggregate each period's historical returns, weighted by the relative size of the position. This is where the method gets its name – "simulation". We calculate returns using historical data, but using today's weights. Suppose for example that we hold today positions in three equity portfolios – indexed to the S&P 500 index, the FTSE index and the Nikkei 225 index – in equal amounts. These equal weights are going to be used to calculate the return we would have gained J days ago if we were to hold this equally weighted portfolio. This is regardless of the fact that our equity portfolio J days ago may have been completely different. That is, we pretend that the portfolio we hold today is the portfolio we held up to K days into the past (where K is our lookback window size) and calculate the returns that would have been earned.

From an implementation perspective this is very appealing and simple. This approach has another important advantage – note that we do not estimate any parameters whatsoever. For a portfolio involving N positions the VarCov approach requires the estimation of N volatilities and $N(N - 1)/2$ correlations. This is potentially a very large number, exposing the model to estimation error. Another important issue is related to the estimation of correlation. It is often argued that when markets fall, they fall together. If, for example, we see an abnormally large decline of 10 percent in the S&P index on a given day, we strongly believe that other components of the portfolio, e.g., the Nikkei position and the FTSE position, will also fall sharply. This is regardless of the fact that we may have estimated a correlation of, for example, 0.30 between the Nikkei and the other two indexes under more normal market conditions (see Longin and Solnik (2001)).

The possibility that markets move together at the extremes to a greater degree than what is implied by the estimated correlation parameter poses a serious problem to the risk manager. A risk manager using the VarCov approach is running the risk that his VaR estimate for the position is understated. At the extremes the benefits of diversification disappear. Using the HS approach with the initial aggregation step may offer an interesting solution. First, note that we do not need to estimate correlation parameters (nor do we need to estimate volatility parameters). If, on a given day, the S&P dropped 10 percent, the Nikkei dropped 12 percent and the FTSE dropped 8 percent, then an equally weighted portfolio will show a drop of 10 percent – the average of the three returns. The following step of the HS methods is to order the observations in ascending order and pick the fifth of 100 observations (for the 5 percent VaR, for example). If the tails are extreme, and if markets co-move over and above the estimated correlations, it will be taken into account through the aggregated data itself.

Figure 2.12 provides a schematic of the two alternatives. Given a set of historical data and current weights we can either use the variance-covariance matrix in the VarCov approach, or aggregate the returns and then order them in the HS approach. There is an obvious third alternative methodology emerging from this figure. We may estimate the volatility (and mean) of the vector of aggregated returns and assuming normality calculate the VaR of the portfolio.

Is this approach sensible? If we criticize the normality assumption we should go with the HS approach. If we believe normality we should take the VarCov approach. What is the validity of this intermediate approach of aggregating first, as in the HS approach, and only then assuming normality as in the VarCov approach? The answer lies in one of the most important theorems in statistics, the strong law of large numbers. Under certain assumptions it is the case that an average of a very large number of random variables will end up converging to a normal random variable.

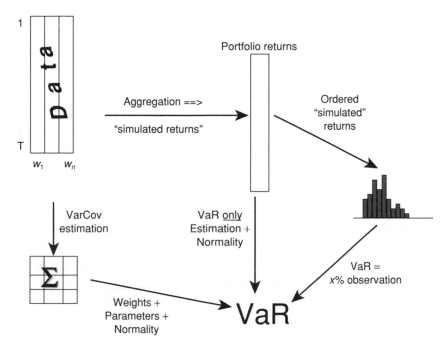

Figure 2.12 VaR and aggregation

It is, in principle, possible, for the specific components of the portfolio to be non-normal, but for the portfolio as a whole to be normally distributed. In fact, we are aware of many such examples. Consider daily stock returns for example. Daily returns on specific stocks are often far from normal, with extreme moves occurring for different stocks at different times. The aggregate, well-diversified portfolio of these misbehaved stocks, could be viewed as normal (informally, we may say the portfolio is more normal than its component parts – a concept that could easily be quantified and is often tested to be true in the academic literature). This is a result of the strong law of large numbers.

Similarly here we could think of normality being regained, in spite of the fact that the single components of the portfolio are nonnormal. This holds only if the portfolio is well diversified. If we hold a portfolio comprised entirely of oil- and gas-related exposures, for example, we may hold a large number of positions that are all susceptible to sharp movements in energy prices.

This last approach – of combining the first step of aggregation with the normality assumption that requires just a single parameter estimate – is gaining popularity and is used by an increasing number of risk managers.

2.4 IMPLIED VOLATILITY AS A PREDICTOR OF FUTURE VOLATILITY

Thus far our discussion has focused on various methods that involve using historical data in order to estimate future volatility. Many risk managers describe managing risk this way as similar to driving by looking in the rear-view mirror. When extreme circumstances arise in financial markets an immediate reaction, and preferably even a preliminary indication, are of the essence. Historical risk estimation techniques require time in order to adjust to changes in market conditions. These methods suffer from the shortcoming that they may follow, rather than forecast risk events. Another worrisome issue is that a key assumption in all of these methods is stationarity; that is, the assumption that the past is indicative of the future.

Financial markets provide us with a very intriguing alternative – option-implied volatility. Implied volatility can be imputed from derivative prices using a specific derivative pricing model. The simplest example is the Black–Scholes implied volatility imputed from equity option prices. The implementation is fairly simple, with a few technical issues along the way. In the presence of multiple implied volatilities for various option maturities and exercise prices, it is common to take the at-the-money (ATM) implied volatility from puts and calls and extrapolate an average implied; this implied is derived from the most liquid (ATM) options. This implied volatility is a candidate to be used in risk measurement models in place of historical volatility. The advantage of implied volatility is that it is a forward-looking, predictive measure.

A particularly strong example of the advantage obtained by using implied volatility (in contrast to historical volatility) as a predictor of future volatility is the GBP currency crisis of 1992. During the summer of 1992, the GBP came under pressure as a result of the expectation that it should be devalued relative to the European Currency Unit (ECU) components, the deutschmark (DM) in particular (at the time the strongest currency within the ECU). During the weeks preceding the final drama of the GBP devaluation, many signals were present in the public domain. The British Central Bank raised the GBP interest rate. It also attempted to convince the Bundesbank to lower the DM

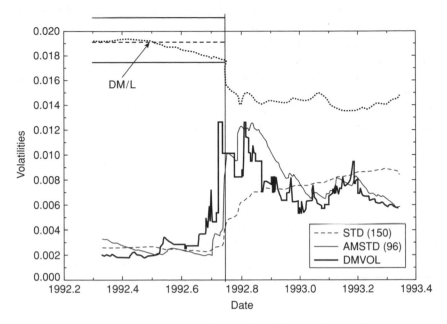

Figure 2.13 Implied and historical volatility: the GBP during the ERM crisis of 1992

interest rate, but to no avail. Speculative pressures reached a peak toward summer's end, and the British Central Bank started losing currency reserves, trading against large hedge funds such as the Soros fund.

The market was certainly aware of these special market conditions, as shown in figure 2.13. The top dotted line is the DM/GBP exchange rate, which represents our "event clock." The event is the collapse of the exchange rate. Figure 2.13 shows the Exchange Rate Mechanism (ERM) intervention bands. As was the case many times prior to this event, the most notable predictor of devaluation was already present – the GBP is visibly close to the intervention band. A currency so close to the intervention band is likely to be under attack by speculators on the one hand, and under intervention by the central banks on the other. This was the case many times prior to this event, especially with the Italian lira's many devaluations. Therefore, the market was prepared for a crisis in the GBP during the summer of 1992. Observing the thick solid line depicting option-implied volatility, the growing pressure on the GBP manifests itself in options prices and volatilities. Historical volatility is trailing, "unaware" of the pressure. In this case, the situation is particularly problematic since historical volatility happens to decline as implied volatility rises. The fall in historical volatility is due to the fact that movements close to the intervention band are bound to be smaller by the fact of the intervention bands' existence and the nature of intervention, thereby dampening the historical measure of volatility just at the time that a more predictive measure shows increases in volatility.

As the GBP crashed, and in the following couple of days, RiskMetrics™ volatility increased quickly (thin solid line). However, simple STDEV ($K = 50$) badly trailed events – it does not rise in time, nor does it fall in time. This is, of course, a particularly sharp example, the result of the intervention band preventing markets from fully reacting to information. As such, this is a unique example. Does it generalize to all other assets? Is it the case that implied volatility is a superior predictor of future volatility, and hence a superior risk measurement tool, relative to historical? It would seem as if the answer must be affirmative, since implied volatility can react immediately to market conditions. As a predictor of future volatility this is certainly an important feature.

Implied volatility is not free of shortcomings. The most important reservation stems from the fact that implied volatility is model-dependent. A misspecified model can result in an erroneous forecast. Consider the Black–Scholes option-pricing model. This model hinges on a few assumptions, one of which is that the underlying asset follows a continuous time lognormal diffusion process. The underlying assumption is that the volatility parameter is constant from the present time to the maturity of the contract. The implied volatility is supposedly this parameter. In reality, volatility is not constant over the life of the options contract. Implied volatility varies through time. Oddly, traders trade options in "vol" terms, the volatility of the underlying, fully aware that (i) this vol is implied from a constant volatility model, and (ii) that this very same option will trade tomorrow at a different vol, which will also be assumed to be constant over the remaining life of the contract.

Yet another problem is that at a given point in time, options on the same underlying may trade at different vols. An example is the *smile effect* – deep out of the money (especially) and deep in the money (to a lesser extent) options trade at a higher vol than at the money options.[15]

The key is that the option-pricing model provides a convenient nonlinear transformation allowing traders to compare options with different maturities and exercise prices. The true underlying process is not a lognormal diffusion with constant volatility as posited by the model. The underlying process exhibits stochastic volatility, jumps, and a non-normal conditional distribution. The vol parameter serves as a "kitchen-sink" parameter. The market converses in vol terms, adjusting for the possibility of sharp declines (the smile effect) and variations in volatility.

The latter effect – stochastic volatility, results in a particularly difficult problem for the use of implied volatility as a predictor of future volatility. To focus on this particular issue, consider an empirical exercise repeatedly comparing the 30-day implied volatility with the empirically measured volatility during the following month. Clearly, the forecasts (i.e., implied) should be equal to the realizations (i.e., measured return standard deviation) only on average. It is well understood that forecast series are bound to be smoother series, as expectations series always are relative to realization series. A reasonable requirement is, nevertheless, that implied volatility should be equal, on average, to realized volatility. This is a basic requirement of every forecast instrument – it should be unbiased.

Empirical results indicate, strongly and consistently, that implied volatility is, on average, greater than realized volatility. From a modeling perspective this raises many interesting questions, focusing on this empirical fact as a possible key to extending and improving option pricing models. There are, broadly, two common explanations. The first is a market inefficiency story, invoking supply and demand issues. This story is incomplete, as many market-inefficiency stories are, since it does not account for the presence of free entry and nearly perfect competition in derivative markets. The second, rational markets, explanation for the phenomenon is that implied volatility is greater than realized volatility due to stochastic volatility. Consider the following facts: (i) volatility is stochastic; (ii) volatility is a priced source of risk; and (iii) the underlying model (e.g., the Black–Scholes model) is, hence, misspecified, assuming constant volatility. The result is that the premium required by the market for stochastic volatility will manifest itself in the forms we saw above – implied volatility would be, on average, greater than realized volatility.

From a risk management perspective this bias, which can be expressed as $\sigma_{implied} = \sigma_{true} + Stoch.Vol.Premium$, poses a problem for the use of implied volatility as a predictor for future volatility. Correcting for this premium is difficult since the premium is unknown, and requires the "correct" model in order to measure precisely. The only thing we seem to know about this premium is that it is on average positive, since implied volatility is on average greater than historical volatility.

It is an empirical question, then, whether we are better off with historical volatility or implied volatility as the predictor of choice for future volatility. Many studies have attempted to answer this question with a consensus emerging that implied volatility is a superior estimate. This result would have been even sharper if these studies were to focus on the responsiveness of implied and historical to sharp increases in conditional volatility. Such times are particularly important for risk managers, and are the primary shortcoming associated with models using the historical as opposed to the implied volatility.

In addition to the upward bias incorporated in the measures of implied volatility, there is another more fundamental problem associated with replacing historical volatility with implied volatility measures. It is available for very few assets/market factors. In a covariance matrix of 400 by 400 (approximately the number of assets/markets that RiskMetrics™ uses), very few entries can be filled with implied volatilities because of the sparsity of options trading on the underlying assets. The use of implied volatility is confined to highly concentrated portfolios where implied volatilities are present. Moreover, recall that with more than one pervasive factor as a measure of portfolio risk, one would also need an implied correlation. Implied correlations are hard to come by. In fact, the only place where reliable liquid implied correlations could be imputed is in currency markets.[16]

As a result, implied volatility measures can only be used for fairly concentrated portfolios with high foreign exchange rate risk exposure. Where available, implied volatility can always be compared in real time to historical (e.g., RiskMetrics™) volatility. When implied volatilities get misaligned by more than a certain threshold level (say, 25 percent difference), then the risk manager has an objective "red light" indication. This type of rule may help in the decision making process of risk limit readjustment in the face of changing market conditions. In the discussion between risk managers and traders, the comparison of historical to implied can serve as an objective judge.[17]

2.5 LONG HORIZON VOLATILITY AND VaR

In many current applications, e.g., such as by mutual fund managers, there is a need for volatility and VaR forecasts for horizons longer than a day or a week. The simplest approach uses the "square root rule," discussed briefly in Chapter 1. Under certain assumptions, to be discussed below, the rule states that an asset's *J*-period return volatility is equal to the square root of J times the single period return volatility

$$\sigma(r_{t,t+J}) = \surd(J) \times \sigma(r_{t,t+1}).$$

Similarly for VaR this rule is

$$J\text{-period VaR} = \surd(J) \times 1\text{-period VaR}.$$

The rule hinges on a number of key assumptions. It is important to go through the proof of this rule in order to examine its limits. Consider, first, the multiperiod continuously compounded rate of return. For simplicity consider the two-period return:

$$r_{t,t+2} = r_{t,t+1} + r_{t+1,t+2}.$$

The variance of this return is

$$\text{var}(r_{t,t+2}) = \text{var}(r_{t,t+1}) + \text{var}(r_{t+1,t+2}) + 2{*}\text{cov}(r_{t,t+1}, r_{t+1,t+2}).$$

Assuming:

$$A1: \quad \text{cov}(r_{t,t+1}, r_{t+1,t+2}) = 0,$$

$$A2: \quad \text{var}(r_{t,t+1}) = \text{var}(r_{t+1,t+2}),$$

we get

$$\text{var}(r_{t,t+2}) = 2{*}\text{var}(r_{t,t+1}),$$

and hence

$$\text{STD}(r_{t,t+2}) = \surd(2){*}\text{STD}(r_{t,t+1}).$$

Which is the square root rule for two periods. The rule generalizes easily to the J period rule.

The first assumption is the assumption of non-predictability, or the random walk assumption. The term $\text{cov}(r_{t,t+1}, r_{t+1,t+2})$ is the autocovariance of returns. Intuitively the autocovariance being zero means that knowledge that today's return is, for example, positive, tells us nothing with respect to tomorrow's return. Hence this is also a direct result of the random walk assumption, a standard market efficiency

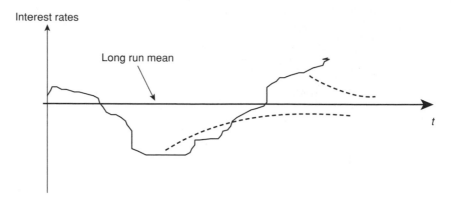

Figure 2.14   Mean reverting process

assumption. The second assumption states that the volatility is the same in every period (i.e., on each day).

In order to question the empirical validity of the rule, we need to question the assumptions leading to this rule. The first assumption of non-predictability holds well for most asset return series in financial markets. Equity returns are unpredictable at short horizons. The evidence contrary to this assertion is scant and usually attributed to luck. The same is true for currencies. There is some evidence of predictability at long horizons (years) for both, but the extent of predictability is relatively small. This is not the case, though, for many fixed-income-related series such as interest rates and especially spreads.

Interest rates and spreads are commonly believed to be predictable to varying degrees, and modeling predictability is often done through time series models accounting for autoregression. An autoregressive process is a stationary process that has a long run mean, an average level to which the series tends to revert. This average is often called the "Long Run Mean" (LRM). Figure 2.14 represents a schematic of interest rates and their long run mean. The dashed lines represent the expectations of the interest rate process. When interest rates are below their LRM they are expected to rise and vice versa.

Mean reversion has an important effect on long-term volatility. To understand the effect, note that the autocorrelation of interest rate changes is no longer zero. If increases and decreases in interest rates (or spreads) are expected to be reversed, then the serial covariance is negative. This means that the long horizon volatility is overstated using the zero-autocovariance assumption. *In the presence of mean reversion in*

Table 2.4 Long horizon volatility

Mean reversion	$\sqrt{J}$ rule using today's volatility
In returns	overstates true long horizon volatility
In return volatility	If today's vol. > LRM vol. then overstated
	If today's vol. < LRM vol. then understated

the underlying asset's long horizon, volatility is lower than the square root times the short horizon volatility.

The second assumption is that volatility is constant. As we have seen throughout this chapter, this assumption is unrealistic. Volatility is stochastic, and, in particular, autoregressive. This is true for almost all financial assets. Volatility has a long run mean – a "steady state" of uncertainty. Note here the important difference – most financial series have an unpredictable series of returns, and hence no long run mean (LRM), with the exception of interest rates and spreads. However, most volatility series are predictable, and do have an LRM.

When current volatility is above its long run mean then we can expect a decline in volatility over the longer horizon. Extrapolating long horizon volatility using today's volatility will overstate the true expected long horizon volatility. On the other hand, if today's volatility is unusually low, then extrapolating today's volatility using the square root rule may understate true long horizon volatility. The bias – upwards or downwards, hence, depends on today's volatility relative to the LRM of volatility. The discussion is summarized in table 2.4.

2.6 MEAN REVERSION AND LONG HORIZON VOLATILITY

Modeling mean reversion in a stationary time series framework is called the analysis of autoregression (AR). We present here an AR(1) model, which is the simplest form of mean reversion in that we consider only one lag. Consider a process described by the regression of the time series variable X_t:

$$X_{t+1} = a + bX_t + e_{t+1}.$$

This is a regression of a variable on its own lag. It is often used in financial modeling of time series to describe processes that are mean reverting, such as the real exchange rate, the price/dividend or price/earnings ratio, and the inflation rate. Each of these series can be modeled using an assumption about how the underlying process is predictable. This time series process has a finite long run mean under certain restrictions, the most important of which is that the parameter b is less than one. The expected value of X_t as a function of period t information is

$$E_t[X_{t+1}] = a + bX_t.$$

We can restate the expectations as follows

$$E_t[X_{t+1}] = (1 - b)*[a/(1 - b)] + bX_t.$$

Next period's expectations are a weighted sum of today's value, X_t, and the long run mean $a/(1 - b)$. Here b is the key parameter, often termed "the speed of reversion" parameter. If $b = 1$ then the process is a random walk – a nonstationary process with an undefined (infinite) long run mean, and, therefore, next period's expected value is equal to today's value. If $b < 1$ then the process is mean reverting. When X_t is above the LRM, it is expected to decline, and vice versa.

By subtracting X_t from the autoregression formula we obtain the "return", the change in X_t

$$X_{t+1} - X_t = a + bX_t + e_{t+1} - X_t$$
$$= a + (b - 1)X_t + e_{t+1}.$$

and the two period return is

$$X_{t+2} - X_t = a + ab + b^2X_t + be_{t+1} + e_{t+2} - X_t$$
$$= a(1 + b) + (b^2 - 1)X_t + be_{t+1} + e_{t+2}.$$

The single period conditional variance of the rate of change is

$$\text{var}_t(X_{t+1} - X_t) = \text{var}_t(a + bX_t + e_{t+1} - X_t)$$
$$= \text{var}_t(e_{t+1})$$
$$= \sigma^2.$$

The volatility of e_{t+1} is denoted by σ. The two period volatility is

$$\mathrm{var}_t(X_{t+2} - X_t) = \mathrm{var}_t(a(1 + b) + (b^2 - 1)X_t + be_{t+1} + e_{t+2})$$

$$= \mathrm{var}_t(be_{t+1} + e_{t+2})$$

$$= (1 + b^2)*\sigma^2.$$

This is the key point – the single period variance is σ^2. The two period variance is $(1 + b^2)\sigma^2$ which is less than $2\sigma^2$, note that if the process was a random walk, i.e., $b = 1$, then we would get the standard square root volatility result. The square root volatility fails due to mean reversion. That is, with no mean reversion, the two period volatility would be $\sqrt{(2)}\sigma = 1.41\sigma$. With mean reversion, e.g., for $b = 0.9$, the two period volatility is, instead, $\sqrt{(1 + 0.9^2)}\sigma = 1.34\sigma$.

The insight, that mean reversion effects conditional volatility and hence risk is very important, especially in the context of arbitrage strategies. Risk managers often have to assess the risk of trading strategies with a vastly different view of risk. The trader may view a given trade as a convergence trade. Convergence trades assume explicitly that the spread between two positions, a long and a short, is mean reverting. If the mean reversion is strong, than the long horizon risk is smaller than the square root volatility. This may create a sharp difference of opinions on the risk assessment of a trade. It is common for risk managers to keep a null hypothesis of market efficiency – that is, that the spread underlying the convergence trade is random walk.

2.7   CORRELATION MEASUREMENT

Thus far, we have confined our attention to volatility estimation and related issues. There are similar issues that arise when estimating correlations. For example, there is strong evidence that exponentially declining weights provide benefits in correlation estimation similar to the benefits in volatility estimation. There are two specific issues related to correlation estimation that require special attention. The first is correlation breakdown during market turmoil. This will be discussed in chapter 3, in the context of stress testing and scenario analysis. The second issue is an important technical issue – the problem of using nonsynchronous data.

The problem arises when sampling daily data from market closing prices or rates, where the closing time is different for different series. We use here the example of US and Japanese interest rate changes, where the closing time in the US is 4:00 p.m. EST, whereas the Japanese market closes at 1:00 a.m. EST, fifteen hours earlier. Any information that is relevant for global interest rates (e.g., changes in oil prices) coming out after 1:00 a.m. EST and before 4:00 p.m. EST will influence today's interest rates in the US and tomorrow's interest rates in Japan.

Recall that the correlation between two assets is the ratio of their covariance divided by the product of their standard deviations

$$\text{corr}(\Delta i_{t,t+1}{}^{US}, \Delta i_{t,t+1}{}^{Jap})$$

$$= \text{cov}(\Delta i_{t,t+1}{}^{US}, \Delta i_{t,t+1}{}^{Jap})/\{\text{STD}(\Delta i_{t,t+1}{}^{US})*\text{STD}(\Delta i_{t,t+1}{}^{Jap})\}.$$

Assume that the daily standard deviation is estimated correctly irrespective of the time zone. The volatility of close-to-close equites covers 24 hours in any time zone. However, the covariance term is *underestimated* due to the nonsynchronisity problem.

The problem may be less important for portfolios of few assets, but as the number of assets increases, the problem becomes more and more acute. Consider for example an equally weighted portfolio consisting of n assets, all of which have the same daily standard deviation, denoted σ and the same cross correlation, denoted ρ. The variance of the portfolio would be

$$\sigma_p^2 = (1/n)\sigma^2 + (1 - 1/n)\rho\sigma^2.$$

The first term is due to the own asset variances, and the second term is due to the cross covariance terms. For a large n, the volatility of the portfolio is $\rho\sigma^2$, which is the standard deviation of each asset scaled down by the correlation parameter. The bias in the covariance would translate one-for-one into a bias in the portfolio volatility.

For US and Japanese ten year zero coupon rate changes for example, this may result in an understatement of portfolio volatilities by up to 50 percent relative to their true volatility. For a global portfolio of long positions this will result in a severe understatement of the portfolio's risk. Illusionary diversification benefits will result in lower-than-true VaR estimates.

There are a number of solutions to the problem. One solution could be sampling both market open and market close quotes in order to make the data more synchronous. This is, however, costly because more data are required, quotes may not always be readily available and quotes may be imprecise. Moreover, this is an incomplete solution since some nonsynchronicity still remains. There are two other alternative avenues for amending the problem and correcting for the correlation in the covariance term. Both alternatives are simple and appealing from a theoretical and an empirical standpoint.

The first alternative is based on a natural extension of the random walk assumption. The random walk assumption assumes consecutive daily returns are independent. In line with the independence assumption, assume intraday independence – e.g., consecutive hourly returns – are independent. Assume further, for the purpose of demonstration, that the US rate is sampled without a lag, whereas the Japanese rate is sampled with some lag. That is, 4:00 p.m. EST is the "correct" time for accurate and up to the minute sampling, and hence a 1:00 a.m. EST. quote is stale. The true covariance is

$$\text{cov}^{tr}(\Delta i_{t,t+1}{}^{US}, \Delta i_{t,t+1}{}^{Jap})$$
$$= \text{cov}^{obs}(\Delta i_{t,t+1}{}^{US}, \Delta i_{t,t+1}{}^{Jap}) + \text{cov}^{obs}(\Delta i_{t,t+1}{}^{US}, \Delta i_{t+1,t+2}{}^{Jap}),$$

a function of the contemporaneous observed covariance plus the covariance of today's US change with tomorrow's change in Japan.

The second alternative for measuring true covariance is based on another assumption in addition to the independence assumption; the assumption that the intensity of the information flow is constant intraday, and that the Japanese prices/rates are 15 hours behind US prices/rates. In this case

$$\text{cov}^{tr}(\Delta i_{t,t+1}{}^{US}, \Delta i_{t,t+1}{}^{Jap}) = [24/(24 - 15)]*\text{cov}^{obs}(\Delta i_{t,t+1}{}^{US}, \Delta i_{t,t+1}{}^{Jap}).$$

The intuition behind the result is that we observe a covariance which is the result of a partial overlap, of only 9 out of 24 hours. If we believe the intensity of news throughout the 24 hour day is constant than we need to inflate the covariance by multiplying it by $24/9 = 2.66$. This method may result in a peculiar outcome, that the correlation is greater than one, a result of the assumptions. This factor will transfer directly to the correlation parameter – the numerator of which increases by a factor of 2.66, while the denominator remains the same. The factor by which we need to inflate the covariance term falls as the level of nonsynchronicity declines. With London closing 6 hours prior to New York, the factor is smaller – $24/(24 - 6) = 1.33$.

Both alternatives rely on the assumption of independence and simply extend it in a natural way from interday to intraday independence.

This concept is consistent, in spirit, with the kind of assumptions backing up most extant risk measurement engines. The first alternative relies only on independence, but requires the estimation of one additional covariance moment. The second alternative assumes in addition to independence that the intensity of news flow is constant throughout the trading day. Its advantage is that it requires no further estimation.[18]

2.8   SUMMARY

This chapter addressed the motivation for and practical difficulty in creating a dynamic risk measurement methodology to quantify VaR. The motivation for dynamic risk measurement is the recognition that risk varies through time in an economically meaningful and in a predictable manner. One of the many results of this intertemporal volatility in asset returns distributions is that the magnitude and likelihood of tail events changes though time. This is critical for the risk manager in determining prudent risk measures, position limits, and risk allocation.

Time variations are often exhibited in the form of fat tails in asset return distributions. One attempt is to incorporate the empirical observation of fat tails is to allow volatility to vary through time. Variations in volatility can create deviations from normality, but to the extent that we can measure and predict volatility through time we may be able to recapture normality in the conditional versions, i.e., we may be able to model asset returns as conditionally normal with time-varying distributions.

As it turns out, while indeed volatility is time-varying, it is not the case that extreme tails events disappear once we allow for volatility to vary through time. It is still the case that asset returns are, even conditionally, fat tailed. This is the key motivation behind extensions of standard VaR estimates obtained using historical data to incorporate scenario analysis and stress testing. This is the focus of the next chapter.

APPENDIX 2.1   BACKTESTING METHODOLOGY AND RESULTS

In Section 2.2, we discussed the MSE and regression methods for comparing standard deviation forecasts. Next, we present a more detailed discussion of the methodology for backtesting VaR methodologies. The dynamic VaR estimation algorithm provides an estimate of the x percent VaR for the sample period for each of the methods. Therefore, the probability of observing a return lower than the calculated VaR should be x percent:

$$\text{prob}[r_{t-1,t} < -VaR_t] = x\%.$$

There are a few attributes which are desirable for VaR_t. We can think of an indicator variable I_t, which is 1 if the VaR is exceeded, and 0 otherwise. There is no direct way to observe whether our VaR estimate is precise; however, a number of different indirect measurements will, together, create a picture of its precision.

The first desirable attribute is *unbiasedness*. Specifically, we require that the VaR estimate be the x percent tail. Put differently, we require that the average of the indicator variable I_t should be x percent:

$$\text{avg}[I_t] = x\%.$$

This attribute alone is an insufficient benchmark. To see this, consider the case of a VaR estimate which is constant through time, but is also highly precise unconditionally (i.e., achieves an average VaR probability which is close to x percent). To the extent that tail probability is cyclical, the occurrences of violations of the VaR estimate will be "bunched up" over a particular state of the economy. This is a very undesirable property, since we require dynamic updating which is sensitive to market conditions.

Consequently, the second attribute which we require of a VaR estimate is that extreme events do not "bunch up." Put differently, a VaR estimate should increase as the tail of the distribution rises. If a large return is observed today, the VaR should rise to make the probability of another tail event exactly x percent tomorrow. In terms of the indicator variable, I_t, we essentially require that I_t be independently and identically distributed (i.i.d.). This requirement is similar to saying that the VaR estimate should provide a filter to transform a serially dependent return volatility and tail probability into a serially independent I_t series.

The simplest way to assess the extent of independence here is to examine the empirical properties of the tail event occurrences, and compare them to the theoretical ones. Under the null that I_t is independent over time

$$\text{corr}[I_{t-s} * I_t] = 0 \quad \forall s,$$

that is, the indicator variable should not be autocorrelated at any lag. Since the tail probabilities that are of interest tend to be small, it is very difficult to make a distinction between pure luck and persistent error in the above test for any individual correlation. Consequently, we consider a joint test of whether the first five daily autocorrelations (one trading week) are equal to zero.

Note that for both measurements the desire is essentially to put all data periods on an equal footing in terms of the tail probability. As such, when we examine a number of data series for a given method, we can aggregate across data series, and provide an average estimate of the unbiasedness and the independence of the tail event probabilities. While the different data series may be correlated, such an aggregate improves our statistical power.

The third property which we examine is related to the first property – the biasedness of the VaR series, and the second property – the autocorrelation of tail events. We calculate a rolling measure of the absolute percentage error. Specifically, for any given period, we look forward 100 periods and ask how many tail events were realized. If the indicator variable is both unbiased and independent, this number is supposed to be the VaR's percentage level, namely x. We calculate the average absolute value of the difference between the actual number of tail events and the expected number across all 100-period windows within the sample. Smaller deviations from the expected value indicate better VaR measures.

The data we use include a number of series, chosen as a representative set of "interesting" economic series. These series are interesting since we *a priori* believe that their high order moments (skewness and kurtosis) and, in particular, their tail behavior, pose different degrees of challenge to VaR estimation. The data span the period from January 1, 1991 to May 12, 1997, and include data on the following:

- DEM   the dollar/DM exchange rate;
- OIL   the spot price for Brent crude oil;
- S&P   the S&P 500 Index;
- BRD   a general Brady bond index (JP Morgan Brady Broad Index).

We have 1,663 daily continuously compounded returns for each series.

In the tables, in addition to reporting summary statistics for the four series, we also analyze results for:

- EQW   an equally weighted portfolio of the four return series
- AVG   statistics for tail events averaged across the four series.

The EQW results will give us an idea of how the methods perform when tail events are somewhat diversified (via aggregation). The AVG portfolio simply helps us increase the effective size of our sample. That is, correlation aside, the AVG statistics may be viewed as using four times more data. Its statistics are therefore more reliable, and provide a more complete picture for general risk management purposes. Therefore, in what follows, we shall refer primarily to AVG statistics, which include 6,656 observations.

In the tables we use a 250-trading day window throughout. This is, of course, an arbitrary choice, which we make in order to keep the tables short and informative. The statistics for each of the series include 1,413 returns, since 250 observations are used as back data. The AVG statistics consist of 5,652 data points, with 282 tail events expected in the 5 percent tail, and 56.5 in the 1 percent tail.

In table 2.5 we document the percentage of tail events for the 5 percent and the 1 percent VaR. There is no apparent strong preference among the models for the 5 percent VaR. The realized average

Table 2.5 Comparison of methods – results for empirical tail probabilities

	Historical STD	Historical simulation	EXP		Hybrid	
			0.97	0.99	0.97	0.99
5% Tail						
DEM	5.18	5.32	5.74	5.18	5.25	5.04
OIL	5.18	4.96	5.60	5.39	5.18	5.18
S&P	4.26	5.46	4.68	4.18	6.17	5.46
BRD	4.11	5.32	4.47	4.40	5.96	5.46
EQW	4.40	4.96	5.04	4.26	5.67	5.39
AVG	**4.62**	**5.21**	**5.11**	**4.68**	**5.65**	**5.30**
1% Tail						
DEM	1.84	1.06	2.20	1.63	1.84	1.28
OIL	1.84	1.13	1.77	1.77	1.70	1.35
S&P	2.06	1.28	2.20	2.13	1.84	1.42
BRD	2.48	1.35	2.70	2.41	1.63	1.35
EQW	1.63	1.49	1.42	1.42	1.63	1.21
AVG	**1.97**	**1.26**	**2.06**	**1.87**	**1.73**	**1.32**

Table 2.6   Rolling mean absolute percentage error of VaR

	Historical STD	Historical simulation	EXP		Hybrid	
			0.97	0.99	0.97	0.99
5% Tail						
DEM	2.42	2.42	1.58	2.11	1.08	1.77
OIL	2.84	2.62	2.36	2.67	1.93	2.44
S&P	1.95	1.91	1.52	1.85	1.72	1.68
BRD	3.41	3.53	3.01	3.34	2.54	2.97
EQW	2.43	2.36	2.48	2.33	1.50	2.20
AVG	**2.61**	**2.57**	**2.19**	**2.46**	**1.76**	**2.21**
1% Tail						
DEM	1.29	0.87	1.50	1.12	1.02	0.88
OIL	1.71	0.96	1.07	1.39	0.84	0.80
S&P	1.45	1.14	1.40	1.42	0.99	0.82
BRD	2.15	1.32	1.98	2.06	1.03	1.12
EQW	1.57	1.52	1.25	1.25	0.72	0.87
AVG	**1.63**	**1.16**	**1.44**	**1.45**	**0.92**	**0.90**

varies across methods, between 4.62 percent and 5.65 percent.[19] A preference is observed, however, when examining the empirical performance for the 1 percent VaR across methods. That is, HS and Hybrid ($\lambda = 0.99$) appear to yield results that are closer to 1 percent than the other methods. Thus, the nonparametric methods, namely HS and Hybrid, appear to outperform the parametric methods for these data series, perhaps because nonparametric methods, by design, are better suited to addressing the well known tendency of financial return series to be fat tailed. Since the estimation of the 1 percent tail requires a lot of data, there seems to be an expected advantage to high smoothers ($\lambda = 0.99$) within the hybrid method.

In table 2.6 we document the mean absolute error (MAE) of the VaR series. The MAE is a conditional version of the previous statistic (percentage in the tail from table 2.4). The MAE uses a rolling 100-period window. Here again, we find an advantage in favor of the nonparametric methods, HS and Hybrid, with the hybrid method performing best for high λ ($\lambda = 0.99$) (note, though, that this is not always true: $\lambda = 0.97$ outperforms for the 5 percent for both the hybrid and the EXP). Since a statistical error is inherent in this statistic, we

Table 2.7 First-order autocorrelation of the tail events

	Historical STD	Historical simulation	EXP		Hybrid	
			0.97	0.99	0.97	0.99
5% Tail						
DEM	0.39	0.09	−2.11	−1.06	−2.63	−2.28
OIL	1.76	2.29	2.11	1.25	3.20	0.31
S&P	0.77	1.09	−0.15	0.94	0.77	2.46
BRD	11.89	12.69	13.60	12.27	10.12	12.08
EQW	5.52	2.29	3.59	4.26	−2.04	−0.14
AVG	**4.07**	**3.69**	**3.41**	**3.53**	**1.88**	**2.49**
1% Tail						
DEM	2.04	−1.08	1.05	2.76	−1.88	−1.29
OIL	−1.88	−1.15	2.27	2.27	−1.73	1.37
S&P	4.94	9.96	7.65	8.04	2.04	8.70
BRD	15.03	9.30	10.75	12.60	−1.66	3.97
EQW	2.76	3.32	3.63	3.63	2.76	4.73
AVG	**4.58**	**4.07**	**5.07**	**5.86**	**−0.09**	**2.95**

cannot possibly expect a mean absolute error of zero. As such, the 38 percent improvement of the hybrid method with λ of 0.99 (with MAE of 0.90 percent for the AVG series' 1 percent tail) relative to the EXP method with the same λ (with MAE of 1.45), is an understatement of the level of improvement. A more detailed simulation exercise would be needed in order to determine how large this improvement is. It is worthwhile to note that this improvement is achieved very persistently across the different data series.

The adaptability of a VaR method is one of the most critical elements in determining the best way to measure VaR. When a large return is observed, the VaR level should increase. It should increase, however, in a way that will make the next tail event's probability precisely x percent. We can therefore expect these tail event realizations to be i.i.d. (independent) events with x percent probability. This independence can be examined using the autocorrelation of tail events, with the null being that autocorrelation is zero. As we see in table 2.7, the hybrid method's autocorrelation for the AVG series is closest to zero. Interestingly, this is especially true for the more fat-tailed series, such as BRD and OIL. As such, the hybrid method is very well suited for fat tailed, possibly skewed series.

Table 2.8(a) Test statistic for independence (autocorrelations 1–5)

	Historical STD	Historical simulation	EXP		Hybrid	
			0.97	0.99	0.97	0.99
5% Tail						
DEM	7.49	10.26	3.80	8.82	3.73	6.69
OIL	9.58	12.69	5.82	4.90	4.71	3.94
S&P	8.09	8.32	0.88	4.31	0.81	3.87
BRD	66.96	87.80	88.30	78.00	46.79	69.29
EQW	16.80	6.30	11.66	14.75	4.87	12.10
AVG	**21.78**	**25.07**	**22.09**	**22.16**	**12.18**	**19.18**
1% Tail						
DEM	3.34	5.33	4.56	4.39	7.58	3.83
OIL	33.98	8.29	3.82	18.89	8.53	3.54
S&P	14.67	36.15	22.68	25.18	3.26	24.10
BRD	88.09	29.37	41.60	82.77	11.26	11.36
EQW	41.55	14.69	16.85	16.85	5.08	13.05
AVG	**36.32**	**18.77**	**17.90**	**29.61**	**7.14**	**11.18**

Table 2.8(b) p-value for independence (autocorrelations 1–5)

	Historical STD	Historical simulation	EXP		Hybrid	
			0.97	0.99	0.97	0.99
5% Tail						
DEM	0.19	0.07	0.58	0.12	0.59	0.24
OIL	0.09	0.03	0.32	0.43	0.45	0.56
S&P	0.15	0.14	0.97	0.51	0.98	0.57
BRD	0.00	0.00	0.00	0.00	0.00	0.00
EQW	0.00	0.28	0.04	0.01	0.43	0.03
AVG	**0.09**	**0.10**	**0.38**	**0.21**	**0.49**	**0.28**
1% Tail						
DEM	0.65	0.38	0.47	0.49	0.18	0.57
OIL	0.00	0.14	0.58	0.00	0.13	0.62
S&P	0.01	0.00	0.00	0.00	0.66	0.00
BRD	0.00	0.00	0.00	0.00	0.05	0.04
EQW	0.00	0.01	0.00	0.00	0.41	0.02
AVG	**0.13**	**0.11**	**0.21**	**0.10**	**0.28**	**0.25**

In tables 2.8a and b we test the statistical significance of the auto-correlations in table 2.7. Specifically, we examine the first through fifth autocorrelations of the tail event series, with the null being that all of these autocorrelations should be zero. The test statistic is simply the sum of the squared autocorrelations, appropriately adjusted to the sample size. Under the null this statistic is distributed as $\chi^2(5)$. These test statistics are generally lower for the hybrid method relative to the EXP. For the specific series four rejections out of a possible eight are obtained with the hybrid method, relative to seven out of eight for the EXP method.

CHAPTER THREE

PUTTING VaR TO WORK

3.1 THE VaR OF DERIVATIVES – PRELIMINARIES

The pricing and risk management of derivatives are intimately related. Since a derivative's price depends on an underlying asset, they both share the same risk factors. For example, a call option on the S&P 100 index changes in value as a function of the underlying factor – the S&P 100 index. The value of a convertible bond depends on two factors – interest rates and the value of the asset into which the bond is convertible.

In order to analyze the risk of a derivative one needs a *pricing model* that specifies the value of the derivative as a function of the underlying factor(s). In addition, one must specify how the risk factor may vary through time; that is, what are reasonable scenarios for the underlying factor? In the case where there are a few relevant underlying factors, one must specify how the underlying factors may co-vary.

In reality, some complex derivatives (e.g., mortgage-backed securities) cannot be priced with a reasonable level of precision of the relevant pricing factors. Therefore, even though we may know some of the relevant factors, some of the variation is asset-specific or asset-class-specific. We can break down derivatives' return volatility along these lines into risk factor-related volatility and asset-specific volatility. Asset-specific or asset-class-specific risk can be attributed to factors that are unknown to the financial economist or the trader, but are known to the market. Asset-specific risk can also be viewed as being a result of modeling errors.

In this chapter, we initially focus on factor-related risk, assuming that derivatives' returns are fully attributable to variations in known risk factors. This assumption is exact only in a theoretical world, for example, when we price an option in a Black–Scholes world using the Black–Scholes option pricing formula. In reality, pricing models do not describe the world perfectly. As a result, actual derivatives prices incorporate some element of asset-specific risk.[1] Later on in the chapter, we will discuss asset-specific and asset class risk.

3.1.1 Linear derivatives

We distinguish, broadly, between two types of derivatives, *linear derivatives* and *nonlinear derivatives*. A linear derivative is linear in the sense that the relationship between the derivative and the underlying pricing factor(s) is linear. It does not need to be one-for-one, but the "transmission parameter," the delta, needs to be constant for all levels of the underlying factor.[2] This is (approximately) the case, for example, for a futures contract on the S&P 500 index, as we explain below. This is not the case for an option on the S&P 500 – a given change in the underlying factor will result a change in the value of the option that depends on the option's "moneyness," i.e., the degree to which an option is in or out of the money.

A futures contract on the S&P 500 is defined as a dollar multiple of the index level. The S&P 500 option traded on the Chicago Mercantile Exchange is defined as a $250 index. An increase (decrease) of one point in the S&P 500 index will result in a gain of $250 on the long (short) futures contract, regardless of the level of the S&P 500. That is, the sensitivity parameter, the delta, is not a function of the level of the index:

$$F_t = \$250 * S_t,$$

where F_t is the futures contract and S_t is the S&P index. If the S&P rises by one point, the futures contract rises by $250 (e.g., a margin account with a long position in one futures contract receives $250). This is regardless of the *level* of the index.

Many so-called linear derivatives are only approximately linear. We often ignore the fact that there may be other underlying factors, whose relevance is much lower, and the linearity of the derivative with respect to those factors may not hold true. Consider, for example, a foreign currency forward. The standard pricing formula of a forward is

$$F_{t,T} = S_t(1 + i_{t,T})/(1 + i^*_{t,T}),$$

where $F_{t,T}$ is the $T - t$ period forward rate at t. forward rate, S_t is the spot exchange rate, $i_{t,T}$ is the domestic and interest rate, and $i^*_{t,T}$ is the foreign interest rate.

The formula is derived by arbitrage, using the fact that the following positions are equivalent:

- purchase an FX forward;
- short a dollar-denominated bond at $i_{t,T}$, convert the proceeds into foreign currency, and long a foreign currency-denominated bond at $i^*_{t,T}$.

The synthetic forward (the latter position) has the same payoff as the forward, hence the arbitrage formula.

The VaR of a forward is, therefore, related to the spot rate and the two interest rates. If interest rates were fixed and we were looking at very short intervals the following would be a good approximation:

$$F_{t,T} = (1 + i_{t,T})/(1 + i^*_{t,T})S_t \approx KS_t.$$

That is, the interest rate differential is a constant K which is not a function of time. The continuously compounded return on the forward, $\Delta f_{t,t+1}$, is approximately equal to the return on the spot, $\Delta s_{t,t+1}$.

$$\Delta f_{t,t+1} = \ln(F_{t+1,T-1}/F_{t,T})$$

$$= \ln(S_{t+1}/S_t) + \ln(\text{change in the interest rate differential})$$

$$\approx \ln(S_{t+1}/S_t).$$

Thus, if to a first approximation the only relevant factor is the exchange rate, then the VaR of a spot position and a forward position (notional amount) are similar. It is not unreasonable to focus on exchange rate fluctuations to the exclusion of interest rate fluctuations because the typical exchange rate volatility is about 80bp/day, ten times larger than the typical interest rate volatility of about 8bp/day.

In principle, though, accounting for the change in the two interest rates is more precise, and this would result in a nonlinear relationship. The nonlinearity can be viewed in light of the arbitrage pricing relationship as a result of the nonlinear relation between bond prices and interest rates. Since the forward position can be thought of as a short/long position in domestic/foreign bonds, as we showed above, the nonlinearity would carry through.

It is important to note that linearity or nonlinearity depends on the definition of the underlying risk factors. An interest rate swap contract can be thought of as equivalent to holding a long position in a floating rate note and a short position in a fixed rate bond. It is hence linear with respect to these underlying assets. These underlying assets, in turn, are nonlinear in interest rates.

Another such example is a currency swap. A currency swap can be thought of as a portfolio of foreign exchange forward contracts. Being a sum of forwards, a currency swap is, hence, linear in the underlying forward contracts. Forwards are linear in the underlying exchange rate, as we saw above, but are also sensitive to interest rate changes. For short maturity forwards the interest rate sensitivity is second order to the exchange rate dependence. Linearity falls apart, however, for long dated forwards that involve longer-term interest rates. As a result, currency swaps are nonlinear in interest rates, since some of the underlying forwards are long dated, and are hence affected by interest rate changes in a meaningful way.

The duration effect plays the role of a magnifying glass. Consider, for example, a ten-year swap. The last exchange on the swap is similar to a ten-year currency forward contract. Interest rate fluctuations are magnified by the duration effect since a ten-year bond underlies the synthetic ten-year currency forward. Thus, even relatively small interest rate fluctuations represent large potential price movements for long duration bonds (see Appendix 3.1 for a more detailed discussion of duration and its effect on prices). To conclude, thinking of a foreign exchange swap with a medium to long maturity as exposed to exchange rates alone may be a bad categorization. It may be a reasonable approximation, though, for a short-dated forward or swap.

3.1.2 Nonlinear derivatives

The primary example for a nonlinear derivative is an option. Consider for example an at-the-money (ATM) call option with six months to expiration written on a non-dividend-paying stock worth $100, with a volatility of 20 percent per annum. The value of the call option is $6.89 according to the Black–Scholes option pricing formula. If the underlying were to fall by $1.00 to $99.00, the option would fall by $0.59 to $6.30. In percentage terms a decline of 1 percent in the underlying would cause a decline of 8.5 percent in the option. The "$Delta" here is $0.59 – a decline of $0.59 in the option of a $1.00 decline in the underlying. The "Delta" is 8.5 – a 1 percent decline in the underlying generates an 8.5 percent decline in the option.

Consider now an option with a higher exercise price, $110, on the same underlying asset. The Black–Scholes value of this option is $2.91, and if the underlying fell by 1 percent to $99, the option value would decline to $2.58, a decline of 11 percent, hence a Delta of 11. For the same percentage decline in the underlying, we see a larger percentage decline for the more levered out-of-the-money option. This difference exemplifies the nonlinearity of options. More generally, the change in the value of the derivative as a function of the change in the value of the underlying is state dependent. In our case the state can be summarized as a function of S/X, the level of moneyness of the option.

3.1.3 Approximating the VaR of derivatives

Calculating the VaR of a linear derivative is straightforward. Consider, again, the futures example:

$$F_t = \$250 * S_t.$$

Then the VaR of the futures contract is at the VaR of the underlying index. To see this, assume the underlying does move by its VaR during the trading day t to $t + 1$, then the VaR of the futures contract is

$$\mathrm{VaR}(F_t) =$$
$$= F_{t+1} - F_t$$
$$= \$250 * (S_{t+1} - S_t)$$
$$= \$250 * (S_t + \mathrm{VaR}(S_t) - S_t)$$
$$= \$250 * \mathrm{VaR}(S_t).$$

In words, the VaR of the futures is the number of index point movements in the underlying index, times the contract's multiple – $250.

More generally, the VaR of the underlying factor (denoted as VaR_f) is defined as a movement in the factor that is related to its current volatility times some multiple that is determined by the desired VaR percentile. The VaR of a linear derivative on this underlying factor would then be the factor VaR times the sensitivity of the derivative's price to fluctuations in the underlying factor. The latter term is simply the derivative's delta. Thus, for the case of linear derivative, we can express the derivative's VaR (denoted VaR_p) as:

$$VaR_p = Delta * VaR_f. \tag{3.1}$$

That is, the VaR of the derivative is delta times the VaR of the underlying risk factor.

An important caveat should be noted here. Our derivation assumes implicitly that the delta is positive. A positive delta implies a long position or a positive exposure to the underlying. If the delta is negative, a loss of *VaR* on the underlying generates a *gain* of *Delta*VaR* on the derivative. It is hence the case that one needs to look for cases of extreme gain in the underlying in order to find extreme cases of loss in the derivative when the delta is negative.

Turning to nonlinear derivatives we should first note that every asset is locally linear. That is, for small enough moves we could extrapolate given the *local delta* of the derivative, where the local delta is taken to mean the percentage change in the derivative for a 1 percent change in the underlying factor.

Table 3.1 Call option prices and deltas*

Stock price	$90	$99	$99.9	$100	$100.1	$101	$110
Call	$2.35	$6.30	$6.83	$6.89	$6.95	$7.50	$14.08
Change in stock							
Price DS(%)	−10.0%	−1.0%	−0.1%		0.1%	1.0%	10.0%
Change in call							
Value DC(%)	−65.9%	−8.5%	−0.9%		0.9%	8.9%	104.3%
DC(%)/DS(%)	6.59	8.48	8.66		8.70	8.87	10.43

*   Assume a strike price of $X = 100$, time to expiration of $1/2$ year $t = 0.5$, a riskfree rate $r = 5\%$, and stock price volatility $\sigma = 20\%$.

Consider for example, the at-the-money call option shown in table 3.1. As we saw, the delta of the option is 8.48: a decline of 1 percent in the underlying will generate a decline of 8.48 percent in the option. Suppose now that we wish to calculate the one-day VaR of this option. Recall that the underlying asset has an annualized volatility of 20 percent. This annual volatility corresponds to, roughly, 1.25 percent per day[3]. The 5 percent VaR of the underlying asset corresponds, under normality, to 1.65 standard deviation move, where the standard deviation on a daily basis is 1.25 percent. Assuming a zero mean return, this implies that the 5 percent VaR of the underlying is 0 − 1.25*1.65 = −2.06%. This, in turn, implies a decline in the value of the call option of:

$$5\% VaR(call) = -2.06\%*delta = -2.06\%*8.48 = -17.47\%.$$

That is, there is a 5 percent probability that the option value will decline by 17.47 percent or more. Recall that this is only an approximation, because as the asset declines in value the delta changes. The precise change can be calculated using the Black–Scholes formula (assuming that is the correct model to price the option exactly) to evaluate the option when the underlying declines from a current value of $100 by 2.06 percent, to $97.94. The precise value of the option is $5.72, implying a decline in value of 17.0 percent. While there is some imprecision, the extent of imprecision could be thought of as relatively small.

Consider the case where we want the VaR of the option for the one week horizon. The weekly volatility of the underlying is

20%/√(52) = 2.77%. Still assuming normality and a mean of zero, the 1 percent VaR is calculated as 0 − 2.33*2.77% = −6.46%. That is, a decline of 6.46 percent in the underlying corresponds, using our delta-linear approximation, to (8.48)(−6.46) = −54.78%. That is, given a one week 1 percent VaR of 6.46 percent for the underlying, the one-week 1 percent VaR of the call is 54.78 percent. In order to evaluate the precision of the linear approximation in this case, we need to price the option given a decline in the underlying of 6.46 percent. That is, we should reprice the option with an exercise price of $100 assuming that the underlying asset falls in value to $93.54. The value of the option in this case would decline from $6.83, the at-the-money value, to $3.62. This is a decline of 47.4 percent.

The level of imprecision in the one-day VaR can be quantified by taking the ratio of the linear VaR to the correct, full revaluation, VaR. For the 5 percent daily VaR, this ratio is 17.4%/17% = 1.023. The bias resulting from the linear approximation is 2.3 percent. We can compare this ratio to the accuracy ratio for the one-week 99th percentile VaR. This ratio is 54.78%/47.4% = 1.15. The linear VaR is much more biased for a larger move relative to the "true" full revaluation VaR. The bias grows from 2.3 percent to 15 percent as the VaR percentile goes from 5 percent to 1 percent and as the time period increases from one day to one week.

Figures 3.1 and 3.2 provide a schematic of this effect. Figure 3.1 graphs the value of the call option on the Y-axis as a function of the option's moneyness on the X-axis. The option is convex in the value of the underlying. For small enough moves, though, the linear approximation should work well. The slope of the call's price as a function of the underlying is a close approximation to the changes in value we would see for small enough moves in the underlying. The nonlinearity results in the slope changing for different level of moneyness.

The change in the slope coefficient is the result of the option's non-linearity in the underlying. This nonlinearity is also the culprit for the imprecision in the linear approximation, and the increasing degree of imprecision as we consider larger moves of the underlying. In particular, as figure 3.2 shows, for larger moves we can see a clear bias in the linear approximation of the change in the value of the call option. In fact, the bias will always be positive; that is, whether the underlying rises or falls, the linear approximation will underestimate the true value of the option. In other words, the required correction term is always positive. In figure 3.2 this is visible from the fact that the straight

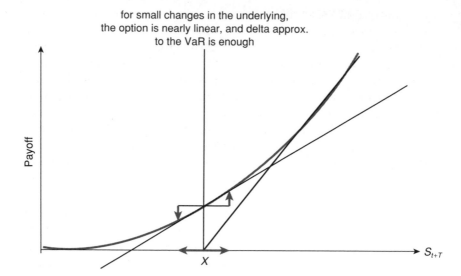

Figure 3.1 The VaR of options: small moves

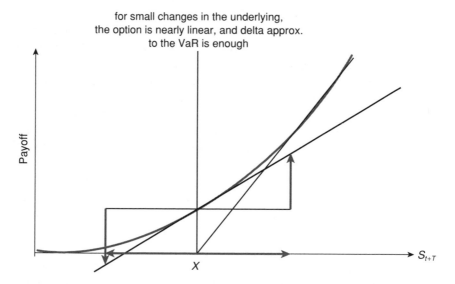

Figure 3.2 The VaR of options: large moves

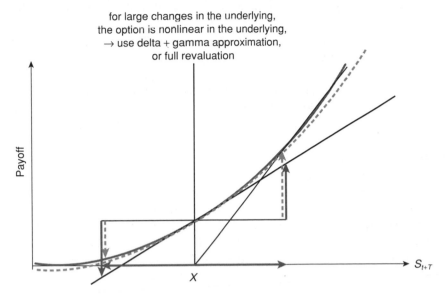

for large changes in the underlying,
the option is nonlinear in the underlying,
→ use delta + gamma approximation,
or full revaluation

Figure 3.3 The VaR of options: convexity correction

line, corresponding to the linear approximation, lies underneath the
true option value (using the Black–Scholes option pricing formula).

The bias is a result of the fact that the slope changes as the underlying changes. The further the underlying asset moves away from
its original value, where the slope was correct, the more the slope
changes, and the worse the linear approximation with the given fixed
slope becomes. Since the value of the option is convex in the underlying (i.e., the second derivative is positive), we will get a positive bias
assuming linearity.

Figure 3.3 describes one way to mitigate the problem, by approximating the curvature of the pricing function using a convexity correction. The premise is related to what is known in mathematics as a
Taylor Series approximation. Simply put, the approximation says that
any "well behaved" function can be approximated by a polynomial of
order two (i.e., a quadratic) as follows:

$$f(x) \approx f(x_0) + f'(x_0)(x - x_0) + 1/2f''(x_0)(x - x_0)^2. \qquad (3.2)$$

This means that the value of a function $f(x)$ for any value of x is approximated by starting with the value of the function at a given point x_0
(which is assumed to be known), and then approximating the change
in the value of the function from $f(x_0)$ to $f(x)$ by accounting for:

- the slope of the function at x_0, $f'(x_0)$, times the change in the x-variable, $(x - x_0)$;
- plus the curvature of the function at x_0, $f''(x_0)$, times the change squared divided by two;

the first term is exactly the linear approximation, while the second term is the convexity correction.

The improvement in the convexity correction turns out to be important in application. This correction is implemented by calculating the option's second derivative with respect to the underlying factor and the option's gamma.

One particularly well-known example of the need to approximate a nonlinear relation is, in fact, not from the derivative securities area. The example is the nonlinear relation between interest rates and the value of a pure discount bond. The value of a zero coupon bond with one year to maturity as a function of the one-year rate y is:

$$d = 1/r.$$

This is clearly a nonlinear relation. The graph of this function is a hyperbola. Figure 3.4 describes the relationship. The straight line marked by "duration" is the linear approximation to the price change as a function of the interest rate (see Appendix 3.1 for a detailed discussion

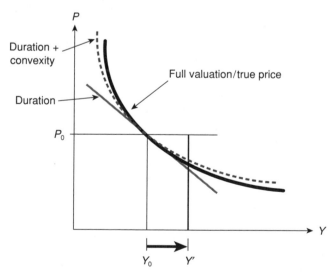

Figure 3.4 Duration and convexity in bond pricing

of duration). Duration apparently falls apart as an approximation for the bond's price change for large moves in interest rates. To this end we have the convexity correction to the duration approximation.

The idea behind the duration–convexity approximation of the impact of interest rate fluctuations on bond prices is identical to the idea behind the delta–gamma approximation of the impact of fluctuations in the underlying on the value of an option. Both rely on:

- the knowledge of the pricing model and the existence of an explicit pricing formula;
- the ability to provide a first and second derivative to this pricing formula as a function of the underlying;
- the use of the Taylor Series approximation.

This approach is not unique. There are many types of derivatives where a pricing relation can be derived analytically or via computations. Examples include:

- convertible bonds which are nonlinear in the value of the underlying asset into which the bonds are convertible;
- defaultable bonds that are nonlinear in changes in the default probability;
- mortgage backed securities, which are nonlinear in the refinancing incentive (the difference between the mortgage pool's rate and the current refinancing rate).

3.1.4 Fixed income securities with embedded optionality

The Taylor Series approximation described in section 3.1.3 does not perform well in the case of derivatives with extreme nonlinearities. For example, mortgage backed securities (MBS) represent fixed income securities with embedded options; that is, the mortgagor (the borrower) can choose to prepay the mortgage at any time, particularly, when mortgage rates are declining. Figure 3.5 depicts the sensitivity of three different mortgage pools, Government National Mortgage Association (GNMA) 8 percent, 9 percent and 10 percent, as a function of the long rate.[4] The Y-axis is the conditional regression beta – regressing MBS prices on interest rate changes. The coefficient is conditional in the sense that the estimate is for the local sensitivity of prices to rates in the vicinity of a given interest rate (i.e., small rate changes). For all

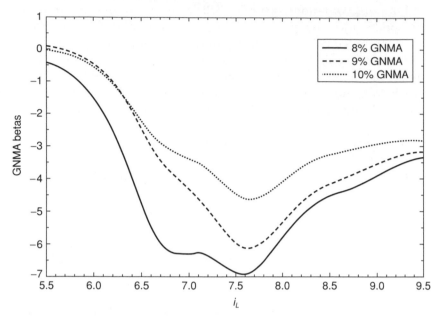

Figure 3.5 Empirical interest rate sensitivity of MBSs
Source: Boudoukh, Richardson, Stanton, and Whitelaw (1997)

three mortgage pools the regression beta is negative. This is intuitive
– as interest rates rise the value of all three mortgage pools drop, and
vice versa. The beta can be interpreted as the duration of the pools
(with the reverse sign).

The interesting point is that the beta/duration is not constant and
changes in a remarkable way for different long-term rates. As rates
fall from higher levels of, say, 9.5 percent, duration increases (i.e.,
the beta becomes more negative). This is an effect common to many
ordinary fixed income securities such as bonds – that duration rises
as interest rates fall. As interest rates fall further duration starts to
fall. This is the result of an actual and anticipated rise in prepayment
activity. As rates fall a high coupon mortgage is likely to be refinanced
by a homeowner. This causes the life of the MBS to shorten – a security that was supposed to pay fixed interest payments for a long period
now pays down the full face amount, exercising the option to prepay.

Such shifts in duration result in a security that is not simple to price
or hedge. A similar effect is also observed in other fixed income
securities with embedded derivatives such as callable debt. Callable
debt will also exhibit an initial rise in duration as rates fall, but then,

as the option to call back the debt enters into the money the expected call will shorten the life of the callable bond.

These securities pose a problem for risk managers. First, it is clearly the case that such securities require fairly sophisticated models for pricing, and hence for risk management. These may not be compatible with simple risk measurement techniques that may be suitable for linear assets. Moreover, the sharp changes in duration may make the duration–convexity approximation weaker. For these securities the rate of change in duration changes for different interest rates, making the convexity correction much less accurate. Thus, convexity alone cannot be used to correct for the change in duration.

3.1.5   "Delta normal" vs. full-revaluation

There are two primary approaches to the measurement of the risk of nonlinear securities. The first is the most straightforward approach – the full revaluation approach. The approach is predicated on the fact that the derivative moves one-for-one, or one-for-delta with the underlying factor. Assuming a positive delta, i.e., that the derivative moves in the same direction as the factor, we use a valuation expression to price the derivative at the VaR tail of the underlying factor. For example, the 1 percent VaR of an option on the S&P 500 index can be calculated by first finding out the 1 percent VaR of the index. This step can be done using any approach – be it parametric (e.g., assuming normality) or nonparametric (e.g., historical simulation). The VaR of the option is just the value of the option evaluated at the value of the index after reducing it by the appropriate percentage decline that was calculated as the 1 percent VaR of the index itself.

This approach has the great advantage of accuracy. It does not involve any approximations. However, this approach can be computationally very burdensome. Specifically, we may be able to reprice a bond or an option easily, but repricing a portfolio of complex derivatives of MBSs, swaptions, exotic options and so on can require many computations. In particular, as we will see later on, we may want to evaluate thousands of different scenarios. Thousands of revaluations of a portfolio consisting of hundreds of exotic securities using simulations or binomial trees may require computing power that takes days to generate the results, thereby rendering them useless.

The alternative is the approach known as the "delta–normal" approach, which involves the delta (linear) approximation, or the delta–gamma (Taylor Series) approximation. The approach is known as "delta–normal" because the linear approximation shown in equation (3.1) is often used in conjunction with a normality assumption for the distribution of fluctuations in the underlying factor value. The approach can be implemented relatively simply. First we calculate the VaR of the underlying. Then we use equation (3.1) to revalue the derivative according to its delta with respect to the underlying times the change in the underlying. Clearly the first step – finding out the VaR of the underlying, does not need to be calculated necessarily using the normality assumption. We could just as well use historical simulation for example. The key is that the approach uses the delta approximation.

This approach is extremely inexpensive computationally. Calculating the risk of a complex security can be almost "free" as far as computational time in concerned. In particular, consider a fixed income derivative that is priced today, for simplicity, at $100 for $100 of par. Suppose we used a binomial interest rate tree to price and hedge this derivative given a current interest rate of 6 percent p.a. Assume further that the security matures in 10 years, and that our binomial interest rate tree is built with a time step of one month. There are, hence, 120 one-month periods to maturity. Suppose the first one-month step involves a change in interest rates of 10bp up or down. That is, the binomial tree that we use for pricing takes today's rate of 6 percent and after the first time step rates can be either 6.1 percent or 5.9 percent. Binomial pricing involves spanning a complete tree of interest rates to the maturity of the derivative, discounting back through the tree the derivative's cash flows.

As we work our way back through the tree when pricing this security we can note the prices the security can take next period, i.e., in one month. Suppose that the bond prices were $101 for the down-state of interest rates, 5.9 percent, and $99.2 for the up-state of 6.1 percent. If we are willing to ignore that one-month time value, these two numbers give us an approximate interest rate sensitivity measure. Specifically, we know that the following is approximately true:

$$Y = 5.9\% \rightarrow P = \$99.2, \ Y = 6\% \rightarrow P = \$100, \ Y = 6.1\% \rightarrow P = \$101.$$

This information provides us with an estimate of the derivative's interest rate sensitivity. In particular, for a difference in rates of 20bp (6.1% − 5.9%) we know that the price of the security would fall by $1.80, the difference between the up-state price of $99.2, and the down-state price of $101. A linear approximation would imply that a rise of 100bp in rates would result in a change in value of $9. Given a par value of $100, this means that a rise of 1 percent would result in approximately $9 drop in price.

Note that this calculation did not require full revaluation. In the full revaluation approach if we wanted to price the security for a 100bp shift up in rates, we would have to rebuild the binomial interest rate tree starting from a current rate of 7 percent instead of 6 percent. The empirical duration method presented here provides us with a linear approximation to the price change. In particular, we would expect a drop in value of 9 percent for a rise of 1 percent in rates. In our case this also corresponds to a drop in value of $9, since we assumed the security trades at par value.

3.2   STRUCTURED MONTE CARLO, STRESS TESTING, AND SCENARIO ANALYSIS

3.2.1   Motivation

The calculation of VaR can be an easy task if the portfolio consists of linear securities. Practical issues remain with respect to the implementation and accuracy of the VaR estimate, but conceptually there are no obstacles left. As we have seen in this chapter, this is certainly not the case for nonlinear derivatives. Moreover, portfolios of nonlinear derivatives will pose a special challenge to the risk manager. To see the problem consider an options straddle position – a long position in a call and a put with the same exercise price. The cash flow diagram of the straddle appears in figure 3.6.

How can we calculate the VaR of this option position? Since this is a portfolio of derivatives, we need to first come up with the VaR of the underlying, and then either revalue the derivative at this underlying value or use a delta approximation approach. If the derivative involves an implicit short position, then we need to examine an extreme rise in the underlying as the relevant VaR event rather than an extreme decline. Suppose our example involves a straddle on the S&P 500 index. Suppose further that the standard deviation of the index is 100bp/day, and that the 1 percent one-day VaR under normality is a decline of 233bp. The mirror image case assuming that returns are symmetric would be an increase of 233bp. With an at-the-money straddle it is clearly the case that we make money in either case. Straddles, being a bullish bet on volatility, pay off when the underlying moves

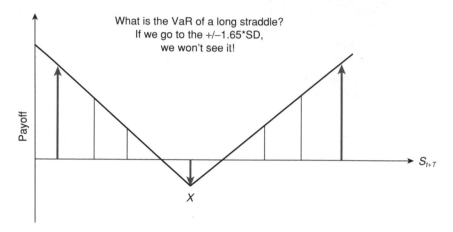

Figure 3.6   The VaR of options: a straddle

sharply. Loss scenarios for straddles, precisely what VaR is supposed to deliver, involve the underlying remaining close to its current value. How do we generalize our derivative approach to VaR calculation to accommodate such a complication?

3.2.2   Structured Monte Carlo

For the straddle, large loss scenarios involve small, not large, moves in the underlying. The methodology described so far clearly cannot handle this situation. There is, however, a distribution of possible values for the portfolio given possible values for the underlying. By definition, there exists a VaR. One way to derive this VaR is to simulate thousands of possible values for the underlying given its distribution (e.g., under the normality assumption).

Suppose that we generate, say, 10,000 values for the S&P 500 index tomorrow based on a standard deviation of 100bp/day. Then we re-evaluate the straddle for each of these 10,000 values of the underlying. As a result we have 10,000 values that the straddle might take by the end of tomorrow's trading, based, of course, on our statistical assumptions about the price distribution of the underlying S&P 500. Ordering the 10,000 simulated values for the straddle from smallest to largest would generate a distribution for the straddle, and the 9,900th value would be the simulated 1st percentile. This value corresponds to the 1 percent VaR.

More generally, suppose that one needs to generate scenarios for an asset whose returns are distributed normally with a mean of μ and a standard deviation of σ^2. The simulation requires a random-number generator that generates draws from a normal distribution with a mean of zero and a standard deviation of one. Denote these $N(0,1)$ draws by $z_1, z_2, \ldots, z_{NSIM}$. The NSIM scenarios are, hence $\mu + \sigma z_1$, $\mu + \sigma z_2$, $\ldots, \mu + \sigma z_{NSIM}$. Since we use continuously compounded returns, the index's simulated value for a given random normal draw z_i is denoted $S_{t+1,i}$ and can be expressed as:

$$S_{t+1,i} = S_t^* exp\{\mu + \sigma^* z_i\}.$$

For each of these values we revalue the entire derivative portfolio. Next, we order the NSIM simulated value and pick the $(1 - X/100)*NSIMth$ value as the $X\%$ VaR.

We can extend the Monte Carlo approach to the more relevant case facing real world risk managers in financial institutions – the case of multiple assets with multiple risk exposures. The extension is conceptually straightforward, although some technical issues arise. Briefly, for K risk factors and $NSIM$ simulations we need to generate $K*NSIM$ independent variables distributed as $N(0,1)$. These can be stacked as $NSIM$ vectors of size K. Each such vector is distributed as multivariate normal with a mean vector which is a $K*1$ vector of zeros, and a variance covariance matrix which is an identity matrix of size $K*K$. Similar to the one dimensional, single factor case we generate $NSIM$ scenarios for K underlying factors

$$Ln(\mathbf{S}_{t+1}/\mathbf{S}_t) = exp\{\mu + A'^*\mathbf{Z}_t\},$$

where

$Ln(\mathbf{S}_{t+1}/\mathbf{S}_t)$ is a $K*1$ vector of lognormal returns;
μ is a $\mathbf{K}*1$ vector of mean returns;
$\mathbf{Z}_t$ is a $\mathbf{K}*1$ vector of $N(0,1)$'s;
and A' is the Cholesky decomposition[5] of the factor return covariance matrix Σ, that is $\mathbf{A'A} = \Sigma$.

Simulated factor returns are distributed with a mean and a covariance matrix that can be estimated from live market data, or postulated based on a model or theory.

The main advantage of the use of structured Monte Carlo (SMC) simulation is that we can generate correlated scenarios based on a statistical distribution. To see this advantage one needs to compare this approach to the standard scenario analysis approach, of, say, revaluing the portfolio given a 100bp rise in rates. Analyzing the effect of a parallel shift of 100bp on the portfolio's value tells us something about its interest rate risk, but nothing about the overall risk of the portfolio. The SMC approach to portfolio risk measurement addresses most of the relevant issues.

The first issue is that while a 100bp parallel shift in rates is a possible scenario, there is no guidance as to how likely this event is. There is no probability attached to scenario analysis that is performed based on scenarios that are pulled from thin air. As such, it is not clear what to do about the result. It is clearly the case that an institution would want to protect itself from a 1:100 event, but it is not clear what it is supposed to do about a 1:1,000,000 event, if anything. What are the odds of a 100bp move, then?

Second, the 100bp parallel shift scenario is a test of the effect of a single risk factor – the level of domestic rates. It is not clear what is the relevance of such a scenario, especially in the context of a globally diversified portfolio. A more complete risk model would recognize that statistically the likelihood of a 100bp rise in rates in isolation is a remote likelihood scenario, relative to a scenario in which rates rise across many countries. This is a critical point for a global fixed income portfolio.

Consider a simple example of a speculative position that is long US Bonds and short UK bonds. An increase in US interest rates will make the position look very risky. While the long side of the position – US bonds, will fall in value, there will be no commensurate fall in the short-gilts UK side of the portfolio. However, chances are that a sharp increase in US interest rates will coincide with a rise in UK rates. Under those circumstances, the resulting decline in UK bond prices on the short side would generate a profit that will compensate for the loss in the long US bond position. Of course, there is no absolute certainty that interest rates will move in tandem across countries, but a sharp increase in interest rates is often attributable to a global rise in inflationary expectations and political instability that make such co-movement more likely to occur.

SMC copes effectively with these two issues. The scenarios that will be generated using the estimated variance–covariance matrix will be generated based on a set of correlations estimated from real data. As such, the scenarios will be as likely in the simulation as they are in reality. With respect to the first point, regarding the likelihood of a given scenario, in an SMC we have a clear interpretation of the distribution of the *NSIM* simulations we generate. Each is as likely. It is hence the case that the 1 percent VaR according to the SMC is the first percentile of the distribution of the simulated scenario portfolio values.

With respect to the manner in which various risk factors co-vary with one another, the use of the covariance matrix of the scenarios as an input guarantees that the economic nature of the events driving the simulation is plausible. It is important to note, though, that the economic content is only as sound as our ability to model co-movements of the factors through the covariance matrix (see Boyle, Broadie, and Glasserman, 1997).

3.2.3   Scenario analysis

As we have seen in the previous discussion, structured Monte Carlo simulation may be used to solve the special problems associated with estimating the VaR of a portfolio of nonlinear derivatives. However, the approach is not free of shortcomings. In particular, generating scenarios in simulation and claiming that their distribution is relevant going forward is as problematic as estimating past volatility and using it as a forecast for future volatility. Generating a larger number of simulations cannot remedy the problem. As we will see in the remainder of this section, scenario analysis may offer an alternative that explicitly considers future events.

3.2.3.1   *Correlation breakdown*

Consider the case of a global bond portfolio investment. Such a portfolio is often predicated on the notion of diversification. Specifically, global bond portfolios often achieve excess risk-adjusted performance by taking on sovereign risk, taking advantage of the "fact" that sovereign risk premiums are too high. Historical estimation of the co-movement of portfolios of sovereign bonds, e.g., Brady Bonds, generate unusually low correlations. These correlations, in turn, imply strong risk-reduction due to diversification.

It is possible to use these risk estimates to demonstrate that the yield enhancement of taking on sovereign credit risk comes at little cost as far as pervasive risk is concerned. However, low cross-country correlations are likely to be exhibited by the data, as long as there were no global crises within the estimation window. However, during times of crisis a *contagion* effect is often observed. Consider two specific examples.

First, consider the correlation of the rates of return on Brady Bonds issued by Bulgaria and the Philippines. These two countries are, loosely speaking, as unrelated as can be as far as their creditworthiness. Their geographic regions are distinct, their economic strengths and weaknesses rely on unrelated factors, and so forth. Indeed, the correlation of the return series of bonds issued by these countries is low – around 0.04. A portfolio comprised of bonds issued by these two countries would show little pervasive volatility. However, during the economic crisis in east Asia in 1997/8 the correlation between these bonds rose dramatically, from 0.04 to 0.84!

The second example is the statistical link between the yield change series of US government bonds and JGBs (Japanese Government Bonds). These two bonds tend to exhibit low correlation during normal times. In particular, while the correlation of the two series may vary through time, prior to August 1990 the estimated correlation was 0.20. During the war in the Gulf region in the summer of 1990 and early 1991 the correlation increased to 0.80. A common factor of global unrest and inflationary fears due to rising oil prices may have caused a global rise in yields.

These events of breakdown in historic correlation matrices occur when the investor needs the diversification benefit the most. In particular, note that the increase in volatility that occurs during such crises would require an even stronger diversification effect in order not to generate extreme returns. The opposite is true in the data. Spikes in volatility occur at the same time that correlations approach one because of an observed contagion effect. A rise in volatility and correlation generates an entirely different return generating process. Table 3.2 includes a few examples of stress events and the "before" and "during" correlations between relevant variables.

In addition to the Asian crisis of 1997/8 and the Gulf War of 1990/1 there are a few other examples of correlation breakdown:

- the GBP/USD exchange rate and the GBP LIBOR rate before and during the collapse of the period that the UK dropped out of the ERM;
- the Peso/USD and the Peso rate during the 1994/5 Mexican crisis;
- yield changes (returns) on low grade and high grade debt before and during the 1987 stock market crash.

Table 3.2 Correlation breakdown

Event	Date	Correlations between variables	Prior to	During
ERM crisis	Sep 92	GBP/USD, GBP LIBOR	−0.10	0.75
Mexican crisis	Dec 94	Peso/USD, 1mo Cetes	0.30	0.80
Crash of 1987	Oct 87	Junk yield, 10yr Treasury	0.80	−0.70
Gulf War	Aug 90	10yr JGBs, 10yr Treasury	0.20	0.80
Asian crisis	1997/8	Brady debt of Bulgaria and the Philippines	0.04	0.84

3.2.3.2   Generating reasonable stress

Our discussion of correlation breakdown carries strong implications for our interpretation of results from an SMC simulation. A simulation using SMC based on a covariance matrix that was estimated during normal times cannot generate scenarios that are economically relevant for times of crisis. A common, but potentially erroneous, remedy is to increase the number of simulations and go further out in the tail to examine more "severe stress." For example, it is common to see a mention of the 0.01 percentile of the simulation, e.g., the 10th out of 100,000 simulations. It is not uncommon for financial institutions to run an especially long portfolio simulation over the weekend to come up with such numbers. Unfortunately the 10th out of 100,000 simulations, while strictly speaking is indeed the 0.01 percent VaR given the covariance matrix, has little to do with the 1 in 10,000 event. The 1 in 10,000 event on a daily basis is an event that we are likely to see only once in 40 years (the odds of 1:10,000 divided by 250 trading days per year). It would be dangerous to assert that an SMC as described above can provide a reasonable assessment of losses on such a day (or week, or month, for that matter).

Table 3.3 demonstrates the problem further. A four or more standard deviation event should occur, according to the normal benchmark in expectation, 6.4 times in 100,000. It is a 1 in 15,625 event, or an event that is expected to occur once every 62 years. Consider now the S&P 500 index. This broad well-diversified index exhibits daily returns that are four or more standard deviation events at a rate that is equivalent to 440 in 100,000 (over a smaller post-WWII sample, or course). The true likelihood of a four or more standard deviation event is once every 0.9 years. An extreme move that a

Table 3.3   Empirical stress

SDs	Normal distribution	S&P 500	Yen/$	10yr rate
2	4500	3700	5600	5700
3	270	790	1300	1300
4	6.4	440	310	240
5	0	280	78	79
6	0	200	0	0

normal-distribution-based SMC would predict should occur once in a blue moon is, in reality, a relatively common event.

We obtain results similar to those shown in table 3.3 for common risk factors such as the ten-year interest rate and the USD/JPY exchange rate. This is a simple extension of the fat tails effect for single assets and risk factors. The difficulty here is twofold – the spikes in returns and the collapse of low correlations during financial crises. While there is a lively debate in the literature on whether the contagion effect is an example of irrationality or a result of rational behavior in the presence of a spike in the volatility of global risk factors, the fact remains that covariance matrices cannot generate stress in SMC simulations, regardless of the number of simulations.[6]

One approach is to stress the correlation matrix that generates the SMC scenarios. Stressing a correlation matrix is an attempt, intuitively, to model the contagion effect that may occur, and how it may affect volatilities and correlations. The exercise of stressing a correlation matrix is not straightforward in practice. A covariance matrix should have certain properties that may be lost when tinkering with the correlations of this matrix. In particular, the variance–covariance matrix needs to be invertible, for example. Significant work has been done on the subject of how to increase contagion given an estimated covariance matrix without losing the desirable properties of the covariances that were estimated using historical data.[7]

3.2.3.3   Stress testing in practice

It is safe to say that stress testing is an integral component of just about every financial institution's risk management system. The common practice is to provide two independent sections to the risk report:

(i) a VaR-based risk report; and (ii) a stress testing-based risk report. The VaR-based analysis includes a detailed top-down identification of the relevant risk generators for the trading portfolio as a whole. The stress testing-based analysis typically proceeds in one of two ways: (i) it examines a series of historical stress events; and (ii) it analyzes a list of predetermined stress scenarios. In both cases we need to assess the effect of the scenarios on the firm's current portfolio position.

Historical stress events may include such events as the crash of 1987, the 1990/1 Gulf War, the Mexican crisis of 1994, the east Asian crisis of 1996 and the near collapse of LTCM in 1998. The alternative approach is to examine predetermined stress scenarios as described above. For example, we may ask what is the effect of such extreme scenarios as a 200bp shift up in rates, an increase in volatility to 25 percent p.a. and so on, on the portfolio's value. The latter approach is a standard requirement in many regulatory risk reports (e.g., the Office of Thrift Supervision's requirement for savings banks to report periodically the effect of parallel shifts in the yield curve on the institution's asset–liability portfolio).

These approaches to stress testing provide valuable information. The analysis of past extreme events can be highly informative about the portfolio's points of weakness. The analysis of standard scenarios can illuminate the relative riskiness of various portfolios to standard risk factors and as such may allow the regulator to get a notion of the financial system's aggregate exposure to, say, interest rate risk. Nevertheless, the approach of analyzing pre-prescribed scenarios may generate unwarranted red flags on the one hand, and create dangerous loopholes on the other.

In particular, consider the analysis of specific term structure scenarios. While the analysis of parallel shift scenarios and perhaps a more elaborate analysis of both parallel shift as well as tilt scenarios may give us an idea of the interest rate risk exposure of the bank's portfolio with respect to changes in domestic interest rates, this risk measure may be deceiving for a number of reasons.

The first was discussed in detail in section 3.2.2 above when structured Monte Carlo was introduced and motivated. Briefly, to the extent that interest rates move in tandem around the world, at least when it comes to large moves, then large losses in the domestic bond portfolio are likely to occur together. This effect may cause a severe error in risk estimation – with a long and short position risk may be overstated, with a long-only portfolio risk may be understated.

Another problem with this approach is the issue of asset-class-specific risk. It is often argued that some asset classes may have asset-class-specific risks. For example, emerging market debt could suffer from contagion risk – the complete loss of investor sentiment for investment in sovereign debt. Another example is the mortgage backed securities market, where interest rate risk factors explain only a portion of the total risk. There are, apparently, other pervasive risk factors governing returns in this sector. These factors are not well understood or modeled (see Boudoukh, Richardson, Stanton, and Whitelaw, 1997).

From an academic perspective it is important to sort out whether such co-movements within an asset class are rational or irrational. Using terms such as "investor sentiment" and "contagion" as reasons for co-movements within an asset class may allude to some form of market irrationality. Alternatively, however, co-movements within the asset class may be rational and attributable to explanatory variables that are erroneously omitted from our models. Moreover, the models may be misspecified – that is, that the right functional form or structural model was not correctly identified. Which one of these possible explanations is correct is probably unimportant from a risk management perspective. What is important is that these pricing errors can undermine the accuracy of stress tests.

Note that asset-specific risk is extremely important for financial institutions that are not well diversified across many lines of business. Specialized financial institutions may carry large inventory positions relative to their capital in their area of specialization or focus. Such institutions may be able to assess, report, and risk-manage their known risk (e.g., interest rate risk), but often cannot measure and manage their total risk exposure.

Total risk is rightfully thought of as unimportant in asset pricing. Asset pricing theory states that the asset or firm specific risks are not priced – it is only systematic risk that is priced (whether it is market risk, interest risk or any other systematic form of risk). However, from the perspective of the risk manager both systematic risk and asset specific risk may matter, in particular if asset specific risk is not diversified through a large portfolio of different assets that are drawn from different asset classes.

3.2.3.4 Stress testing and historical simulation

As discussed above, the common approach in stress testing is to choose past events that are known to be periods of financial market volatility as the relevant stress tests. This approach could be problematic since it might miss the true relevant risk sources that may be specific to an institution. An alternative approach is an approach based on the same intuition of historical simulation. The idea is to let the data decide which scenarios fit the definition "extreme stress."

In particular, consider, for example, examining the returns on all the factors that are relevant for our trading portfolio over one-week horizons for the last 20 years. The last 20 years provide a sample of 1,040 weekly periods, including a few of the well-known crises that are often used as stress tests. However, a fixed income portfolio, for example, may experience extreme movements during different periods than an equity portfolio, and that may differ from a currency portfolio. Thus, the definition of stress periods may differ from asset to asset. It is always inferior to base the analysis on a prespecified set of events rather than examining all possible events in order to identify those with extreme returns.

Unlike the case of historical simulation as a counterpart to VaR, here we are not interested in the 5 percent VaR – the 5th of 100 trading periods or the 52nd of 1,040 trading weeks. We are going to focus our attention on the five or ten worst weeks of trading, given today's portfolio. These will help us determine the true risk exposures of our portfolio. To the extent the LTCM crash is the relevant stress event, this will show up in the data. To the extent the east Asian crisis is relevant, this will show up as an extreme move. But it is also possible that an entirely different period may become the focal point through this examination. The difference here is that the extreme events are assumed to be extreme valuations, as opposed to extreme movements in underlying risk factors.

The decline in rates during the 1994–5 period that resulted in extreme refinancing activity may not be thought of as a major stress event. Consider, however, a mortgage portfolio's risk. For a holder of a portfolio of CMOs this may be the most relevant stress event. It will show up as such only using the historical simulation-based approach we discussed in this section.

3.2.3.5   Asset concentration

No discussion of risk management would be complete without reiterating the first rule of prudent risk management – diversification. The effect of diversification is a mathematical fact, not a theory.[8] The question is how do we achieve "true" diversification? Long Term Capital

Management, for example, may have had reasons to believe that the different trades run by the different "desks" in the firm had little in common. After the fact, it is clear that there was a strong pervasive factor to all the trades; that is, they were all exposed to liquidity crises. This is a factor that is difficult to quantify or forecast. In particular, unlike most other factors where live quotes exist and risk estimates can hence be provided, liquidity is hard to measure, and spikes in liquidity occur seemingly "out of the blue."

The trigger event of stress is hard to predict. Worse than that, financial markets find a way of discovering different triggers for each new crisis; thus, the list of triggers keeps getting longer. The inflation spiral of 1973–4 was triggered by the war in the Middle East in October 1973, the crash of 1987 had no apparent trigger, the Asian crisis was triggered by sharp currency moves in Thailand, the collapse of the internet bubble, some would argue, was the March 2000 verdict in the Microsoft case, and the list goes on.

The only solution to the problem may seem rather simple minded and arbitrary. The solution comes in the form of explicit dollar limits on specific counterparty exposure and limits on total notional amount exposure per asset or asset class. For example, it is standard practice for financial institutions to set limits on the maximal amount of outstanding credit exposure to any single counterparty. These limits may be a function of the total loan amount and/or the total notional outstanding and/or the total mark to market of positions. The limit would often be quoted as a percentage of both the counterparty as well as the institution's capital.[9]

This solution may, at first, seem arbitrary, and even overly simplistic. For example, one might argue that while setting limits on total mark-to-market exposure may make sense, setting limits on aggregate notional outstanding makes no sense at all. Consider, for example writing at-the-money vs. out-of-the-money options. If we want to fix the mark-to-market exposure and compare across exercise prices it is clearly the case that the notional amount of out-of-the-money options would be much greater, since their value is smaller. This is, however, the point of this approach. The limit on the notional amount makes sense as the only possible indicator of an extreme exposure.

As an example, consider the liability of two put option writers shown in table 3.4. One writes at the money (ATM) put options and the other out-of-the-money (OTM) put options. Consider options with one year to maturity on an underlying with a volatility of 16 percent p.a. and

Table 3.4   Theoretical stress and position limits*

	X	S_0	P_0	S_{VaR}	P_{VaR}	S_{Xtrm}	P_{Xtrm}
ATM	100	100	4.08	98	4.82	80	16.11
OTM	80	100	0.25	98	0.34	80	3.27

* $S = 16\%$p.a., $r = 5\%$p.a.; $T = 365$ days.

a risk free rate of 5 percent p.a. Today's value of the underlying is 100. The value of an ATM put with an exercise price of 100 is 4.08, while a deep OTM put has a value of 0.25.

The daily standard deviation is approximately 1 percent, and for simplicity we will consider a 2 percent decline in the underlying to 98 as the VaR, corresponding to the 2.5 percent VaR tail. A decline of the underlying to 98 would increase the ATM liability by 18 percent from 4.08 to 4.82, while the OTM liability would rise by 36 percent, from 0.25 to 0.34. It is clearly the case that the OTM option is riskier in percentage terms for an equal size move in the underlying. A VaR-sensitive risk limit system would be sensitive to that effect.

VaR limits are often set in terms of dollar amounts. Suppose we fix the "quality" of the counterparty and normalize by assuming that the ATM counterparty is allowed to write one put option, and hence a VaR of 4.82 − 4.08 = 0.74. The per-unit VaR of the OTM put writer is 0.34 − 0.25 = 0.09. The OTM writer may, hence, write 8.22 OTM options that will generate a VaR of:

8.22options*0.09 VaR per option = 0.74 total VaR.

Now consider an extreme decline in the underlying, from 100 to 80. The liability of the ATM writer would rise from 4.08 to 16.11, a rise of 295 percent. The OTM writer would see his liability rising from 0.25 to 3.27, a rise of 1,200 percent. When we add to this the fact that the OTM position was allowed to be 8.22 times larger due to equating VaR limits across the two positions, we would get a liability that rises from $0.25 \times 8.22 = 2.06$ to $3.27 \times 8.22 = 26.87$. The rise in percentage terms is still 1,200 percent, of course, but the risk should be measured in monetary, not percentage units. The loss, defined as the increase in the liability, in the extreme stress scenario, of the ATM writer is 16.11 − 4.08 = 12.03. The loss in the case of the OTM writer is 26.87 − 2.06 = 24.81.

The stress event loss inherent in the two seemingly equal risk (from a VaR perspective) positions is vastly different. The OTM writer has a stress event risk approximately twice as large as that of the ATM writer. This loophole in the VaR limit system may be caught by setting limits per counterparty. Recall, the OTM put writer was allowed the same VaR as the ATM writer. As a result he was allowed to have a position in 8.22 options rather than just one that the ATM writer was allowed. The idea carries through to other types of derivatives and levered positions.[10]

3.3   WORST-CASE SCENARIO (WCS)

3.3.1   WCS vs. VaR

In this section[11] a complementary measure to VaR is offered which is related to stress testing. It is the "worst-case scenario" (WCS) measure. WCS asks the following question "What is the worst that can happen to the value of the firm's trading portfolio over a given period (e.g., the next 20 or 100 trading days)?" This is to be compared with VaR's focus on the 5th or 1st *percentile* of the distribution.

To understand why WCS may be a more appropriate risk measure than VaR, consider the example above, where the firm's portfolio return is normally distributed with a mean μ_p and volatility σ_p. VaR tells us that losses greater than $\mu_p - 2.33\sigma_p$ will occur, on average, once over the next 100 trading periods, and that losses greater than $\mu_p - 1.65\sigma_p$ will occur, on average, once over the next 20 trading periods. From a risk management perspective, however, managers care more about the magnitude of losses given that a large loss occurs (WCS), rather than the number of times they should expect to face a loss of a given amount or greater (VaR).

In contrast to VaR, WCS focuses on the distribution of the loss during the worst trading period ("period" being, e.g., one day or two weeks), over a given horizon ("horizon" being, e.g., 100 days or one year). *The key point is that a worst period will occur with probability one. The question is how bad will it be?* As shown in figure 3.7, WCS analysis will show that the expected loss during the worst period is far greater than the corresponding VAR. Of more importance, there is a substantial probability of a much more severe loss.

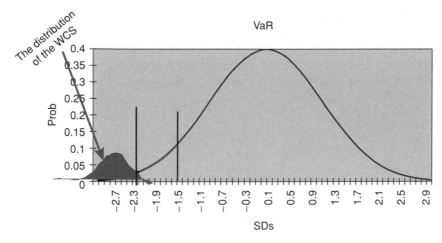

Figure 3.7   "The worst will happen"

3.3.2   A comparison of VaR to WCS

We assume that the firm's portfolio return is normally distributed with a mean of 0 and a volatility of 1. This is without loss of generality because we can always scale the portfolio up and down, both as far as mean as well as variance is concerned. Over N of these intervals, VaR states how many times one might expect to exceed a particular loss. In contrast, WCS states what the distribution of the maximum loss will be. That is, it focuses on $F(min[Z_1, Z_2, \ldots, Z_N])$, denoted $F(Z)$, where $F(\cdot)$ denotes the distribution function and Z_i denotes the normalized return series, corresponding to the change in the portfolio's value over interval i.

Table 3.5 shows the expected number of trading periods in which VaR will be exceeded. For example, the 5 percent VaR corresponds to 1.65 in the normalized units in the table and is expected to be exceeded once over a horizon of length 20, and five times over a horizon of length 100. This is the "classical" notion of VaR.

Table 3.5 also provides information regarding the WCS measures over different horizons. The distribution is obtained via a simulation of 10,000 random normal vectors (using antithetic variates) of lengths N, corresponding to the various horizons. The WCS distribution indicates that the expected worst loss over the next 20 periods is 1.86, while over the next 100 periods it is 2.51. More importantly, over the next

Table 3.5 The distribution of the minimum*

	H = 5	H = 20	H = 100	H = 250
E[number of $Z_i < -2.33$]	.05	.20	1.00	2.50
E[number of $Z_i < -1.65$]	.25	1.00	5.00	12.50
Expected WCS	−1.16	−1.86	−2.51	2.82
Percentile of Z				
1%	−2.80	−3.26	−3.72	−3.92
5%	−2.27	−2.77	−3.28	−3.54
10%	−2.03	−2.53	−3.08	−3.35
50%	−1.13	−1.82	−2.47	−2.78

* The WCS denoted Z is the lowest observation of a vector of $N(0,1)$'s of size H.

20 periods there is a 5 percent and a 1 percent probability of losses exceeding 2.77 and 3.26 respectively. The corresponding losses for a 100-period horizon are 3.28 and 3.72 respectively.

Looking at the results from a different perspective, for the 1 percent, 100-period VaR measure, the VaR is 2.33 while the expected WCS is 2.51 and the first percentile of the WCS distribution is 3.72. If the fraction of capital invested throughout the 100 periods is maintained, then WCS is the appropriate measure in forming risk management policies regarding financial distress. If the firm maintains capital at less than 160 percent of its VaR, there is a 1 percent chance that the firm will face financial distress over the 100 periods.

To summarize, consider a horizon of $H = 100$. The expected number of events where Z is less than −2.33 is 1 out of 100 (1 percent VaR). The distribution of the worst case, $\underline{Z}$, is such that its average is −2.51, and its 5th and 1st percentiles are −3.28 and −3.72 respectively. That is, over the next 100 trading periods a return worse than −2.33 is expected to occur once, when it does, it is expected to be of size −2.51, but with probability 1 percent it might be −3.72 or worse (i.e., we focus on the 1%tile of the Z's).

3.3.3   Extensions

Our analysis indicates the importance of the information in the WCS over and above VaR. In practice, the WCS analysis has some natural extensions and caveats, which also pertain to VaR.

First, our analysis was developed in the context of a specific model of the firm's investment behavior; that is, we assumed that the firm, in order to remain "capital efficient," increases the level of investment when gains are realized. There are alternative models of investment behaviour, which suggest other aspects of the distribution of returns should be investigated. For example, we might be interested in the distribution of "bad runs," corresponding to partial sums of length J periods for a given horizon of H.

Second, the effect of time-varying volatility has been ignored. Assuming that the risk capital measures are adjusted to reflect this, e.g., via RiskMetrics, GARCH, density estimation, implied volatility, or another method, there is the issue of model risk. That is, to the extent that volatility is not captured perfectly, there may be times when we understate it. Consequently, the probability of exceeding the VAR and the size of the 1 percent tail of the WCS will be understated.

Third, and related to model risk, there is the issue of the tail behavior of financial series. It is well established that volatility-forecasting schemes tend to understate the likelihood and size of extreme moves. This holds true for currencies, commodities, equities, and interest rates (to varying degrees). This aspect will also tend to understate the frequency and size of extreme losses. For a specific case, one could infer a distribution from the historical series in order to obtain a better description of the relevant distribution and so capture the tails. This caveat extends naturally to the issue of correlations, where the most important question is whether extreme moves have the same correlation characteristics as the rest of the data. Of course, if correlations in the extremes are higher, we face the risk of understating the WCS risk.

In conclusion, the analysis of the WCS, and further investigation of the caveats discussed above, is important for the study of some of the more recent proposals on the use of internal models and the more lenient capital requirements imposed on "sophisticated" banks and major dealers. These issues are even more critical when it comes to estimating credit risk and operational risk exposures.

3.4   SUMMARY

The first section of this chapter focused on the calculation of VaR for derivatives. While linear derivatives are relatively easy to price and hedge, nonlinear derivatives pose a challenge. There are two approaches to calculating the VaR of nonlinear derivatives – the Greeks approach, and the full revaluation approach. The Greeks approach relies on approximating the valuation function of the derivative. The approximation can be rough (linear or delta approximation) or more precise (nonlinear or delta–gamma approximation). The full revaluation approach calls for the revaluation of the derivative at the VaR value of the underlying. That is, in order to assess the risk in the derivative position, the derivatives need to be revalued at an extreme value (e.g., the VaR value) of the underlying.

Difficulty arises in generalizing this approach since some derivative positions may "hide" loss scenarios. For example, an ATM straddle does not lose at extreme values of the underlying but, rather, at current levels. Motivated by this issue, as well as by our discussion of empirical implementation of VaR in chapter 2, we turned to a discussion of structured Monte Carlo (SMC). SMC is an approach that facilitates the generation of a large number of economically meaningful scenarios. In comparison to scenario analysis, SMC-generated scenarios are drawn from the variance–covariance matrix of underlying risk factors. As such, risk factors will be as correlated in SMC scenarios as they are in reality. Moreover, SMC generates a large number of scenarios, thereby giving a probabilistic meaning to extreme scenarios.

In spite of these clear advantages SMC can generate scenarios only as informative as the variance–covariance matrix that was used to generate such scenarios. To the extent that this matrix is not fully representative of risk factor co-movements under extreme market stress, then SMC will fail to generate realistic scenarios. We provide anecdotal evidence that correlations do seem to fall apart during extreme market conditions, motivating a historical-simulation-based approach to stress testing.

We conclude with a discussion of the worst case scenario measure for risk, an alternative to the standard VaR approach. The pros and cons of the two approaches are discussed.

APPENDIX 3.1   DURATION

Consider first a t-period zero coupon bond. For simplicity we will discuss annual compounding, although the convention is often semi-annual compounding. The price-rate relation can be written as follows

$$d_t(r_t) = \frac{1}{(1 + r_t)^t}.$$

For example, compare the value (per $1 of face value) of a one-year vs. a five-year zero, where rates are assumed to be in both cases 5 percent. The value of the one-year zero is $0.9524, and the value of the five-year zero is $0.7835.

In order to discuss the price sensitivity of fixed income securities as a function of changes in interest rates, we first introduce dollar duration, the price sensitivity, and then duration,[12] the percentage sensitivity. We define dollar duration as the change in value in the zero for a given change in interest rates of 1 percent. This is approximately the derivative of the zero with respect to interest rates, or:

$$d'_t(r_t) = \frac{-t}{(1 + r_t)^{t+1}},$$

therefore

$$\$dur_t = -d'_t(r_t) = \frac{t}{(1 + r_t)^{t+1}}.$$

The dollar duration of the one-year zero is $1/(1.05)^2 = 0.9070$ whereas the dollar duration of the five-year zero is $5/(1.05)^6 = 3.73$. What this means is that an increase in rates from 5 percent to 6 percent should generate a loss of $0.00907 in the value of the one-year zero, as compared to a loss of $0.0373 in the value of the five-year zero coupon bond. Thus, the five-year zero is more sensitive to interest rate changes. Its sensitivity is close to being five times as large (if interest rates were 0 percent, then this comparison would be precise).

The expression for duration is actually an approximation.[13] In contrast, the precise calculation would show that if interest rates increased 1 percent from 5 percent to 6 percent, then the new price of the one-year zero would be $1/(1.06) = 0.9434, and $1/(1.06)^5 = 0.7473 for the five-year. Comparing these new prices to the original prices before the interest rate increase (i.e., $0.9524 for the one-year and $0.7835 for the five-year), we can obtain a precise calculation of the price losses due to the interest rate increase. For the one-year zero, the precise calculation of price decline is $0.9524 − 0.9434 = $0.0090 and for the five-year zero, $0.7835 − 0.7472 = $0.0363. Comparing these results to the duration approximation above, we see that the duration approximation overstated price declines for the one-year zero by $0.00007 = 0.00907 − 0.0090. The overstatement was higher for the five-year zero; $0.0010 = 0.0373 − 0.0363. Duration is an overly

Table 3.6 Duration example

t	d(r = 5%)	$Dur	Dur	D-loss	d(r = 6%)	True loss	Duration error
1	**$0.9524**	**$0.9070**	**0.9524**	**$0.0091**	**$0.9434**	**$0.0090**	**–$0.0001**
2	$0.9070	$1.7277	1.9048	$0.0173	$0.8900	$0.0170	–$0.0002
3	$0.8638	$2.4681	2.8571	$0.0247	$0.8396	$0.0242	–$0.0005
4	$0.8227	$3.1341	3.8095	$0.0313	$0.7921	$0.0306	–$0.0007
5	**$0.7835**	**$3.7311**	**4.7619**	**$0.0373**	**$0.7473**	**$0.0363**	**–$0.0010**
6	$0.7462	$4.2641	5.7143	$0.0426	$0.7050	$0.0413	–$0.0014
7	$0.7107	$4.7379	6.6667	$0.0474	$0.6651	$0.0456	–$0.0018
8	$0.6768	$5.1569	7.6190	$0.0516	$0.6274	$0.0494	–$0.0021
9	$0.6446	$5.5252	8.5714	$0.0553	$0.5919	$0.0527	–$0.0025
10	$0.6139	$5.8468	9.5238	$0.0585	$0.5584	$0.0555	–$0.0029
1&5	**$1.7359**	**$4.6381**	**2.6719**	**$0.0464**	**$1.6907**	**$0.0453**	**–$0.0011**

pessimistic approximation of price changes resulting from unanticipated interest rate fluctuations. That is, duration overstates the price decline in the event of interest rate increases and understates the price increase in the event of an interest rate decline. Table 3.6 summarizes our example.

It is easy to generalize this price–rate relationship to coupon bonds and all other fixed cash flow portfolios. Assuming all interest rates change by the same amount (a parallel shift), it is easy to show that

$$\text{portfolio } \$dur = k_1 \times \$dur_{t_1} + k_2 \times \$dur_{t_2} + \ldots$$

where $k_1, k_2, \ldots$ are the dollar cash flows in periods $t_1, t_2, \ldots$

Duration is easy to define now as:

duration

$\approx$ [percent change in value] per [100 bp change in rates]

$$= \left[\frac{\text{dollar change in value per 100 bp}}{\text{initial value}} \right] \bigg/ [1/100]$$

$$= \left[\frac{\text{dollar duration} \times 0.01}{\text{initial value}} \right] \times 100$$

$$= \frac{\text{dollar duration}}{\text{initial value}}.$$

Therefore we get

$$\text{duration} = \frac{\dfrac{t}{(1 + r_t)^{t+1}}}{\dfrac{1}{(1 + r_t)^t}} = \frac{t}{(1 + r_t)},$$

and for a portfolio we get

$$\text{duration} = \frac{\text{dollar duration}}{\text{value}} = \frac{k_1 \times \$dur_{t_1} + k_2 \times \$dur_{t_2} + \ldots}{k_1 \times d_{t_1} + k_2 \times d_{t_2} + \ldots},$$

but since

$$\$dur_t = d_t \times dur_t$$

we get

$$\text{portfolio dur} = \frac{k_1 \times d_{t_1} \times dur_{t_1} + k_2 \times d_{t_2} \times dur_{t_2} + \ldots}{k_1 \times d_{t_1} + k_2 \times d_{t_2} + \ldots}$$

$$\Rightarrow \text{portfolio dur} = w_1 \times dur_{t_1} + w_2 \times dur_{t_2} + \ldots.$$

where $w_i = \dfrac{k_i \times d_{t_i}}{k_1 \times d_{t_1} + k_2 \times d_{t_2} + \ldots}$ is the pv weight of cash flow i.

That is, the duration, or interest rate sensitivity, of a portfolio, under the parallel shift in rates assumption, is just the weighted sum of all the portfolio sensitivities of the portfolio cash flow components, each weighted by its present value (i.e., its contribution to the present value of the entire portfolio).

Going back to our example, consider a portfolio of cash flows consisting of $1 in one year and $1 in five years. Assuming 5 percent p.a. interest rates, the value of this portfolio is the sum of the two bonds, $0.9524 + 0.7835 = $1.7359, and the sum of the dollar durations, $0.9070 + 3.73 = $4.6370. However, the duration of the portfolio is:

$$\$2.18116 = \frac{0.9524}{1.7359}(0.907) + \frac{0.7835}{1.7359}(3.73).$$

This tells us that a parallel shift upwards in rates from a flat term structure at 5 percent to a flat term structure at 6 percent would generate a loss of 2.18116 percent. Given a portfolio value of $1.7359, the dollar loss is 2.18116% × $1.7359 = $0.03786.

The way to incorporate duration into VaR calculations is straightforward. In particular, duration is a portfolio's percentage loss for a 1 percent move in interest rates. The percentage VaR of a portfolio is, hence, its duration multiplied by interest rate volatility. For example, suppose we are interested in the one-month VaR of the portfolio of one-year and five-year zeros, whose value is $1.7359 and duration is 2.18116. Suppose further that the volatility of interest rates is 7bp/day, and there are 25 trading days in a month. The monthly volatility using the square root rule is $\sqrt{(25)} \times 7 = 35$bp/month. The %VaR is therefore 2.18116 × 0.35 = 0.7634%, and the $VaR = 0.007634 × $1.7359 = $0.01325.

There is clearly no question of aggregation. In particular, since we assume a single factor model for interest rates, the assumed VaR shift in rates of 35bp affects all rates along the term structure. The correlation between losses of all cash flows of the portfolio is one. It is, therefore, the case that the VaR of the portfolio is just the sum of the VaRs of the two cash flows, the one-year zero and the five-year zero.

CHAPTER FOUR

EXTENDING THE VaR APPROACH TO NON-TRADABLE LOANS

Market risk exposure arises from unexpected security price fluctuations. Using long histories of daily price fluctuations, chapters 1–3 demonstrated how VaR techniques are used to estimate the tails of the price distribution in order to obtain measures of trading losses on unusually (say, one in 100) bad days. Using this history of daily price fluctuations we can distinguish between "typical" and "atypical" trading days.

Unfortunately, measuring a loan's credit risk exposure is far more difficult. Since loans are not always traded, and even when traded they trade infrequently, there is often no history of daily price fluctuations available to build a (loan) loss distribution. Moreover, credit events such as default or rating downgrades are rare, often non-recurring events. Thus, we often have insufficient statistical power to estimate a daily VaR for credit risk exposure; i.e., data limitations create special challenges in adapting VaR techniques to estimate credit risk exposure. However, we can use VaR techniques to estimate losses due to credit events if the time interval we consider is longer. Indeed, the convention in the new generation of credit risk models is to assume that the credit risk time horizon is one year, thereby estimating losses during the next year if it is a "bad" year, defined according to a specified VaR level; for example, a 99.5 percentile VaR estimates the minimum losses in the worst 5 years out of a thousand.

There are many sources of credit risk exposure ranging from corporate and sovereign debt instruments to credit derivatives to syndicated loans to retail mortgages to other asset-backed securities. In this chapter, we survey some VaR methods used to estimate credit risk exposure. We describe proprietary VaR models such as CreditMetrics and Algorithmics Mark-to-Future. We relate these proprietary VaR models to two basic theoretical approaches: the structural approach and the reduced form or intensity-based approach. However, even before VaR and other methods to estimate credit risk became available, banks and other lenders employed credit risk measurement models. Indeed, many of these models continue to be employed, especially at smaller banks. Therefore, we begin this chapter with a brief survey of those traditional models.

4.1   TRADITIONAL APPROACHES TO CREDIT RISK MEASUREMENT

Traditional methods focus on estimating the probability of default (PD), rather than on the magnitude of potential losses in the event of default (so-called LGD, loss given default, also known as LIED, loss in the event of default). Moreover, traditional models typically specify "failure" to be a bankruptcy filing, default, or liquidation, thereby ignoring consideration of the downgrades and upgrades in credit quality that are measured in so-called "mark to market" models. We consider three broad categories of traditional models used to estimate PD: (i) expert systems, including artificial neural networks; (ii) rating systems; and (iii) credit scoring models.

4.1.1   Expert systems

Historically, many bankers have relied on the 5 Cs of the credit expert system to assess credit quality. The 5 Cs are:

1 **Character** – a measure of the reputation of the firm, its willingness to repay, and its repayment history.
2 **Capital** – the equity contribution of owners and its ratio to debt (leverage).
3 **Capacity** – the ability to repay, which reflects the volatility of the borrower's earnings. If repayments on debt contracts follow a constant stream over time, but earnings are volatile (or have a high standard deviation), there may be periods when the firm's capacity to repay debt claims is constrained.
4 **Collateral** – in the event of default, a banker has claims on the collateral pledged by the borrower.
5 **Cycle (or economic) conditions** – the state of the business cycle is an important element in determining credit risk exposure. Even firms that appear to be relatively independent of general macro-economic effects become more cycle dependent during economic downturns and financial crises as asset correlations approach one worldwide.

Evaluation of the 5 Cs is performed by human experts (e.g., loan officers), who may be inconsistent and subjective in their assessments. Moreover, traditional expert systems specify no weighting scheme that would order the 5 Cs in terms of their relative importance in forecasting PD. Thus, artificial neural networks have been introduced to evaluate expert systems more objectively and consistently. A neural network is "trained" using historical repayment experiences and default data. Structural matches are found that coincide with defaulting firms and then used to determine a weighting scheme to forecast PD. Each time that the neural network evaluates the credit risk of a new loan opportunity, it updates its weighting scheme so that it continually "learns" from experience. Thus, neural networks are flexible, adaptable systems that can incorporate changing conditions into the decision making process. For example, Kim and Scott (1991) use a supervised artificial neural network to predict bankruptcy in a sample of 190 Compustat firms. While the system performs well (87 percent prediction rate) during the year of bankruptcy, its accuracy declines markedly over time, showing only a 75 percent, 59 percent, and 47 percent prediction accuracy one-year prior, two-years prior, and three-years prior to bankruptcy, respectively. Altman, Marco, and Varetto (1994) examine 1,000 Italian industrial firms from 1982 to 1992 and find that neural networks have about the same level of accuracy as do traditional credit scoring models. Poddig (1994), using data on 300 French firms collected over three years, claims that neural networks outperform traditional credit scoring models in bankruptcy prediction. However, he finds that not all artificial neural systems are equal, noting that the multi-layer perception (or back propagation) network is best suited for bankruptcy prediction. Yang, Platt, and Platt (1999) use a sample of oil and gas company debt to show that the back propagation neural network obtained the highest classification accuracy overall, when compared to the probabilistic neural network, and discriminant analysis. However, discriminant analysis outperforms all models of neural networks in minimizing type 2 classification errors.[1]

During "training" the neural network fits a system of weights to each financial variable included in a database consisting of historical repayment/default experiences. However, the network may be "overfit" to a particular database if excessive training has taken place, thereby resulting in poor out-of-sample estimates. Moreover, neural networks are costly to implement and maintain. Because of the large number of possible connections, the neural network can grow prohibitively large rather quickly. For a set of networks with 10 inputs (say, financial data) and 12 hidden units (endogenously determined by the neural network), the maximum possible number of network configurations[2] is 4.46×10^{43}. Thus, various pruning methods exist to economize on the number of connections in the system. Finally, neural networks suffer from a lack of transparency. Since there is no direct economic interpretation attached to the hidden intermediate steps, the system cannot be checked for plausibility and accuracy. Structural errors will not be detected until PD estimates become noticeably inaccurate.

4.1.2   Rating systems

External credit ratings provided by firms specializing in credit analysis were first offered in the US by Moody's in 1909. White (2002) identifies 37 credit rating agencies with headquarters outside of the US. These firms offer investors access to low cost information about the creditworthiness of bond issuers. The usefulness of this information is not limited to bond investors. Kallberg and Udell (2001) show that access to data gathered by independent credit bureaus, such as Dun and Bradstreet, are useful in improving efficiency in directing trade credit and bank credit card offers.

When using external credit ratings as a measure of credit quality, a distinction must be made between "point-in-time" and "through-the-cycle" risk assessment. This is most relevant in the context of interpreting external credit ratings that are designed to be "through-the-cycle" assessments of the default probability over the life of the loan. Thus, the PD is estimated at the worst point in the cycle expected to prevail over the debt maturity time horizon.[3] In contrast, "point-in-time" assessments of PD respond to changes in cyclical conditions. Crouhy, Galai, and Mark (2001) contend that "through-the-cycle" ratings are a more appropriate input into lending decisions, whereas "point-in-time" ratings are more appropriate for the purposes of capital allocation. For a discussion of cyclicality in credit risk estimates, see Allen and Saunders (2002).

The Office of the Comptroller of the Currency (OCC) in the US has long required banks to use internal ratings systems to rank the credit quality of loans in their portfolios. However, the rating system has been rather crude, with most loans rated as Pass/Performing and only a minority of loans differentiated according to the four non-performing classifications (listed in order of declining credit quality): other assets especially mentioned (OAEM), substandard, doubtful, and loss. Similarly, the National Association of Insurance Commissioners (NAIC) requires insurance companies to rank their assets using a rating schedule with six classifications corresponding to the following credit ratings: A and above, BBB, BB, B, below B, and default.

Many banks have instituted internal ratings systems in preparation for the BIS New Capital Accords scheduled for implementation in 2006 (see discussion in chapter 7). The architecture of the internal rating system can be one-dimensional, in which an overall rating is assigned to each loan based on the probability of default (PD) or expected loss (EL), or two-dimensional, in which each borrower's PD is assessed separately from the loss severity of the individual loan (LGD). Treacy and Carey (2000) estimate that 60 percent of the financial institutions in their survey had one-dimensional rating systems, although they recommend a two-dimensional system. Moreover, the BIS (2000) found that banks were better able to assess the PD of their borrowers in contrast to estimating LGD.[4]

Treacy and Carey (2000) in their survey of the 50 largest US bank holding companies, and the BIS (2000) in their survey of 30 financial institutions across the G-10 countries, found considerable diversity in internal ratings models. Although all used similar financial risk factors, there were differences across financial institutions with regard to the relative importance of each of the factors. Treacy and Carey (2000) found that qualitative factors played more of a role in determining the ratings of loans to small and medium-sized firms, with the loan officer chiefly responsible for the ratings, in contrast with loans to large firms in which the credit staff primarily set the ratings using quantitative methods such as credit-scoring models. Typically, ratings were set with a one-year time horizon, although loan repayment behavior data were often available for 3–5 years.[5]

4.1.3   Credit scoring models

The most commonly used traditional credit risk measurement methodology is the multiple discriminant credit scoring analysis pioneered by Altman (1968). Mester (1997) documents the widespread use of credit scoring models: 97 percent of banks use credit scoring to approve credit card applications, whereas 70 percent of the banks use credit scoring in their small business lending.[6] There are four methodological forms of multivariate credit scoring models: (i) the linear probability model; (ii) the logit model; (iii) the probit model; and (iv) the multiple discriminant analysis model. All of these models identify financial variables that have statistical explanatory power in differentiating defaulting firms from non-defaulting firms. Once the model's parameters are obtained, loan applicants are assigned a Z-score assessing their classification as good or bad. The Z-score itself can also be converted into a PD. For a discussion of advances in credit scoring models, see Wharton (2002).

Credit scoring models are relatively inexpensive to implement and do not suffer from the subjectivity and inconsistency of expert systems. Table 4.1 shows the spread of these models throughout the world, as surveyed by Altman and Narayanan (1997). What is striking is not so much the models' differences across countries of diverse size and in various stages of development, but rather their similarities. Most studies found that financial ratios measuring profitability, leverage, and liquidity had the most statistical power in differentiating defaulted from non-defaulted firms.

Shortcomings of all credit scoring models are data limitations and the assumption of linearity. Discriminant analysis fits a linear function of

Table 4.1 International survey of business failure classification models

Studies cited	Explanatory variables
United States	
Altman (1968)	EBIT/assets; retained earnings/assets; working capital/assets; sales/assets; market value (MV) equity/book value of debt.
Japan	
Ko (1982)	EBIT/sales; working capital/debt; inventory turnover 2 years prior/inventory turnover 3 years prior; MV equity/debt; standard error of net income (4 years).
Takahashi, Kurokawa, and Watase (1979)	Net worth/fixed assets; current liabilities/assets; voluntary reserves plus unappropriated surplus/assets; interest expense/sales; earned surplus; increase in residual value/sales; ordinary profit/assets; sales − variable costs.
Switzerland	
Weibel (1973)	Liquidity (near monetary resource asset − current liabilities)/operating expenses prior to depreciation; inventory turnover; debt/assets.
Germany	
Baetge, Huss, and Niehaus (1988)	Net worth/(total assets − quick assets − property & plant); (operating income + ordinary depreciation + addition to pension reserves)/assets; (cash income − expenses)/short-term liabilities.
von Stein and Ziegler (1984)	Capital borrowed/total capital; short-term borrowed capital/output; accounts payable for purchases & deliveries/material costs; (bill of exchange liabilities + accounts payable)/output; (current assets − short-term borrowed capital)/output; equity/(total assets − liquid assets − real estate); equity/(tangible property − real estate); short-term borrowed capital/current assets; (working expenditure − depreciation on tangible property)/(liquid assets + accounts receivable − short-term borrowed capital); operational result/capital; (operational result + depreciation)/net turnover; (operational result + depreciation)/short-term borrowed capital; (operational result + depreciation)/total capital borrowed.

Table 4.1 (*cont'd*)

Studies cited	Explanatory variables
England Marais (1979), Earl and Marais (1982)	Current assets/gross total assets; 1/gross total assets; cash flow/current liabilities; (funds generated from operations – net change in working capital)/debt.
Canada Altman and Lavallee (1981)	Current assets/current liabilities; net after-tax profits/debt; rate of growth of equity – rate of asset growth; debt/assets; sales/assets.
The Netherlands Bilderbeek (1979) van Frederikslust (1978)	Retained earnings/assets; accounts payable/sales; added value/assets; sales/assets; net profit/equity. Liquidity ratio (change in short-term debt over time); profitability ratio (rate of return on equity).
Spain Fernandez (1988)	Return on investment; cash flow/current liabilities; quick ratio/industry value; before tax earnings/sales; cash flow/sales; (permanent funds/net fixed assets)/industry value.
Italy Altman, Marco, and Varetto (1994)	Ability to bear cost of debt; liquidity; ability to bear financial debt; profitability; assets/liabilities; profit accumulation; trade indebtedness; efficiency.
Australia Izan (1984)	EBIT/interest; MV equity/liabilities; EBIT/assets; funded debt/shareholder funds; current assets/current liabilities.
Greece Gloubos and Grammatikos (1988)	Gross income/current liabilities; debt/assets; net working capital/assets; gross income/assets; current assets/current liabilities.
Brazil Altman, Baidya, and Ribeiro-Dias (1979)	Retained earnings/assets; EBIT/assets; sales/assets; MV equity/book value of liabilities.

Table 4.1   (*cont'd*)

Studies cited	Explanatory variables
India Bhatia (1988)	Cash flow/debt; current ratio; profit after tax/net worth; interest/output; sales/assets; stock of finished goods/sales; working capital management ratio.
Korea Altman, Kim, and Eom (1995)	Log(assets); log(sales/assets); retained earnings/assets; MV of equity/liabilities.
Singapore Ta and Seah (1981)	Operating profit/liabilities; current assets/current liabilities; EAIT/paid-up capital; sales/working capital; (current assets − stocks − current liabilities)/EBIT; total shareholders' fund/liabilities; ordinary shareholders' fund/capital used.
Finland Suominen (1988)	Profitability: (quick flow − direct taxes)/assets; liquidity: (quick assets/total assets); liabilities/assets.
Uruguay Pascale (1988)	Sales/debt; net earnings/assets; long-term debt/total debt.
Turkey Unal (1988)	EBIT/assets; quick assets/current debt; net working capital/sales; quick assets/inventory; debt/assets; long-term debt/assets.

Notes: Whenever possible, the explanatory variables are listed in order of statistical importance (e.g., the size of the coefficient term) from highest to lowest.
Source: Altman and Narayanan (1997).

explanatory variables to the historical data on default. Moreover, as shown in table 4.1, the explanatory variables are predominately limited to balance sheet data. These data are updated infrequently and are determined by accounting procedures which permit book rather than market valuation. Finally, there is often limited economic theory as to why a particular financial ratio would be useful in forecasting default. In contrast, modern credit risk measurement models are often more firmly grounded in financial theory.

4.2   THEORETICAL UNDERPINNINGS: TWO APPROACHES

Modern methods of credit risk measurement can be traced to two alternative branches in the asset pricing literature of academic finance: an
options-theoretic structural approach pioneered by Merton (1974) and a
reduced form approach utilizing intensity-based models to estimate
stochastic hazard rates, following a literature pioneered by Jarrow and
Turnbull (1995), Jarrow, Lando, and Turnbull (1997), and Duffie and
Singleton (1998, 1999). These two schools of thought offer differing
methodologies to accomplish the central task of all credit risk measurement models – estimation of default probabilities. Structural models
utilize equity prices and risk-free debt prices in order to obtain
the risk-neutral probability of borrower default. In contrast, reduced
form models input risky debt prices in order to estimate the risk-
neutral default probability.

The default probabilities estimated using either the structural or reduced form approach are then input into a VaR model in order to obtain
estimates of unexpected losses. That is, under a *default mode* (DM) model,
the value of the portfolio is simulated considering only two possible
outcomes for each asset in the portfolio: either default or non-default.
However, most VaR models are *mark-to-market* (MTM) models in
which the value of the portfolio is simulated for all possible credit events,
including upgrade and downgrade, as well as default. Either structural
or intensity-based models can be used to estimate the likelihood of each
credit event in order to estimate the portfolio's value distribution.[7] Since
these probabilities are critical inputs into all VaR credit risk models,
we first summarize the structural and reduced form approaches.[8]

4.2.1   Options-theoretic structural models of
credit risk measurement

Merton (1974) models equity in a levered firm as a call option on the
firm's assets with a strike price equal to the debt repayment amount.
If at expiration (coinciding to the maturity of the firm's liabilities,
assumed to be comprised of pure discount debt instruments) the market value of the firm's assets exceeds the value of its debt (denoted
B), as shown in figure 4.1 when asset values $A_2 > B$, then the firm's
shareholders will exercise the option to "repurchase" the company's
assets by repaying the debt. This is the no default region shown in

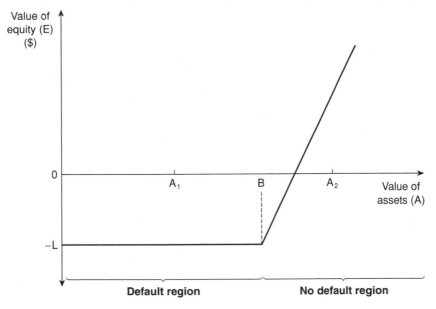

Figure 4.1   Equity as a call option on a firm

figure 4.1. However, if the market value of the firm's assets falls below the value of its debt, as when $A_1 < B$, then the option will expire unexercised and the firm's shareholders will default, shown as the default region in figure 4.1.[9] Thus, the PD until expiration (set equal to the maturity date of the firm's pure discount debt, typically assumed to be one year)[10] is equal to the likelihood that the option will expire out of the money. To determine the PD we value the call option[11] as explained below.

Using standard option valuation models, the value of the equity (E) call option on the firm's value can be expressed as a function of five variables:

1   The value of the option's underlying instrument: A, the *market value* (not the book value) of the firm's assets.
2   The volatility of the market value: σ_A, i.e., the standard deviation of the firm's market value of assets.
3   The risk-free rate: denoted r.
4   The time to expiration: set equal to the debt's maturity date, T, or a given debt horizon such as one year.
5   The exercise price: the face value of the firm's debt, denoted B.

Thus, the option valuation expression for the firm's equity value E is:

$$E = E(A, \sigma_A, r, T, B). \tag{4.1}$$

All values can easily be obtained with the exception of A and σ_A, the *market* value of the firm's assets and its asset volatility. To solve for these two unknowns, we need two equations. Specifically, as the second equation we can use the relationship between the unknown σ_A and the volatility of equity, σ_E (estimated from a time series of equity prices):

$$\sigma_E = (A/E)(\partial E/\partial A)\sigma_A. \tag{4.2}$$

Using equations (4.1) and (4.2) and inserting values for the known or observable variables on the left-hand sides and the right-hand sides of equations (4.1) and (4.2), we can iteratively solve for A and σ_A. These values for A and σ_A are combined with the amount of debt liabilities B (to be repaid at a given horizon date) to calculate the firm's current Distance to Default (the number of standard deviations between current asset values and the debt repayment amount). The greater the Distance to Default, the lower the PD (often called the expected default frequency (EDF) in these models). The Distance to Default (and hence PD) can be calculated for different credit time horizons, e.g., 1 year, 2 years, as shown in figure 4.2.

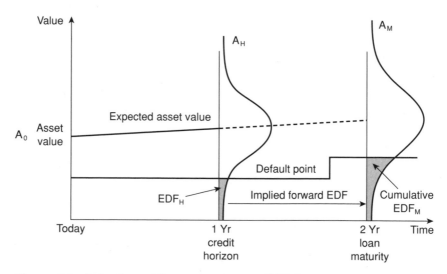

Figure 4.2   Valuation of the term structure of EDF

To convert the Distance to Default into a PD estimate, Merton assumes that asset values are lognormally distributed. Using the well-known properties of the normal distribution, figure 4.2 shows the shaded areas under the asset distribution function as estimates of the PD. However, since asset values display properties not associated with the normal distribution (e.g. fat tails and skewness – see chapters 1–3), proprietary structural models, such as KMV's Credit Monitor and Moody's Public Firm model, use alternative approaches to resolve this practical problem of converting the distance to default into a PD. For example, KMV uses databases containing historical experience, and Moody's uses a neural network to analyze historical experience and current financial data.

A new model called CreditGrades, sponsored jointly by the RiskMetrics Group, Goldman Sachs, JP Morgan and Deutsche Bank, addresses this problem in the context of the option theoretic model by assuming a stochastic default barrier.[12] Since the exact level of leverage is unknown prior to default, CreditGrades assumes that the default barrier is lognormally distributed, allowing for possible discrete jumps in the default point, thereby increasing the estimated PD as compared to the understated estimates obtained by Merton (1974) using the normal distribution. Thus, CreditGrades is able to estimate PD using a closed form function of six observable market parameters, in contrast to KMV's and Moody's approaches that rely on proprietary databases. The survival probability is calculated in CreditGrades as follows:

$$P(t) = \Phi\left(-\frac{A_t}{2} + \frac{\log(d)}{A_t}\right) - d\Phi\left(-\frac{A_t}{2} - \frac{\log(d)}{A_t}\right), \qquad (4.3)$$

where $d \equiv \dfrac{S_0 + LD}{LD}e^{\lambda^2}$

$$A_t^2 = \left(\sigma_S^* \frac{S^*}{S^* + LD}\right)^2 t + \lambda^2,$$

where D = debt per share, calculated from financial statements. Debt is defined to be the principal value of short-term bonds plus long-term bonds plus convertible bonds plus quasi-debts (including capital leases, under-funded pension liabilities and preferred shares). The number of shares (for the denominator of the calculation) are the number of common shares outstanding, including all classes of stock.

L = the mean of the global debt recovery rate;

λ = the standard deviation of the default barrier stochastic distribution. The variables L and λ are calculated from the Portfolio Management Data and the S&P database which contains actual recovery data for 300 non-financial firms that defaulted over the period of 1987–97 (Finger et al. (2002) calculate the values $L = 0.50$ and $\lambda = 0.30$);

S_0 = the initial stock price;

S^* = the current stock price;

σ_S^* = implied stock volatility, which is related to the unobservable implied asset volatility, σ, through the leverage ratio. That is: $\sigma = \sigma_S^*(S^*/(S^* + LD))$. The equity volatility measure is chosen to best match the actual credit default swap (CDS) spreads in the market. Finger et al. (2002) use five-year CDS spreads for 122 firms (with a variety of credit qualities) over the period May 2000 to August 2001 to show that the best fit is obtained using the simple equity volatility computed over the last 1,000 days of equity returns.

Default occurs after ample early warning in Merton's structural model. That is, default occurs only after a gradual decline (diffusion) in asset values to the default point (equal to the debt level). This process implies that the PD steadily approaches zero as the time to maturity declines, something not observed in empirical term structures of credit spreads; e.g., even high rated short-term commercial paper carries a positive spread over the Fed funds rate. CreditGrades resolves this problem by matching equity volatilities to observed spreads on credit default swaps and assuming a stochastic default barrier.[13] Another way to obtain more realistic credit spreads is to use the reduced form or intensity-based model to estimate PD. That is, whereas structural models view default as the outcome of a gradual process of deterioration in asset values,[14] intensity-based models view default as a sudden, unexpected event, thereby generating PD estimates that are more consistent with empirical observations.

4.2.2 Reduced form or intensity-based models of credit risk measurement

In contrast to structural models, intensity-based models do not specify the economic process leading to default. Default is modeled as a point process. Defaults occur randomly with a probability determined by the intensity or "hazard" function. Intensity-based models decompose observed credit spreads on defaultable debt to ascertain both the PD (conditional on there being no default prior to time t) and the LGD (which is 1 minus the recovery rate). Thus, intensity-based models are fundamentally empirical, using observable risky debt prices (and credit spreads) in order to ascertain the stochastic jump process governing default.

Because the observed credit spread (defined as the spread over the risk-free rate) can be viewed as a measure of the expected cost of default, we can express it as follows:

$$CS = PD \times LGD, \tag{4.4}$$

where CS = the credit spread on risky debt = risky debt yield minus
the risk free rate;
PD = the probability of default;
LGD = the loss given default = 1 − the recovery rate.

To illustrate the decomposition of credit spreads into PD and LGD, we first consider a discrete version of reduced form models in order to demonstrate the intuition behind the continuous time versions often used in practice. We proceed from very simple assumptions and gradually add complexity.

Consider a B rated $100 face value, zero coupon debt security with one year until maturity and a fixed recovery rate (which is the same as 1 minus the loss given default, LGD). For simplicity, assume that the LGD = 100%, or that the recovery rate is zero; i.e., the entire loan is lost in the event of default. The current price of this debt instrument can be evaluated in two equivalent ways. First, the expected cash flows may be discounted at the risk-free rate, assumed to be 8 percent p.a. in our example. Since the security is worthless upon default, the expected cash flows are $100(1 − PD), where PD = the probability of default. If the security's price is observed to be $87.96, then we can solve for PD as follows:

$$\frac{100(1 - PD)}{1 + 0.08} = 87.96 \tag{4.5}$$

thereby obtaining a PD of 5 percent p.a. that satisfies the equality in equation (4.5). Equivalently,[15] the security could be discounted at a risk-adjusted rate of return, denoted y such that:

$$\frac{100}{1 + y} = 87.96 \tag{4.6}$$

thereby obtaining a value of $y = 13.69\%$ p.a. that satisfies equation (4.6). The present value of this security is \$87.96.

Under our simplifying assumptions, the relationship between the risk-adjusted return, y, and the risk free rate, denoted r, is:

$$1 + r = (1 - PD)(1 + y) \tag{4.7}$$

$$\text{or,} \quad 1.08 = (1 - 0.05)(1.1369).$$

Since r and y are observable spot rates for traded B rated debt securities, equation (4.7) could be used to solve directly for the probability of default (PD) for B rated corporate bonds.

In general, the PD is not constant, but instead varies over time; therefore, we can express the probability of default as $PD(t)$. If we convert equation (4.7) to its continuous time equivalent, still assuming a zero recovery rate, we have:

$$y = r + PD(t). \tag{4.8}$$

That is, the yield on risky debt is composed of a riskless rate plus a credit spread equal to the probability of default at any point in time t where $PD(t)$ is the stochastic default rate intensity.

Considering other points on the B rated spot yield curve, we can decompose the time-varying credit spread included in the longer maturity zero coupon B rated corporate bond; suppose that the two-year spot rate on the B rated date is 16 percent p.a. In order to divide this rate into its component parts, we must first solve for the one-year forward rate; that is, the rate on a B rated one-year zero coupon corporate bond to be received one year from now, denoted[16] $_1y_1$. Assuming that the expectations hypothesis holds, we can solve for the one-year forward rate on the corporate bond as:

$$(1 + {_0}y_2)^2 = (1 + {_0}y_1)(1 + {_1}y_1),$$

or substituting the values from the B rated spot yield curve:

$$(1 + 0.16)^2 = (1 + 0.1369)(1 + {_1}y_1).$$

Solving for $_1y_1$ yields a one-year forward rate on the one-year B rated corporate bond of 18.36 percent p.a. A similar exercise can be performed to determine the one-year forward rate on the one-year Treasury (risk free) bond as follows:

$$(1 + {}_0r_2)^2 = (1 + {}_0r_1)(1 + {}_1r_1) \tag{4.9}$$

or substituting the values from the risk free Treasury yield curve:

$$(1 + 0.10)^2 = (1 + 0.08)(1 + {}_1r_1).$$

Solving for ${}_1r_1$ yields a one-year forward Treasury rate of 12.04 percent p.a. We can now use these one-year forward rates in order to decompose the risky yield into its risk free and credit risk spread components. Replicating the analysis in equation (4.7) for one-year maturities, but using one-year forward rates instead, we have:

$$1 + r = (1 - PD)(1 + y)$$

$$1 + 0.1204 = (1 - PD)(1 + 0.1836)$$

obtaining the probability of default during the second year (conditional on no default occurring in the first year), PD = 5.34 percent p.a. That is, the probability of default for the B rated corporate bond is 5 percent in the first year and 5.34 percent in the second year, and (assuming independence across time) a two-year cumulative PD of:

$$\text{Cumulative PD} = 1 - [(1 - PD_1)(1 - PD_2)]$$

$$= 1 - [(1 - 0.05)(1 - 0.0534)] = 10.07\%.$$

That is, the B rated corporate bond has a 10.07 percent chance of defaulting sometime over the next two years.

Let us return to the single-period model and remove the simplifying assumption that the recovery rate is zero. Then the expected loss on default, EL, equals the probability of default (PD) times severity or loss given default (LGD). That is, EL = PD × LGD; we can rewrite equation (4.7) as:

$$1 + r = (1 - EL)(1 + y) = (1 - PD \times LGD)(1 + y) \tag{4.7'}$$

or in continuous time form, we can rewrite equation (4.8) as:[17]

$$y = r + [PD(t) \times LGD(t)]. \tag{4.8'}$$

Equation (4.8′) expresses the yield on risky debt as the sum of the riskless rate and the credit spread, comprised of PD × LGD. Using the rates from spot yield curves (in our example, $r = 8\%$ and $y = 13.69\%$), we can solve for PD × LGD = 5%, but there is an identification problem which requires additional equations in order to untangle PD from LGD.[18]

Differing assumptions are used to disentangle the PD from the LGD in the observed credit spread. Das and Tufano (1996) obtain PD using a deterministic intensity function and assume that LGD is correlated with the default risk-free spot rate. Longstaff and Schwartz (1995) utilize a two factor model that specifies a negative relationship between the stochastic processes determining credit spreads and default-free interest rates. Jarrow and Turnbull (1995) assume that the recovery rate is a known fraction of the bond's face value at maturity date. Duffie and Singleton (1998) assume that the recovery rate is a known fraction of the bond's value just prior to default. In Duffie and Singleton (1999), both PD and LGD are modeled as a function of economic state variables. Madan and Unal (1998) and Unal, Madan, and Guntay (2001) model the differential recovery rates on junior and senior debt. Kamakura, in its proprietary model which is based on Jarrow (2001), uses equity as well as debt prices in order to disentangle the PD from the LGD. Credit Risk Plus models the PD as a Poisson process, which stipulates that over a given small time interval, the probability of default is independent across loans and proportional to a fixed default intensity function. The evolution of this intensity process follows a Poisson distribution (see Finger, 2000b).

In the intensity-based approach, default probability is modeled as a Poisson process with intensity h such that the probability of default over the next short time period, Δ, is approximately Δh and the expected time to default is $1/h$; therefore, in continuous time, the probability of survival without default for t years is:

$$1 - PD(t) = e^{-ht}. \tag{4.10}$$

Thus, if an A rated firm has an $h = 0.001$, it is expected to default once in 1,000 years; using equation (4.10) to compute the probability of survival, $1 - PD(t)$, over the next year we obtain 0.999. Thus, the firm's PD over a one-year horizon is 0.001. Alternatively, if a B rated firm has an $h = 0.05$, it is expected to default once in 20 years and substituting into equation (4.10), we find that the probability of survival, $1 - PD(t)$, over the next year is 0.95 and the PD is 0.05.[19] If a portfolio consists of 1,000 loans to A rated firms and 100 loans to B rated firms, then there are 6 defaults expected per year.[20] A hazard rate (or alternatively, the arrival rate of default at time t) can be defined as the arrival time of default, i.e., $-p'(t)/p(t)$ where $p(t)$ is the probability of survival to time t and $p'(t)$ is the first derivative of the survival probability function (assumed to be differentiable with respect to t). Since the probability of survival depends on the intensity h, the terms hazard rate and intensity are often used interchangeably.[21]

Since intensity-based models use observed risky debt prices, they are better able to reflect complex term structures of default than are structural models. However, although the bond market is several times the size of US equity markets,[22] it is not nearly as transparent.[23] One reason is that less than 2 percent of the volume of corporate bond trading occurs on the NYSE or AMEX exchanges. The rest of the trades are conducted over the counter by bond dealers. Saunders, Srinivasan, and Walter (2002) show that this inter-dealer market is not very competitive. It is characterized by large spreads and infrequent trades. Pricing data are often inaccurate, consisting of matrix prices that use simplistic algorithms to price infrequently traded bonds. Even the commercially available pricing services are often unreliable. Hancock and Kwast (2001) find significant discrepancies between commercial bond pricing services, Bloomberg and Interactive Data Corporation, in all but the most liquid bond issues. Bohn (1999) finds that there is more noise in senior issues than in subordinated debt prices. Corporate bond price performance is particularly erratic for maturities of less than one year. The sparsity of trading makes it difficult to obtain anything more frequent than monthly pricing data; see Warga (1999). A study by Schwartz (1998) indicates that even for monthly bond data, the number of outliers (measured relative to similar debt issues) is significant. One can attribute these outliers to the illiquidity in the market.

The considerable noise in bond prices, as well as investors' preferences for liquidity, suggest that there is a liquidity premium built into bond spreads. Thus, if risky bond yields are decomposed into the risk free rate plus the credit spread only, the estimate of credit risk exposure will be biased upward. The proprietary model Kamakura Risk Manager explicitly adjusts for liquidity effects. However, noise from embedded options and other structural anomalies in the default risk free market further distorts risky debt prices, thereby impacting the results of intensity-based models. Other proprietary models control for some of these biases in credit spreads. For example, KPMG's Loan

Analysis System adjusts for embedded options and Credit Risk Plus incorporates macroeconomic, cyclical effects into the specification of the hazard function.

4.2.3   Proprietary VaR models of credit risk measurement

Many of the proprietary models considered in sections 4.2.1 and 4.2.2 are full-fledged credit risk measurement models. Once the default probability for each asset is computed (using either the structural or intensity-based approach),[24] each loan in the portfolio can be valued (using either analytical solutions or Monte Carlo simulation) so as to derive a probability distribution of portfolio values. A loss distribution can then be calculated permitting the computation of VaR measures. We now turn to two proprietary VaR models for credit risk measurement: CreditMetrics and Algorithmics Mark-to-Future.

4.3   CREDITMETRICS

CreditMetrics models default probabilities using the historical default experience of comparable borrowing firms. However, rather than defining comparable firms using an equity-driven distance to default (as in structural models such as KMV and Moody's; see section 4.2.1), CreditMetrics utilizes external credit ratings.[25] That is, the CreditMetrics model is built around a credit migration or transition matrix that measures the probability that the credit rating of any given debt security will change over the course of the credit horizon (usually one year). The credit migration matrix considers the entire range of credit events, including upgrades and downgrades as well as actual default. Thus, CreditMetrics is a mark-to-market (MTM), rather than default mode (DM) model. Since loan prices and volatilities are generally unobservable, CreditMetrics uses migration probabilities to estimate each loan's loss distribution. We describe the model for the individual loan case and then for the entire portfolio.

4.3.1   The distribution of an individual loan's value

CreditMetrics evaluates each loan's cash flows under eight possible credit migration assumptions, corresponding to each of eight credit ratings:

Table 4.2   One-year transition probabilities for BBB-rated borrower

AAA	0.02%	
AA	0.33%	
A	5.95%	
BBB	86.93%	⟵————————— Most likely to stay in the same class
BB	5.30%	
B	1.17%	
CCC	0.12%	
Default	0.18%	

Source: Gupton, Finger, and Bhatia (1997), p. 11.

AAA, AA, A, BBB, BB, B, CCC, and default. For example, suppose that a loan is initially rated the equivalent of BBB. The loan's value over the upcoming year is calculated under different possible scenarios over the succeeding year, e.g., the rating improves to AAA, AA, A, etc. or deteriorates in credit quality (to BBB, BB, B, CCC, etc.) or possibly defaults, as well as under the most likely scenario that the loan's credit rating remains unchanged. Historical data on publicly traded bonds are used to estimate the probability of each of these credit migration scenarios.[26] Putting together the loan valuations under each possible credit migration scenario and their likelihood of occurrence, we obtain the distribution of the loan's value. At this point, standard VaR technology may be utilized.

Consider the following example of a five-year fixed-rate BBB rated loan of $100 million made at 6 percent annual (fixed) interest.[27] Based on historical data on publicly traded bonds (or preferably loans), the probability that a BBB borrower will stay at BBB over the next year is estimated at 86.93 percent. There is also some probability that the borrower will be upgraded (e.g., to A) or will be downgraded (e.g., to CCC or even to default, D). Indeed, eight transitions are possible for the borrower during the next year.[28] Table 4.2 shows the estimated probabilities of these credit migration transitions. The migration process is modeled as a finite Markov chain, which assumes that the credit rating changes from one rating to another with a certain constant probability at each time interval. The credit migration matrix shown in table 4.2 can be estimated from historical experience as tabulated by rating agencies, from Merton options-theoretic default probabilities, from bank internal rating systems, or even from intensity-based models (see Jarrow, Lando, and Turnbull 1997).

The effect of rating upgrades and downgrades is to impact the required credit risk spreads or premiums on the loan's remaining cash flows, and, thus, the implied market (or present) value of the loan. If a loan is downgraded, the required credit spread premium should rise (remember that the contractual loan rate in our example is assumed fixed at 6 percent) so that the present value of the loan should fall. A credit rating upgrade has the opposite effect. Technically, because we are revaluing the five-year, $100 million, 6 percent loan at the end of the first year (the end of the credit event horizon), after a "credit-event" has occurred during that year, then (measured in millions of dollars):[29]

$$P = 6 + \frac{6}{(1 + r_1 + s_1)} + \frac{6}{(1 + r_2 + s_2)^2} + \frac{6}{(1 + r_3 + s_3)^3} + \frac{106}{(1 + r_4 + s_4)^4},$$
(4.11)

where r_i are the risk free rates (the forward risk free rates) on zero-coupon US Treasury bonds *expected* to exist one year into the future. Further, the series of s_i is the annual credit spread on (zero coupon) loans of a particular rating class of one-year, two-year, three-year, and four-year maturities (derived from observed spreads in the corporate bond market over Treasuries). In the above example, the first year's coupon or interest payment of $6 million (to be received on the valuation date at the end of the first year) is undiscounted and can be regarded as equivalent to accrued interest earned on a bond or a loan.

In CreditMetrics, interest rates are assumed to be deterministic.[30] Thus, the risk-free rates, r_i, are obtained by decomposing the current spot yield curve in order to obtain the one-year forward zero curve and then adding fixed credit spreads to the forward zero coupon Treasury yield curve. That is, the risk-free spot yield curve is first derived using US Treasury yields. Pure discount yields for all maturities can be obtained using yields on coupon-bearing US Treasury securities. Once the risk-free spot yield curve is obtained, the forward yield curve can be derived using the expectations hypothesis. The values of r_i are read off this forward yield curve. For example, if today's risk free spot rate were 3.01 percent p.a. for 1 year maturity pure discount US Treasury securities and 3.25 percent for 2 year maturities, then we can calculate r_1, the forward risk free rate expected one year from now on 1-year maturity US Treasury securities using the expectations hypothesis as follows:[31]

$$(1 + 0.0325)^2 = (1 + 0.0301)(1 + r_1)$$
(4.12)

Thereby solving for $r_1 = 3.5\%$ p.a. This procedure can be repeated for the 2-year maturity risk free rate expected in one year r_2, and continuing for as many rates as required to value the multi-year loan (until r_4 for the five-year loan in this example).

CreditMetrics obtains fixed credit spreads s_i for different credit ratings from commercial firms such as Bridge Information Systems. For example, if during the year a credit event occurred so that the five-year loan was upgraded to an A rating (from a BBB), then the value of the credit spread for an A rated bond would be added to the risk free forward rate for each maturity; suppose that the credit spread s_1 was 22 basis points in the first year. Evaluating the first coupon payment after the credit horizon is reached in one year, the risk free forward rate of 3.5 percent p.a. would be added to the one-year credit spread for A rated bonds of 22 basis points to obtain a risk-adjusted rate of 3.72 percent p.a. Using different credit spreads s_i for each loan payment date and the forward rates r_i we can solve for the end of year (i.e., at the end of the first year – the credit horizon) value of a $100 million five-year 6 percent coupon loan that is upgraded from a BBB rating to an A rating within the next year such that:

$$P = 6 + \frac{6}{(1.0372)} + \frac{6}{(1.0432)^2} + \frac{6}{(1.0493)^3} + \frac{106}{(1.0532)^4}$$

$$= \$108.66. \tag{4.13}$$

Table 4.3 shows the loan's value at the credit horizon (one year into the future) for all possible credit migrations. To obtain the distribution

Table 4.3 Value of the loan at the end of year 1, under different ratings (including first-year coupon)

Year-end rating	Value (millions)
AAA	$109.37
AA	109.19
A	108.66
BBB	107.55
BB	102.02
B	98.10
CCC	83.64
Default	51.13

Source: Gupton, Finger, and Bhatia (1997), p. 10.

of loan values, we discount each of the loan's cash flows at the appropriate risk-adjusted forward rate. As shown in equation (4.13), if the loan's credit quality is upgraded from BBB to A over the next year, then the loan's market or present value will increase to $108.66 million. However, table 4.3 shows that if the loan's credit quality deteriorates to CCC, then the loan's value will fall to $83.64 million. Moreover, if the loan defaults, its value will fall to its recovery value, shown in table 4.3 to be $51.13 million.[32] CreditMetrics models recovery values as beta distributed, although the simple model assumes a deterministic recovery value set equal to the mean of the distribution.

The distribution of loan values on the one-year credit horizon date can be drawn using the transition probabilities in table 4.2 and the loan valuations in table 4.3. Figure 4.3 shows that the distribution of

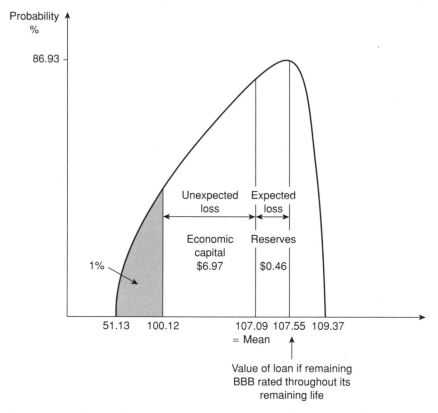

Figure 4.3 Actual distribution of loan values on five-year BBB loan at the end of year 1 (including first-year coupon payment)

loan values is non-normal. CreditMetrics can estimate a VaR measure based on the actual distribution as well as on an approximation using a normal distribution of loan values.[33] The mean of the value distribution shown in figure 4.3 is $107.09 million. If the loan had retained its BBB rating, then the loan's value would have been $107.55 million at the end of the credit horizon. Thus, the expected losses on this loan are $460,000 (=$107.55 minus $107.09 million). However, unexpected losses (to be covered by economic capital) are determined by the unexpected losses over and above expected losses. We measure unexpected losses using the Credit VaR or the minimum possible losses that will occur at a certain (high) confidence level. If we consider the 99th percentile Credit VaR, we can calculate the loan value such that there is only a 1 percent likelihood that the loan's value will fall below that number. Figure 4.3 shows that the 99th percentile loan cutoff value is $100.12 million; that is, there is only a 1 percent chance that loan values will be lower than $100.12 million. Thus, the Credit VaR or unexpected losses total $6.97 million ($107.09 minus $100.12). We obtained the 1 percent maximum loan value assuming that loan values were normally distributed with a standard deviation of loan value of $2.99 million; thus, the 1 percent VaR is $6.97 million (equal to 2.33 standard deviations, or 2.33 × $2.99 million).[34] CreditMetrics estimates that the loan's unexpected losses would exceed $6.97 million in only one year out of a 100.[35]

4.3.2   The value distribution for a portfolio of loans

For simplicity, we retain the (counterfactual) assumption made in section 4.3.1 that a loan portfolio's losses are normally distributed.[36] Appendix 4.1 relaxes this simplifying assumption and illustrates the estimation of the actual loss distribution using an example of a loan portfolio taken from the CreditMetrics technical documents. The major distinction between the single loan case discussed in section 4.3.1 and the portfolio case is the introduction of correlations across loans. CreditMetrics solves for correlations by first regressing equity returns on industry indices. Then the correlation between any pair of equity returns is calculated using the correlations across the industry indices.[37] Once we obtain equity correlations, we can solve for joint migration probabilities to estimate the likelihood that the joint credit quality of the loans in the portfolio will be either upgraded or downgraded. Finally, each loan's value is obtained for each credit migration possibility using the methodology described in section 4.3.1. The first two moments (mean and standard deviation) of the portfolio value distribution are derived from the probability-weighted loan values to obtain the normally distributed portfolio value distribution.[38] We now illustrate the steps in this procedure using a two loan portfolio for simplicity.

4.3.2.1   Calculating the correlation between equity returns and industry indices for each borrower in the loan portfolio

Consider a two loan portfolio consisting of one loan to an American car manufacturer (to protect the innocent, let's call it CAR) and another loan to a US retailer (called BUY). Using each company's daily stock prices, we can construct a series of equity returns that can be regressed on industry index factors.[39] Therefore, in the case of single industry sector specialized firms:

$$R_{CAR} = B_{CAR} R_{AUTO} + e_{CAR} \qquad (4.14)$$

$$R_{BUY} = B_{BUY} R_{RETAIL} + e_{BUY} \qquad (4.15)$$

where R_{CAR}, R_{BUY} = the daily equity returns for the companies CAR and BUY,

$\quad R_{AUTO}$ = the daily returns on an index of auto industry stocks,

$\quad R_{BUY}$ = the daily returns on an index of retail industry stocks,

$\quad B_{CAR}$, B_{BUY} = the sensitivity of each company's stock returns to its industry index,

$\quad e_{CAR}$, e_{BUY} = each company's idiosyncratic risk, unrelated to fluctuations in industry returns.

Suppose that the (regression) estimation of equations (4.14) and (4.15) produces estimates of $B_{CAR} = 0.85$ and $B_{BUY} = 0.70$.

4.3.2.2   Calculating the correlation between borrower equity returns

Using the estimates of industry sensitivities ($B_{CAR} = 0.85$ and $B_{BUY} = 0.70$), we can solve for the correlations between equity returns for the two companies in our loan portfolio: CAR and BUY. However, we first must compute the correlations between the industry indices themselves. Suppose that the correlation between R_{AUTO} and R_{RETAIL} is 0.34; we can now solve for the correlations between R_{CAR} and R_{BUY} as follows:[40]

$$\rho(CAR,BUY) = B_{CAR} B_{BUY} \rho(AUTO,RETAIL). \qquad (4.16)$$

Substituting the values in our example, we obtain $\rho(CAR,BUY) = (0.85)(0.70)(0.34) = 0.20$ for the correlation between the two borrowing firms in the two loan portfolio.

4.3.2.3 Solving for joint migration probabilities

Table 4.2 shows the credit migration probabilities for an individual loan. In order to obtain the joint migration probabilities for loans to the two companies (CAR and BUY) using the correlation coefficient of 0.20 obtained in section 4.3.2.2, we first must link each individual loan's transition matrix (table 4.2) to the standard normal probability distribution.

Suppose that CAR is an A rated borrower. Deducting the mean of CAR's asset values and dividing by the assets' standard deviation, we transform the asset value distribution to the standardized normal distribution. The lower the (standardized) value of the firm's assets, the more likely it is to default; therefore, the loan's credit rating deteriorates (improves) as the firm's asset values decline (increase). As shown in figure 4.4, the most likely outcome (with an 91.05 percent probability) is for the loan's credit rating to remain at A.[41] This will

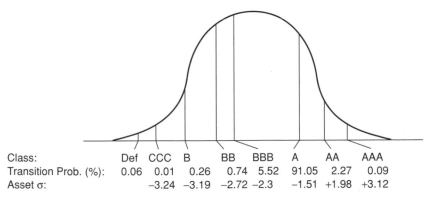

Class:	Def	CCC	B	BB	BBB	A	AA	AAA
Transition Prob. (%):	0.06	0.01	0.26	0.74	5.52	91.05	2.27	0.09
Asset σ:			−3.24	−3.19 −2.72	−2.3	−1.51	+1.98	+3.12

Figure 4.4 The link between asset value volatility (σ) and rating transition for a BB rated borrower
Source: Gupton, Finger, and Bhatia (1997), p. 89.

Table 4.4 Joint migration probabilities with 0.30 asset correlation (%)

Obligor 1 (BBB)	Obligor 2 (A)							
	AAA	AA	A	BBB	BB	B	CCC	Default
	0.09	2.27	91.05	5.52	0.74	0.26	0.01	0.06
AAA	0.02	0.00	0.00	0.02	0.00	0.00	0.00	0.00	0.00
AA	0.33	0.00	0.04	0.29	0.00	0.00	0.00	0.00	0.00
A	5.95	0.02	0.39	5.44	0.08	0.01	0.00	0.00	0.00
BBB	86.93	0.07	1.81	79.69	4.55	0.57	0.19	0.01	0.04
BB	5.30	0.00	0.02	4.47	0.64	0.11	0.04	0.00	0.01
B	1.17	0.00	0.00	0.92	0.18	0.04	0.02	0.00	0.00
CCC	0.12	0.00	0.00	0.09	0.02	0.00	0.00	0.00	0.00
Default	0.18	0.00	0.00	0.13	0.04	0.01	0.00	0.00	0.00

Source: Gupton, Finger, and Bhatia (1997), p. 38.

be the case as long as CAR's assets fall within 1.51 standard deviations below the mean to 1.98 standard deviations above the mean. Alternatively, the default region is defined as the probability that asset values fall 3.24 standard deviations below the mean. These credit rating cutoff points will differ for different loans. For example, a BB rated borrower (say, the company BUY) will experience no change in its credit rating as long as assets fall within 1.23 standard deviations below to 1.37 standard deviations above the mean.[42]

A mapping between rating transitions and asset volatility is performed for each loan in the portfolio (CAR and BUY in our example). The joint migration probability is then calculated for each possible pair of credit ratings. Suppose that BUY is a BB rated borrower and CAR is an A rated borrower. Then the probability that both CAR and BUY retain their original credit ratings (BBB and A, respectively) is:[43]

$$Pr(-1.23 < BBB < 1.37, -1.51 < A < 1.98)$$

$$= \int_{-1.23}^{1.37} \int_{-1.51}^{1.98} f(Y_{CAR} Y_{BUY}; \rho) dY_{CAR} dY_{BUY},$$

$$= 0.7365 \qquad (4.17)$$

where Y_{CAR}, Y_{BUY} = the asset values (at the credit horizon) for BB rated CAR and A rated BUY, respectively,

ρ = the correlation between CAR and BUY (0.2 in the example, as computed in section 4.3.2.2).

Since the two firms (CAR and BUY) are positively correlated (with a correlation coefficient found to be 0.2), the joint credit migration probability is not simply the direct product of each firm's individual credit migration probabilities. Table 4.4 is obtained by estimating equation (4.17) for every possible pair of credit migrations.

4.3.2.4 Valuing each loan across the entire credit migration spectrum

Using its cash flow characteristics, we can evaluate each loan's value for every possible credit migration using the methodology outlined in section 4.3.1. Thus each loan will have a different valuation, V, for each of eight possible credit migrations. Since there are two loans, V_{CAR}

Table 4.5 Loan portfolio values

Obligor 1 (BBB)		All possible 64 year-end values for a two-loan portfolio ($)							
		Obligor 2 (A)							
		AAA	AA	A	BBB	BB	B	CCC	Default
		106.59	106.49	106.30	105.64	103.15	101.39	88.71	51.13
AAA	109.37	215.96	215.86	215.67	215.01	212.52	210.76	198.08	160.50
AA	109.19	215.78	215.68	215.49	214.83	212.34	210.58	197.90	160.32
A	108.66	215.25	215.15	214.96	214.30	211.81	210.05	197.37	159.79
BBB	107.55	214.14	214.04	213.85	213.19	210.70	208.94	196.26	158.68
BB	102.02	208.61	208.51	208.33	207.66	205.17	203.41	190.73	153.15
B	98.10	204.69	204.59	204.40	203.74	210.25	199.49	186.81	149.23
CCC	83.64	190.23	190.13	189.94	189.28	186.79	185.03	172.35	134.77
Default	51.13	157.72	157.62	157.43	156.77	154.28	152.52	139.84	102.26

Source: Gupton, Finger, and Bhatia (1997), p. 12.

and V_{BUY} can be calculated for each of 64 possible joint credit migrations, obtaining $V_{i,CAR}$ and $V_{i,BUY}$ for each $i = 1, \ldots, 64$. Table 4.5 shows
all possible loan values for a portfolio comprised of one loan to a BBB
borrower (CAR) and one loan to an A rated borrower (BUY).

4.3.2.5 Calculating the mean and standard deviation of the normal portfolio value distribution

Using the valuations for each loan from section 4.3.2.4, we can solve
for the portfolio's value at each of the 64 possible joint credit migrations; this is denoted V_i where $i = 1, \ldots, 64$. Obtaining the mean and
variance for the normally distributed portfolio valuation is straightforward as follows:

$$\text{mean} = \mu = \sum_{i=1}^{64} p_i V_i \qquad (4.18)$$

$$\text{variance} = \sum_{i=1}^{64} p_i (V_i - \mu)^2, \qquad (4.19)$$

where p_i = the probability obtained from the joint migration probability table (table 4.5) for each possible pair of credit
migrations, $i = 1, \ldots, 64$.

V_i = the value of the loan portfolio given the joint credit
migration i.

Using the information in tables 4.4 and 4.5, we obtain from the solution of equations (4.18) and (4.19) a mean portfolio value of $213.63
million and a standard deviation – square root of the variance
obtained from the solution to equation (4.19) – of $3.35 million. Thus,
the 99 percent Credit VaR under the normal distribution is: 2.33 ×
$3.35 = $7.81 million.[44] Comparing this VaR estimate to the $6.97
million VaR obtained at the end of section 4.3.1 for a single $100 mil-
lion loan, we can see the power of diversification. Although the
portfolio has doubled in size (from one to two $100 million loans),
the 99 percent VaR has increased by only 12 percent (rather than
100 percent) from $6.97 million to $7.81 million as a result of the
imperfect correlation (an asset correlation of 0.20) between the two
loans in the portfolio.

Table 4.6 Risk drivers in algorithmics mark-to-future

Risk exposure	Risk factors	Time horizon	Type of scenarios	Number of scenarios
Market risk	50–1,000 interest rates, foreign exchange rates, equity prices, commodity prices	1–10 days	Historical; Monte Carlo simulation	100–10,000
Counterparty credit risk	50–100 interest rates, foreign exchange rates, equity prices, commodity prices	1–30 years	Monte Carlo simulation; extreme value analysis	10–5,000
Portfolio credit risk	50–200 systemic market & credit factors, interest rates, exchange rates, equity & commodity prices, macroeconomic factors	1–10 years	Monte Carlo simulation; extreme value analysis	5–5,000
Asset/liability management	20–100 interest rates, foreign exchange rates	6 months–30 years	Historical; Monte Carlo simulation	5–5,000

Source: Dembo, Aziz, Rosen, and Zerbs (2000), p. 11.

4.4   ALGORITHMICS' MARK-TO-FUTURE

CreditMetrics is an MTM credit VaR model that incorporates a static view of market risk.[45] In contrast, Algorithmics Mark-to-Future (MtF) is an MTM credit VaR model that attempts to link market risk, credit risk, and liquidity risk in a scenario-based framework (see Iscoe, Kreinin, and Rosen, 1999). That is, whereas the fundamental risk driver in CreditMetrics is the credit migration matrix, Algorithmics simulates portfolio valuations using hundreds of different risk factors.[46] Table 4.6 summarizes these risk factors. Scenarios are defined by states of the world over time and are comprised of both market factors (interest rates, foreign exchange rates, equity prices and commodity prices) as well as credit drivers (systemic and macroeconomic factors). Each asset in the portfolio is revalued as scenario-driven credit or market events occur, thereby causing credit spreads to fluctuate over time.

MtF is a scenario-based model that focuses on estimating each asset's risk and return characteristics under thousands of different scenarios corresponding to all major risk factors ranging from market risk to liquidity risk to credit risk.[47] For example, MtF can create 5–20 extreme scenarios simulating historical "crashes" using 50–200 systemic market and credit factors in order to estimate VaR. The value of each asset in the portfolio is calculated for each scenario at each point in time in order to trace out the portfolio value distribution. MtF differs from other credit risk measurement models in that it views market risk and credit risk as inseparable.[48] Stress tests show that credit risk measures are quite sensitive to market risk factors.[49] Indeed, it is the systemic risk parameters that drive creditworthiness in MtF.

Dembo et al. (2000) offer an example of this simulation analysis using a BB rated swap obligation. The firm's credit risk is estimated using a Merton options-theoretic model of default; that is, MtF defines a creditworthiness index (CWI) that specifies the distance to default as the distance between the value of the firm's assets and a (nonconstant) default boundary.[50] Figure 4.5 shows the scenario simulation of the CWI, illustrating two possible scenarios of firm asset values: (Scenario 1) the firm defaults in year 3, and (Scenario 2) the firm remains solvent for the next 10 years. The default date under each scenario is represented by the point at which the firm's asset value first hits the default boundary.[51] MtF assumes that the CWI follows a geometric Brownian motion standardized to have a mean of zero and a variance of one. The basic building block of the CWI is the unconditional cumulative

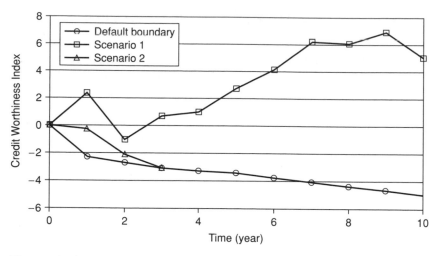

Figure 4.5 Merton model of default
Source: Dembo, Aziz, Rosen, and Zerbs (2000), p. 68

default probabilities for typical BB rated firms obtained using the Merton model (as discussed in section 4.2.1). Using the unconditional default probabilities as a foundation, a conditional cumulative default probability distribution is generated for each scenario. That is, the sensitivity of the default probability to scenario risk factors is estimated for each scenario. For example, suppose that the unconditional likelihood of default within five years for a BB firm is 9.6 percent. Choose a particular scenario of the time path of the S&P500 and six month US Treasury rates over the next 10 years. This is the risk driver. Suppose that in this particular scenario (call it "Scenario 9" or S9), the risk driver decreases about 1.2 standard deviations in five years.

What is the impact of the decline in the risk driver represented in Scenario S9 on the default risk of this BB rated firm? MtF estimates all BB rated firms' historical sensitivity to the risk driver using a multi-factor model that incorporates both systemic and idiosyncratic company specific factors. If the results of the multi-factor model suggest that the obligor has a positive correlation with the risk driver, then the swap's credit quality is expected to decrease (credit risk increase) under Scenario S9. The conditional cumulative default probability is calculated based on the results of the multi-factor model. In this example, the BB firm's five year probability of default increases from 9.6 percent to 11.4 percent under Scenario S9. Figure 4.6 shows the return on the BB swap obligation over the next 10 years using the conditional default probabilities obtained for Scenario S9. This process is replicated for several scenarios. Figure 4.7 shows the conditional default probabilities for ten different risk scenarios. A return distribution can be derived using the full range of possible scenarios.

The results for Scenario S9 depend on the assumption that systemic risk explains 5 percent of the total variance of the CWI, with idiosyncratic risk explaining the remaining 95 percent. If, on the other hand, systemic risk accounted for 80 percent of the variance, the five-year conditional default probability under Scenario S9 would have been 44.4 percent instead of 11.4 percent. Therefore, conditional default probabilities have higher volatility when the systemic risk component is greater.

Integrating different risk factors is critical to obtaining more accurate VaR estimates for credit risk. For example, the Russian debt default in August 1998 was foreshadowed by the devaluation of the ruble. Incorporating data on foreign exchange rates as well as interest rates (during the first few days of August 1998, yields on US Treasury bonds reached historic lows) could have forecast the increased risk of default almost a week before the Russian government announced its debt restructuring plan. Dembo et al. (2000) show that if a "Russian scenario" were used in January 1999 during a similar crisis for Brazilian debt, the 95 percentile Credit VaR estimate would have forecast a 57 percent decline in portfolio value over the two week crisis period. Thus, integrating the market risk drivers into a model of credit risk measurement can improve the quality of the VaR estimates, particularly during crisis periods. Therefore, dichotomizing credit risk and market risk undermines the accuracy of all risk measurement models.

4.5 SUMMARY

In this chapter, VaR techniques are applied to the problem of credit risk measurement. Central to all VaR models is the characterization of default and default probabilities (PD). We outline two approaches to default modeling: the structural options-theoretic approach and the reduced form or intensity-based approach. Both approaches utilize risk-neutral, no-arbitrage pricing techniques in order to estimate default probabilities. Apart from the theoretical differences, structural models utilize equity prices and risk-free debt prices, whereas reduced form models input risky debt prices in order to estimate default probabilities.

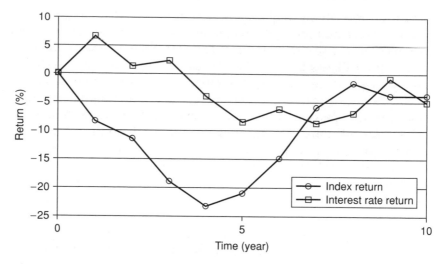

Figure 4.6 Scenario S9 returns
Source: Dembo, Aziz, Rosen, and Zerbs (2000), p. 70

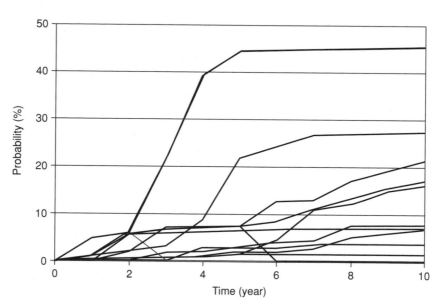

Figure 4.7 Ten scenarios on conditional default probabilities
Source: Dembo, Aziz, Rosen, and Zerbs (2000), p. 70

CreditMetrics and Algorithmics offer proprietary credit risk measurement models to obtain VaR estimates of unexpected losses on a portfolio of defaultable assets. Whereas CreditMetrics focuses on modeling credit risk in a mark-to-market model, Algorithmics integrates credit risk with market risk and liquidity risk exposures in a mark-to-market model. CreditMetrics uses credit migration matrices to evaluate the portfolio's market value under eight possible credit scenarios – ranging from credit upgrades to default. Algorithmics utilizes a scenario analysis approach to value the portfolio under a series of systemic, macroeconomic, and market risk factors.

APPENDIX 4.1   CREDITMETRICS: CALCULATING CREDIT VaR USING THE ACTUAL DISTRIBUTION

The assumption of normality is particularly problematic for portfolios comprised of defaultable assets. Because there is an upper bound on the return on debt (at most the promised interest plus principal), the actual portfolio loss distribution is skewed. Moreover, the large losses associated with rare default events cause the distribution to have fat tails (excessive probability in the extreme outcome ranges). CreditMetrics therefore can be used to estimate the VaR without the counterfactual assumption that the loss distribution is normal. We illustrate the approach first for an individual loan and then for an entire portfolio.

Consider the example of the BBB rated loan presented in section 4.3.1. By combining the loan information in tables 4.2 and 4.3, we obtain table 4.A1 which can be used to calculate the VaR under the actual loss distribution. Ordering the losses starting from the worst possible outcome of default, the biggest loss is $55.96 million (the difference between the loan value of $51.15 million under default and the mean of $107.09 million). There is a 0.18 percent likelihood of this occurrence (from column (2) of table 4.A1, reproduced from table 4.2). Summing the state probabilities in column (2), there is a 1.47 percent likelihood that the loan's value will migrate to a B rating or lower, thereby resulting in a loan value of $98.10 million or less. Therefore, using the actual distribution, the "approximate" 99th percentile (the 98.53 percentile) VaR is $8.99 million ($107.09 million minus $98.10). We can use linear interpolation to calculate the 99th percentile VaR for the example shown in table 4.A1. That is, because the 1.47 percentile equals $98.10 and the 0.3 percentile equals

Table 4.A1 VaR calculations for the BBB loan (benchmark is mean value of loan)

Year-end rating squared	Probability of state (%)	New loan value plus coupon (millions)	Probability weighted value ($)	Difference of value from mean ($)	Probability weighted difference
AAA	0.02	$109.37	0.02	2.28	0.0010
AA	0.33	109.19	0.36	2.10	0.0146
A	5.95	108.66	6.47	1.57	0.1474
BBB	86.93	107.55	93.49	0.46	0.1853
BB	5.30	102.02	5.41	(5.07)	1.3592
B	1.17	98.10	1.15	(8.99)	0.9446
CCC	0.12	83.64	1.10	(23.45)	0.6598
Default	0.18	51.13	0.09	(55.96)	5.6358
			$107.09		8.9477 = variance of value
			mean value		

σ = Standard deviation $2.99

| Assuming normal distribution | 5 percent VaR = | 1.65 × σ = $4.93 |
| | 1 percent VaR = | 2.33 × σ = $6.97 |

Assuming actual distribution*	6.77 percent VaR = 93.23 percent of actual distribution	= $107.09 − $102.02 = $5.07
	1.47 percent VaR = 98.53 percent of actual distribution	= $107.09 − $98.10 = $8.99
	1 percent VaR = 99 percent of actual distribution	= $107.09 − $92.29 = $14.80

Note: Calculation of 6.77% VaR (i.e., 5.3% + 1.17% + 0.12% + 0.18%) and 1.47% VAR (i.e., 1.17% + 0.12% + 0.18%). The 1% VaR is interpolated from the actual distribution of the loan's values under different rating migrations.

Source: Gupton, Finger, and Bhatia (1997), p. 28.

$83.64, the 1.00 percentile equals $92.29. This suggests an actual 99th percentile VaR of $14.80 million ($107.09 minus $92.29).

Using tables 4.4 and 4.5, we can calculate the VaR for the port-folio comprised of the two loans described in section 4.3.2. Counting the probabilities backward, starting with the worst loan outcome and then the next worse and so on, the 99 percentile worst loan value for the portfolio is $204.4 million. Thus, the 99 percentile Credit VaR to cover the portfolio's unexpected losses is $9.23 million (the portfolio mean (derived from the solution to equation (4.18) in section 4.3.2.5) of $213.63 million minus $204.4 million).

The benefits to diversification are striking even for this simple two loan portfolio. Table 4.A1 shows that the 99 percentile VaR using the actual distribution for the individual loan's value is $14.8 million. In con-trast, the two loan portfolio's 99 percentile VaR is only $9.23 million.

CHAPTER FIVE

EXTENDING THE VaR APPROACH TO OPERATIONAL RISKS

CHAPTER OUTLINE

All business enterprises, but financial institutions in particular, are vulnerable to losses resulting from operational failures that undermine the public's trust and erode customer confidence. The list of cases involving catastrophic consequences of procedural and operational lapses is long and unfortunately growing. To see the implications of operational risk events one need only look at the devastating loss of reputation of Arthur Andersen in the wake of the Enron scandal, the loss of independence of Barings Bank as a result of Nick Leeson's rogue trading operation, or UBS' loss of US$100 million due to a trader's error, just to name a few examples.[1] One highly visible operational risk event can suddenly end the life of an institution. Moreover, many, almost invisible individual pinpricks of recurring operational risk events over a period of time can drain the resources of the firm. Whereas a fundamentally strong institution can often recover from market risk and credit risk events, it may be almost impossible to recover from certain operational risk events. Marshall (2001) reports that the aggregate operational losses over the past 20 years in the financial services industry total approximately US$200 billion, with individual institutions losing more than US$500 million each in over 50 instances and over US$1 billion in each of over 30 cases of operational failures.[2] If anything, the magnitude of potential operational risk losses will increase in the future as global financial institutions specialize in volatile new products that are heavily dependent on technology.

Kingsley et al. (1998) define operational risk to be the "risk of loss caused by failures in operational processes or the systems that support them, including those adversely affecting reputation, legal enforcement of contracts and claims" (p. 3). Often this definition includes both strategic risk and business risk. That is, operational risk arises from breakdowns of people, processes, and systems (usually, but not limited to technology) within the organization. Strategic and business risk originate outside of the firm and emanate from external causes such as political upheavals, changes in regulatory or government policy, tax regime changes, mergers and acquisitions, changes in market conditions, etc. Table 5.1 presents a list of operational risks found in retail banking.

Operational risk events can be divided into high frequency/low severity (HFLS) events that occur regularly, in which each event individually exposes the firm to low levels of losses. In contrast, low frequency/high severity (LFHS) operational risk events are quite rare, but the losses to the organization are enormous upon occurrence. An operational risk measurement model must incorporate both HFLS and LFHS risk events. As shown in figure 5.1, there is an inverse relationship between frequency and severity so that high severity risk events are quite rare, whereas low severity risk events occur rather frequently.

In order to calculate expected operational losses (EL), one must have data on the likelihood of occurrence of operational loss events (PE) and the loss severity (loss given event, LGE), such that $EL = PE \times LGE$. Expected losses measure the anticipated operational losses from HFLS events. VaR techniques can be used to measure unexpected losses.

Table 5.1 Operational risk categories

Process risk
  Pre-transaction: marketing risks, selling risks, new connection, model risk
  Transaction: error, fraud, contract risk, product complexity, capacity risk
  Management information
  Erroneous disclosure risk

People risk
  Integrity: fraud, collusion, malice, unauthorized use of information, rogue
    trading
  Competency
  Management
  Key personnel
  Health and safety

Systems risk
  Data corruption
  Programming errors/fraud
  Security breach
  Capacity risks
  System suitability
  Compatibility risks
  System failure
  Strategic risks (platform/supplier)

Business strategy risk
  Change management
  Project management
  Strategy
  Political

External environmental risk
  Outsourcing/external supplier risk
  Physical security
  Money laundering
  Compliance
  Financial reporting
  Tax
  Legal (litigation)
  Natural disaster
  Terrorist threat
  Strike risk

Source: Rachlin (1998), p. 127.

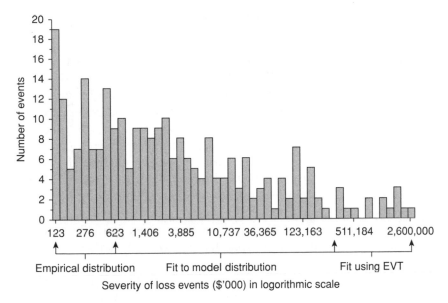

Figure 5.1 Frequency and severity of loss events
Source: Ceske and Hernandez (1999), p. 19.

However, LFHS events typically fall in the area of the extreme tail (the area fit using extreme value theory (EVT) shown in figure 5.1). Analysis of operational risk requires all three measures. The typical risk assessment period in these operational risk measurement models is assumed to be one year.

5.1   TOP-DOWN APPROACHES TO OPERATIONAL RISK MEASUREMENT

Financial institutions have long articulated the truism that "reputation is everything."[3] Particularly in businesses that deal with intangibles that require public trust and customer confidence, such as banking, loss of reputation may spell the end of the institution. Despite this recognition (unfortunately often limited to the firm's advertising campaign), banks and other financial institutions have been slow at internalizing operational risk measurement and management tools to protect their reputational capital. As backward as financial firms have been in this area, nonfinancial firms are often even less sophisticated in assessing potential operational weaknesses.

5.1.1   Top-down vs. bottom-up models

Historically, operational risk techniques, when they existed, utilized a "top-down" approach. The top-down approach levies an overall cost of operational risk to the entire firm (or to particular business lines within the firm). This overall cost may be determined using past data on internal operational failures and the costs involved. Alternatively, industry data may be used to assess the overall severity of operational risk events for similar-sized firms as well as the likelihood that the events will occur. The top-down approach aggregates across different risk events and does not distinguish between HFLS and LFHS operational risk events. In a top-down model, operational risk exposure is usually calculated as the variance in a target variable (such as revenues or costs) that is unexplained by external market and credit risk factors.

The primary advantage of the top-down approach is its simplicity and low data input requirements. However, it is a rather unsophisticated way to determine a capital cushion for aggregate operational losses that may not be covered by insurance. Nonetheless, top-down operational risk measurement techniques may be appropriate for the determination of overall economic capital levels for the firm. However, top-down operational risk techniques tend to be of little use in designing procedures to reduce operational risk in any particularly vulnerable area of the firm. That is, they do not incorporate any adjustment for the implementation of operational risk controls, nor can they advise management about specific weak points in the production process. They over-aggregate the firm's processes and procedures and are thus poor diagnostic tools. Top-down techniques are also backward looking and cannot incorporate changes in the risk environment that might affect the operational loss distribution over time.

In contrast to top-down operational risk methodologies, more modern techniques employ a "bottom-up" approach. As the name implies, the bottom-up approach analyzes operational risk from the perspective of the individual business activities that make up the bank's or firm's "output." That is, individual processes and procedures are mapped to a combination of risk factors and loss events that are used to generate probabilities of future scenarios' occurrence.[4] HFLS risk events are distinguished from LFHS risk events. Potential changes in risk factors and events are simulated, so as to generate a loss distribution that incorporates correlations between events and processes. Standard

Table 5.2 Top-down and bottom-up operational risk measurement models

Operational risk problem	Primarily use top-down or bottom-up model	Operational risk model recommended
Control	Bottom-up	Process approach
Mitigation	Bottom-up	Process approach
Prevention	Bottom-up	Process approach
Economic capital	Top-down	Multi-factor, scenario analysis
Regulatory capital	Top-down	Risk profiling
Efficiency optimization	Top-down and bottom-up	Risk profiling and process approach

Source: Adapted from Doerig (2000), p. 95.

VaR and extreme value theory are then used to represent the expected and unexpected losses from operational risk exposure.

Bottom-up models are useful to many constituencies within the firm – from the internal risk auditor to the line area middle managers to the operations staff. Results of the analysis may be utilized to correct weaknesses in the organization's operational procedures. Thus, bottom-up models are forward looking in contrast to the more backward looking top-down models. The primary disadvantages of bottom-up models are their complexity and data requirements. Detailed data about specific losses in all areas of the institution must be collected so as to perform the analysis. Industry data are required to assess frequencies both for LFHS and HFLS events. Moreover, by overly disaggregating the firm's operations, bottom-up models may lose sight of some of the interdependencies across business lines and processes. Therefore, neglecting correlations may lead to inaccurate results since many of the operational risk factors have a systematic component. Most firms that have operational risk measurement programs use both top-down and bottom-up operational risk measurement models.[5] Table 5.2 shows how both top-down and bottom-up models can be used to address different operational risk problems.

5.1.2 Data requirements

The operational risk measurement methodology that is chosen is often determined by data availability. Senior (1999) interviewed top managers at financial firms and found that the biggest impediment to the implementation of precise operational risk measurement models is the absence of accurate data on operational risk events. Ceske and Hernandez (1999) present four choices for obtaining data inputs: internal collection of data, external data, simulating data using educated estimates, and extrapolating data based on limited samples.

Internal data are most applicable to the individual institution and are therefore the most useful in determining the firm's operational loss distribution. However, internal data are biased toward HFLS events. It is likely that there will be no LFHS events at all in the internal database, simply because many firms do not survive the catastrophic losses associated with this type of operational risk events. Moreover, it is extremely costly and time-consuming to develop a historical internal database on operational risk events. Thus, internal data should be supplemented with external data obtained from other institutions. This expands the database to include more LFHS events, particularly if the scope of the external database is industry-wide. However, external data must be scaled and adjusted to reflect institutional differences in business unit mix, activity level, geography and risk control mechanisms across firms. Moreover, competing firms are reluctant to release sensitive and detailed information about their internal processes and procedures to competitors. Ceske and Hernandez (1999) advocate the creation of a data consortium for financial institutions along the lines of the insurance and energy industries.[6] "The database would contain information on non-public, internal, operational loss events, with the sources of the losses concealed. This would help financial institutions to learn the lessons from operational risk failures at other institutions" (Ceske and Hernandez, 1999, p. 18). Thus, individual firm confidentiality would be preserved while minimizing the cost of developing a comprehensive database on operational risk events for financial institutions.[7] However, Ong (1998) argues against this emphasis on data collection because it would only encourage "follow the pack" decision making that would not necessarily improve risk management.

Another source of data is obtained from management-generated loss scenarios. These scenarios emanate from either educated estimates by operational line managers or from extrapolation from smaller databases. Using either of these methods, management must construct frequency and severity estimates from individual operational risk events across individual business lines using bootstrapping and jackknife methodologies in order to construct "synthetic data points."[8] The operational risk loss distribution is then obtained by considering all possible imaginable scenarios. The distribution can be specified using either parametric models or may be based on non-parametric, empirical distributions. Empirical distributions may not be representative and the results may be driven by outliers. In practice, loss severity is typically modeled using lognormal, gamma or Pareto distributions, although the uniform, exponential, Weibull, binomial and beta distributions are sometimes used.[9] For catastrophic losses (in the fat tails of the distribution), extreme value theory is used. Loss frequency parametric distributions such as Poisson, beta, binomial, and negative binomial are most often used (see discussion in section 5.2.2.2). However, the current state of data availability still does not permit long run backtesting and validation of most operational risk measurement models.

5.1.3   Top-down models

The data requirements of top-down models are less onerous than for bottom-up models.[10] Top-down models first identify a target variable, such as earnings, profitability or expenses. Then the external risk (e.g., market and credit risk) factors that impact the target variable are modeled, most commonly using a linear regression model in which the target variable is the dependent variable and the market and credit risk factors are the independent variable. Operational risk is then calculated as the variance in value of the target variable that is unexplained by the market and credit risk factors (i.e., the variance in the residual of the regression that is unexplained by the independent variables).[11] Sometimes operational risk factors are directly modeled in the regression analysis. Then operational risk is calculated as the portion of the target variable's variance explained by the operational risk independent variable.

5.1.3.1   Multi-factor models

One top-down model that can be estimated for publicly traded firms is the multi-factor model. A multi-factor stock return generating function is estimated as follows:

$$R_{it} = \alpha_{it} + \beta_{1i} I_{1t} + \beta_{2i} I_{2t} + \beta_{3i} I_{3t} + \ldots + \varepsilon_{it}, \tag{5.1}$$

where R_{it} is the rate of return on firm i's equity; I_{1t}, I_{2t}, and I_{3t} are the external risk factor indices (i.e., the change in each market and credit risk factor at time t); β_{1i}, β_{2i} and β_{3i} are firm i's sensitivity to changes in each external risk factor; and ε_{it} is the residual term. The risk factors are external to the firm and include as many market and credit risk factors as possible (i.e., interest rate fluctuations, stock price movements, macroeconomic effects, etc.). The multi-factor model measures operational risk as $\sigma_\varepsilon^2 = (1 - R^2)\sigma_i^2$ where σ_i^2 is the variance of firm i's equity return from equation (5.1) and R^2 is the regression's explanatory power.

The multi-factor model is easy and inexpensive to estimate for publicly traded firms. However, as in most top-down models, it cannot be used as a diagnostic tool because it does not identify specific risk exposures. More importantly, however, the multi-factor model is useful in estimating the firm's stock price reaction to HFLS operational risk events only. In contrast, LFHS events often have a catastrophic impact on the firm (often leading to bankruptcy or forced merger) as opposed to the marginal decline in equity returns resulting from the HFLS operational risk events that are measured by equation (5.1). Thus, the multi-factor model does not perform well when large scale events (such as mergers or catastrophic operational risk events) break the continuity of equity returns.[12]

5.1.3.2   Income-based models

Also known as Earnings at Risk models, income-based models extract market and credit risk from historical income volatility, leaving the residual volatility as the measure of operational risk. A regression model similar to equation (5.1) is constructed in which the dependent variable is historical earnings or revenues. Since long time series of historical data are often unavailable, income-based models can be estimated using monthly earnings data, in which annualized earnings are inferred under that assumption that earnings follow a Wiener process. Thus, monthly earnings volatility can be annualized by multiplying the monthly result by $\sqrt{t}$ where $t = 12$.

Since earnings for individual business lines can be used in the income-based model, this methodology permits some diagnosis of concentrations of operational risk exposure. Diversification across business lines can also be incorporated. However, there is no measure of opportunity cost or reputation risk effects. Moreover, this methodology is sensitive to HFLS operational risk events, but cannot measure LFHS risk events that do not show up in historical data.

5.1.3.3   Expense-based models

The simplest models are expense-based approaches that measure operational risk as fluctuations in historical expenses. Historical expense data are normalized to account for any structural changes in the organization.[13] Unexpected operational losses are calculated as the volatility of adjusted expenses. The primary disadvantage of expense-based models is that they ignore all operational risk events that do not involve expenses, e.g., reputational risk, opportunity costs, or risks that reduce revenues. Moreover, improving the operational risk control environment may entail *increased* expenses. Thus, expense-based models would consider the implementation of costly risk control mechanisms as an increase, rather than a decrease in operational risk exposure. Finally, since organizational changes are factored out of the analysis, expense-based models do not consider structural operational risk exposure (e.g., the operational risks of new business ventures).

5.1.3.4   Operating leverage models

A class of models that joins both the income-based and expense-based approaches is the operating leverage model. Operating leverage measures the relationship between operating expenses (variable costs) and total assets. Marshall (2001) reports that one bank estimated its operating leverage to be 10 percent multiplied by the fixed assets plus 25 percent multiplied by three months of operating expenses. Another bank calculated its operating leverage to be 2.5 times the monthly fixed expenses for each line of business. Operating leverage risk results from fluctuations from these steady state levels of operating leverage because of increases in operating expenses that are relatively larger than the size of the asset base. Data are readily available and thus the model is easy to estimate. However, as is the case with income-based and expense-based models, the operational risk measure does not measure nonpecuniary risk effects, such as the loss of reputation or opportunity costs.

5.1.3.5   Scenario analysis

Scenario analysis requires management to imagine catastrophic operational shocks and estimate the impact on firm value. These scenarios focus on internal operations and try to estimate the impact of LFHS operational risk events, such as a critical systems failure, major regulatory changes, losses of key personnel, or legal action. Marshall (2001) enumerates some possible scenarios: (i) the bank's inability to reconcile a new settlement system with the original system, thereby preventing its implementation (such as in the case of the TAURUS system cancellation by the London Stock Exchange in 1993 resulting in a US$700 million loss); (ii) a class action suit alleging incomplete disclosure (such as in Merrill Lynch's exposure to allegations about conflicts of interest affecting the accuracy of its stock recommendations resulting in a US$100 million fine plus pending legal action); (iii) a significant political event (such as the overthrow and reinstatement of Venezuela's president); (iv) massive technology failure (such as eBay's internet auction failure that reduced market value by US$5 billion in 1999); (v) non-authorized trading (such as Barings Bank's losses of US$1.6 billion in 1995); and many others. The enumeration of scenarios is only limited by management's imagination.[14]

The primary advantage of scenario analysis is its incorporation of LFHS operational risk events that may not have transpired as of yet. This is also the model's primary disadvantage, however. Scenario analysis is by its very nature subjective and highly dependent on management's subjective assessment of loss severity for each operational risk scenario. Moreover, it comprises a laundry list of operational risk events without attaching a likelihood estimate to each event. Thus, scenario analysis is often used to sensitize management to risk possibilities, rather than strictly as an operational risk measure.

5.1.3.6   Risk profiling models

Risk profiling models directly track operational risk indicators. Thus, they do not use income or expenses as proxies for operational risk, but rather measure the incidence of risk events directly. For example, commonly used operational risk indicators are: trading volume, the number of mishandling errors or losses, the number of transaction fails or cancellations, the staff turnover rate, the percentage of staff vacancies, the number of incident reports, the amount of overtime, the ratio of supervisors to staff, the pass–fail rate in licensing exams for the staff, the number of limit violations, the number of process "fails," the number of personnel errors, the average years of staff experience, backlog levels, etc. Risk indicators can be divided into two categories: performance indicators and control indicators. Performance indicators (such as the number of failed trades, staff turnover rates, volume and systems downtime) monitor operational efficiency. Control indicators

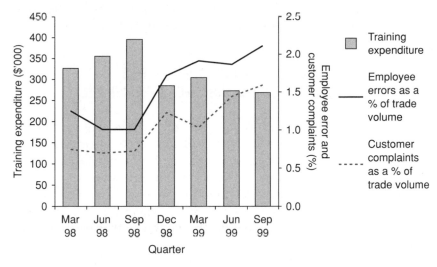

Figure 5.2 Composite risk indicators: training dollars vs. employee error
rate vs. customer complaints
Source: Taylor and Hoffman (1999), p. 15.

measure the effectiveness of controls, e.g., the number of audit
exceptions and the number of outstanding confirmations.

Risk profiling models can track operational risk changes over time. The
results can be used as a diagnostic tool to target operational risk weaknesses. The results can be incorporated into an operational risk scorecard
(see discussion in section 5.2.1.1).[15] However, risk profiling models
assume that there is a direct relationship between operational risk indicators and target variables such as staff turnover rate. If this is not true,
then the risk indicators may not be relevant measures of operational
risk. Moreover, risk profiling may concentrate on the symptom (say,
increased overtime), not the root cause of the operational risk problem.
Finally, risk profiling models should analyze the relationships among
different indicator variables to test for cross correlations that might
yield confounding results. For example, figure 5.2 shows the inverse
relationship between training expenditures and employee errors and
employee complaints. A composite risk indicator can be determined
using, say, the average expenditure required to reduce errors or
customer complaints by 1 percent. Thus, a risk profiling model will
examine several different risk indicators in order to obtain a risk profile
for the company. Doerig (2000) states that each business unit uses approximately 10–15 risk indicators to assess its operational risk exposure.

It is a matter of judgment, however, which risk indicators are most relevant to the overall operational risk exposure of the firm.[16]

5.2   BOTTOM-UP APPROACHES
TO OPERATIONAL RISK MEASUREMENT

Top-down models use various statistical techniques (e.g., regression analysis) to take a "bird's eye view" of the firm's operational risk. Bottom-up models may use the same techniques, but instead apply them to the nuts and bolts of the firm's operational processes and procedures. Thus, bottom-up models are more precise and targeted to the measurement of specific operational risk problems, but at the same time, are more complicated and difficult to estimate than are top-down models.

Bottom-up models use two different approaches to estimate the operational risk of a particular business line or activity: (i) the process approach and (ii) the actuarial approach.[17] The process approach focuses on a step-by-step analysis of the procedures used in any activity. This can be used to identify operational risk exposures at critical stages of the process. In contrast, the actuarial approach concentrates on the entire distribution of operational losses, comprised of the severity of loss events and their frequency. Thus, the actuarial approach does not identify specific operational risk sources, but rather identifies the entire range of possible operational losses taking into account correlations across risk events.

5.2.1   Process approaches

The process approach maps the firm's processes to each of the component operational activities.[18] Thus, resources are allocated to causes of operational losses, rather than to where the loss is realized, thereby emphasizing risk prevention. There are three process models: causal networks or scorecards, connectivity and reliability analysis.

5.2.1.1   Causal networks or scorecards

Causal networks, also known as scorecards, break down complex systems into simple component parts to evaluate their operational risk exposure. Then data are matched with each step of the process map

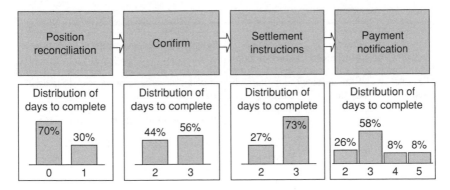

Figure 5.3   Process map for a transaction settlement
Source: Smithson (2000), p. 58.

to identify possible behavioral lapses. Data are obtained using incident reports, direct observation and empirical proxies. For example, figure 5.3 shows a process map for a transaction settlement. The transaction is broken into four steps. Then data regarding the number of days needed to complete the step is integrated into the process map to identify potential weak points in the operational cycle.

Scorecards require a great deal of knowledge about the nuts and bolts of each activity. However, the level of detail in the process map is a matter of judgment. If the process map contains too much detail, it may become unwieldy and provide extraneous data, detracting from the main focus of the analysis. Thus, the process map should identify the high risk steps of the operational process that are the focus of managerial concern. Then all events and factors that impact each high risk step are identified through interviews with employees and observation. For example, the high risk steps in the transaction settlement process map shown in figure 5.3 relate to customer interaction and communication. Thus, the process map focuses on the customer-directed steps, i.e., detailing the steps required to get customer confirmation, settlement instructions and payment notification. In contrast, the steps required to verify the price and position are not viewed by management as particularly high in operational risk and thus are summarized in the first box of the process map shown in figure 5.3.

Mapping the procedures is only the first step in the causal network model. Data on the relationship between high risk steps and component risk factors must be integrated into the process map. In the process map shown in figure 5.3, the major operational risk factor is

Time progression →

Event occurrence	Event detection	Response identification	Response implementation	Outcome
External event occurs	Staff detects event	Staff correctly diagnoses response	Staff implements appropriate response	Success
			Staff implements inappropriate response	Failure
		Staff misdiagnoses response		Failure
	Staff fails to detect event.			Failure

Figure 5.4   Generic event tree
Source: Marshall (2001), p. 259.

assumed to be time to completion. Thus, data on completion times for each stage of the process are collected and input into the process map in figure 5.3. In terms of the number of days required to complete each task, figure 5.3 shows that most of the operational risk is contained in the last two steps of the process – settlement instructions and payment notification. However, there may be several different component risk factors for any particular process. If another operational risk factor were used, say the number of fails and errors at each stage of the process, then the major source of operational risk would be at another point of the process, say the position reconciliation stage.

Another technique used in causal networks is the event tree. The event tree evaluates each risk events' direct and indirect impacts to determine a sequence of actions that may lead to an undesirable outcome. For example, figure 5.4 shows a generic event tree triggered by some external event. As an example, we can apply the generic event tree to Arthur Andersen's operational risk in the wake of the external event of Enron's bankruptcy declaration and the resulting SEC investigation into Enron's financial reporting. One can argue that Arthur Andersen employees, while detecting the event, failed to correctly interpret its significance for Arthur Andersen's reputation as Enron's auditor. In directing employees to shred documents, the staff misdiagnosed the appropriate response, resulting in a failed outcome.

Event trees are particularly useful when there are long time lags between an event's occurrence and the ultimate outcome. They help identify chronological dependencies within complex processes. However, both event trees and process maps are somewhat subjective. Management has to identify the critical risk factors, break down the process into the appropriate level of detail and apply the correct data proxies. Moreover, by focusing on individual processes at the microlevel, the analysis omits macrolevel interdependencies that may result from a single failed activity that produces many failed processes. Moreover, there is no analysis of the likelihood of each external risk event.[19]

5.2.1.2   Connectivity models

Connectivity models are similar to causal networks, but they focus on cause rather than effect. That is, they identify the connections between the components in a process with an emphasis on finding where failure in a critical step may spread throughout the procedure. Marshall (2001) shows that one technique used in connectivity models is fishbone analysis. Each potential problem in a process map is represented as an arrow. Each problem is then broken down into contributing problems. An example of fishbone analysis for errors in a settlement instruction is shown in figure 5.5. The root cause of

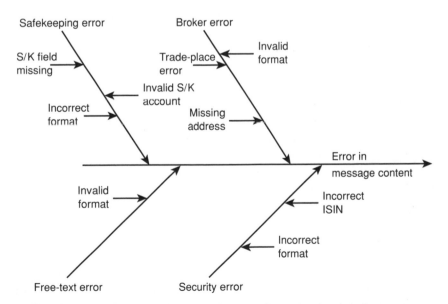

Figure 5.5   Example of a fishbone diagram for errors in a settlement instruction
Source: Marshall (2001), p. 252.

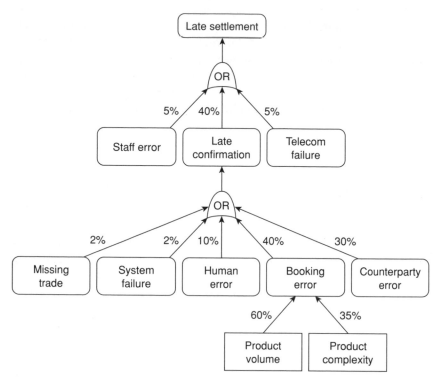

Figure 5.6   Causal structure of late settlement losses
Source: Marshall (2001), p. 95.

the error message is traced to either a safekeeping error, a broker error, a free-text error, or a security error. Within each of these possible problems, the specific cause of the error is identified.

Another technique used in connectivity models is fault tree analysis. A fault tree integrates an event tree with fishbone analysis in that it links errors to individual steps in the production process. Management specifies an operational risk event to trigger the analysis. Then errors are identified at each stage of the process. In both fishbone and fault tree analysis, as well as for causal networks, care should be taken to avoid over-disaggregation which will make the analysis unnecessarily complex, thereby losing its focus. Connectivity models suffer from some of the same disadvantages as do causal networks. They are subjective and do not assess probabilities for each risk event. However, when combined with a scorecard to assess subjective probabilities, one obtains the fault tree shown in figure 5.6. This is taken from Marshall's (2001) example of the analysis of late settlement losses for a financial institution. As shown in figure 5.6, late settlement occurs because of late confirmation (with a 40 percent probability), staff error (5 percent probability) or telecom failure (5 percent probability); the remainder of the cause of the late settlement operational risk event is the result of unknown factors (occurring with a 50 percent probability).[20] However, late confirmations themselves can be the result of several errors: missing trades, system failures, human errors, booking errors, or counterparty errors. Each of these operational risk events is assigned a probability in figure 5.6. Finally, the booking error cause can be the result of product complexity or product volume. Thus, the fault tree measures the extent of interdependencies across steps that make up complex processes.

5.2.1.3   Reliability models

Reliability models use statistical quality control techniques to control for both the impact and the likelihood of operational risk events. They differ from causal networks and connectivity models in that they focus on the likelihood that a risk event will occur. Reliability models estimate the times between events rather than their frequency (the event failure rate).[21] This methodology is similar to intensity-based models of credit risk measurement (see chapter 4, section 4.2.2). If $p(t)$ is the probability that a particular operational risk event will occur at time t, then the time between events, denoted $\lambda(t)$, can be calculated as follows:

$$\lambda(t) = \frac{p(t)}{\displaystyle\int_0^t p(t)dt}. \tag{5.2}$$

Thus, the reliability of a system is the probability that it will function without failure over a period of time t, which can be expressed as:

$$R(t) = 1 - \int_0^t p(t)dt. \tag{5.3}$$

External as well as internal data are needed to estimate the reliability function $R(t)$. Thus, the data requirements may be daunting. Moreover, the model must be estimated separately for LFHS events in contrast to HFLS events. However, by focusing only on frequency and not on impact, reliability models do not measure the severity of the risk event.

5.2.2   Actuarial approaches

The actuarial approach combines estimation of loss severity and frequency in order to construct operational loss distributions. Thus, the actuarial approach is closest to the VaR models discussed in the remainder of this book. There are three actuarial approaches: empirical loss distributions, explicit parametric loss distributions and extreme value theory.

5.2.2.1   Empirical loss distributions

Both internal and external data on operational losses are plotted in a histogram in order to draw the empirical loss distribution. External industry-wide data are important so as to include both LFHS and HFLS operational risk events. The relationship shown in figure 5.1 represents an empirical loss distribution. This model assumes that the historical operational loss distribution is a good proxy for the future loss distribution. Gaps in the data can be filled in using Monte Carlo simulation techniques. Empirical loss distribution models do not require the specification of a particular distributional form, thereby avoiding potential errors that impact models that make parametric distributional assumptions. However, they tend to understate tail events and overstate the importance of each firm's idiosyncratic operational loss history. Moreover, there is still insufficient data available to back-test and validate empirical loss distributions.

5.2.2.2   Parametric loss distributions

Examining the empirical loss distribution in figure 5.1 shows that in certain ranges of the histogram, the model can be fit to a parametric loss distribution such as the exponential, Weibull or the beta distribution. In contrast to the methodology used in market risk measurement,[22] parametric operational loss distributions are often obtained using different assumptions of functional form for the frequency of losses and for the severity of operational losses. Typically, the frequency of operational risk events is assumed to follow a Poisson distribution. The distribution of operational loss severity is assumed to be either

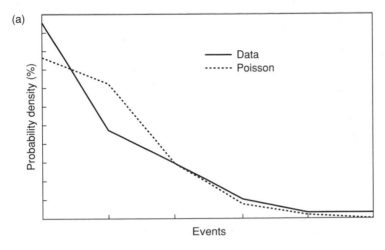

Figure 5.7(a)   Distribution of mishandling events per day
Source: Laycock (1998), p. 138.

lognormal or Weibull in most studies. The two distributions are then combined into a single parametric operational loss distribution using a process called convolution.

An example of the procedure used to fit actual data[23] to empirical distributions is given by Laycock (1998), who analyzes mishandling losses and processing errors that occur because of late settlement of cash or securities in financial transactions. Figure 5.7(a) shows that the likelihood of daily mishandling events can be modeled as a Poisson distribution, with the caveat that actual events are more likely to be correlated than those represented by the theoretical distribution. That is, when it is a bad day, many mishandling events will be bunched together (as shown in the extreme right tail region of the data observations which lies above the Poisson distribution values). Moreover, there are more no-event days than would be expected using the Poisson distribution (as shown by the higher probability density for the observed data in the extreme low-event section of the distributions). Laycock (1998) then plots the loss severity distribution for mishandling events and finds that the Weibull distribution is a "good" fit, as shown in figure 5.7(b). Finally, the likelihood and severity distributions are brought together to obtain the distribution of daily losses shown in figure 5.7(c). Separating the data into likelihood and severity distributions allows risk managers to ascertain whether operational losses from mishandling stem from infrequent, large value losses

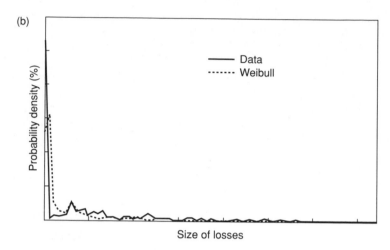

Figure 5.7(b)   Mishandling loss severity distribution
Source: Laycock (1998), p. 139.

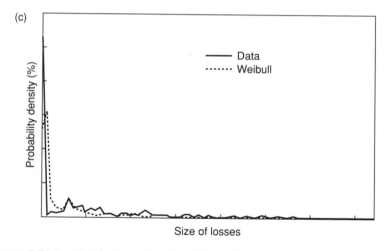

Figure 5.7(c)   Distribution of daily mishandling operational losses
Source: Laycock (1998), p. 140.

or from frequent, small value losses. However, the data required to conduct this exercise are quite difficult to obtain. Moreover, this must be repeated for every process within the firm.

Even if the operational loss distribution can be estimated for a specific business unit or risk variable, there may be interdependencies across risks within the firm. Therefore, operational losses cannot be simply aggregated in bottom-up models across the entire firm. For example, Ceske and Hernandez (1999) offer the simplified example of measuring the operational risk on a trading desk comprised of operational losses on foreign exchange (denoted X) and operational losses on precious metals (denoted Y).[24] If X and Y are independent, then $S \equiv X + Y$ can be represented as:

$$F_S(S) = \int F_X(S - Y)f_Y(Y)dY,$$

where F denotes distribution functions and $f_Y(Y)$ is the probability density function for the random variable Y. However, X and Y are generally not independent. Thus, one must specify the interdependencies between the two random variables in order to specify the (joint) operational loss distribution. This requires a large amount of information that is generally unavailable. Ceske and Hernandez (1999) suggest the use of a copula function that represents the joint distribution as a function of a set of marginal distributions. The copula function can be traced out using Monte Carlo simulation to aggregate correlated losses. (See Appendix 5.1 for a discussion of copula functions.)

5.2.2.3   Extreme value theory

As shown in figure 5.1, it is often the case that the area in the extreme tail of the operational loss distribution tends to be greater than would be expected using standard distributional assumptions (e.g., lognormal or Weibull). However, if management is concerned about catastrophic operational risks, then additional analysis must be performed on the tails of loss distributions (whether parametric or empirical) comprised almost entirely of LFHS operational risk events. Put another way, the distribution of losses on LFHS operational risk events tends to be quite different from the distribution of losses on HFLS events.

The Generalized Pareto Distribution (GPD) is most often used to represent the distribution of losses on LFHS operational risk events.[25] As will be shown below, using the same distributional assumptions for LFHS events as for HFLS events results in understating operational risk exposure. The Generalized Pareto Distribution (GPD) is a two parameter distribution with the following functional form:

$$G_{\xi,\beta}(x) = 1 - (1 + \xi x/\beta)^{-1/\xi} \qquad \text{if } \xi \neq 0, \qquad (5.4)$$

$$= 1 - \exp(-x/\beta) \qquad \text{if } \xi = 0.$$

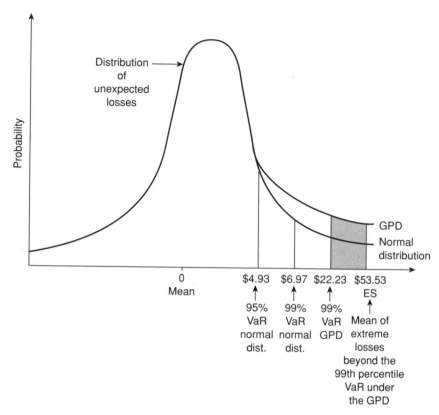

Figure 5.8   Estimating unexpected losses using Extreme Value Theory (ES = the expected shortfall assuming a Generalized Pareto Distribution (GPD) with fat tails)

The two parameters that describe the GPD are ξ (the shape parameter) and β (the scaling parameter). If $\xi > 0$, then the GPD is characterized by fat tails.[26]

Figure 5.8 depicts the size of losses when catastrophic events occur.[27] Suppose that the GPD describes the distribution of LFHS operational losses that exceed the 95th percentile VaR, whereas a normal distribution best describes the distribution of values for the HFLS operational risk events up to the 95th percentile, denoted as the "threshold value" u, shown to be equal to US$4.93 million in the example presented in figure 5.8.[28] The threshold value is obtained using the assumption that losses are normally distributed. In practice, we observe that loss distributions are skewed and have fat tails that are inconsistent with the assumptions of normality. That is, even if the HFLS operational losses that make up 95 percent of the loss distribution are normally distributed, it is unlikely that the LFHS events in the tail of the operational loss distribution will be normally distributed. To examine this region, we use extreme value theory.

Suppose we had 10,000 data observations of operational losses, denoted $n = 10,000$. The 95th percentile threshold is set by the 500 observations with the largest operational losses; that is $(10,000 - 500)/10,000 = 95\%$; denoted as $N_u = 500$. Suppose that fitting the GPD parameters to the data yields $\xi = 0.5$ and $\beta = 7$.[29] McNeil (1999) shows that the estimate of a VaR beyond the 95th percentile, taking into account the heaviness of the tails in the GPD (denoted $\overline{VaR}_q$) can be calculated as follows:

$$\overline{VaR}_q = u + (\beta/\xi)[(n(1 - q)/N_u)^{-\xi} - 1]. \tag{5.5}$$

Substituting in the parameters of this example for the 99th percentile VaR, or $\overline{VaR}_{0.99}$, yields:

$$US\$22.23 = \$4.93 + (7/0.5)[(10,000(1 - 0.99)/500)^{-0.5} - 1]. \tag{5.6}$$

That is, in this example, the 99th percentile VaR for the GPD, denoted $\overline{VaR}_{0.99}$, is US\$22.23 million. However, $\overline{VaR}_{0.99}$ does not measure the severity of catastrophic losses beyond the 99th percentile; that is, in the bottom 1 percent tail of the loss distribution. This is the primary area of concern, however, when measuring the impact of LFHS operational risk events. Thus, extreme value theory can be used to calculate the Expected Shortfall to further evaluate the potential for losses in the extreme tail of the loss distribution.

The Expected Shortfall, denoted $\overline{ES}_{0.99}$, is calculated as the mean of the excess distribution of unexpected losses beyond the threshold \$22.23 million $\overline{VaR}_{0.99}$. McNeil (1999) shows that the expected shortfall (i.e., the mean of the LFHS operational losses exceeding $\overline{VaR}_{0.99}$) can be estimated as follows:

$$\overline{ES}_q = (\overline{VaR}_q/(1 - \xi)) + (\beta - \xi u)/(1 - \xi), \tag{5.7}$$

where q is set equal to the 99th percentile. Thus, in our example, $\overline{ES}_q = ((\$22.23)/0.5) + (7 - 0.5(4.93))/0.5 = US\$53.53$ million to obtain the values shown in figure 5.8. As can be seen, the ratio of the extreme (shortfall) loss to the 99th percentile loss is quite high:

$$\overline{ES}_{0.99}/\overline{VaR}_{0.99} = \$53.53/\$22.23 = 2.4.$$

This means that nearly $2^1/_2$ times more capital would be needed to secure the bank against catastrophic operational risk losses compared to (unexpected) losses occurring up to the 99th percentile level, even when allowing for fat tails in the $VaR_{0.99}$ measure. Put another way, coverage for catastrophic operational risk would be considerably underestimated using standard VaR methodologies.

The Expected Shortfall would be the capital charge to cover the mean of the most extreme LFHS operational risk events (i.e., those in the 1 percent tail of the distribution). As such, the $\overline{ES}_{0.99}$ amount can be viewed as the capital charge that would incorporate risks posed by extreme or catastrophic operational risk events, or alternatively, a capital charge that internally incorporates an extreme, catastrophic stress-test multiplier. Since the GPD is fat tailed, the increase in losses is quite large at high confidence levels; that is, the extreme values of $\overline{ES}_q$ (i.e., for high values of q, where q is a risk percentile) correspond to extremely rare catastrophic events that result in enormous losses.[30]

5.2.3   Proprietary operational risk models[31]

The leading[32] proprietary operational risk model currently available is OpVar, offered by OpVantage which was formed in April 2001 by a strategic alliance between NetRisk, Inc. and PricewaterhouseCoopers (PwC). OpVar integrates NetRisk's Risk Ops product with an operational risk event database originally developed by PwC to support its in-house operational risk measurement product. The operational loss database currently contains more than 7,000 publicly disclosed operational risk events, each amounting to a loss of over US$1 million for a total of US$272 billion in operational losses. In addition, the database contains over 2,000 smaller operational risk events amounting to less than US$1 million each. The data cover a period exceeding 10 years, with semiannual updates that add approximately 500 new large operational risk events to the database each half year. Figure 5.9(a) shows the distribution of operational risk events by cause. Clients, products and business practices overwhelmingly account for the majority (71 percent) of all operational losses in the OpVar database. However, this database may not be relevant for a particular financial institution with distinctive characteristics and thus OpVar's accuracy hinges on its ability to scale the external data and create a customized database for each financial firm. OpVar is currently installed at more than 20 financial institutions throughout the world,

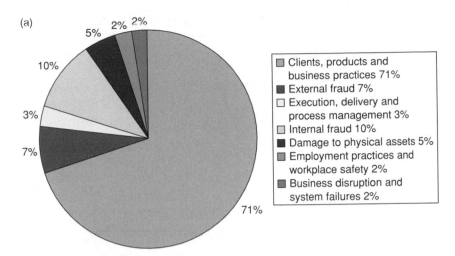

Figure 5.9(a) Total operational losses by cause amount
Source: www.opvantage.com

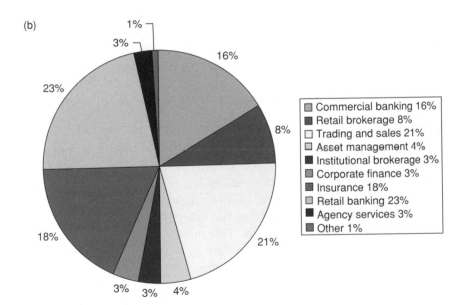

Figure 5.9(b) Total operation losses by business unit type
Source: www.opvantage.com

including Bank of America, Banco Sabadell, CIBC, ING, Sanwa, Societe Generale and Swiss Re. Figure 5.9(b) shows that most operational losses originate in the banking sector (16 percent in commercial banking and 22 percent in retail banking).

OpVar is a bottom-up model that uses several different methodologies. It features multiple curve fitting techniques employing both parametric (e.g., lognormal) and empirical models of severity distributions, frequencies, and operational losses. Moreover, OpVar uses actuarial methods and Monte Carlo simulation to fill in gaps in the data. Graphical displays of causes and effects of operational risk events incorporate the process approach through the analysis of fault trees, causal networks, and risk profiles.

Another major proprietary operational risk measurement model, Algorithmics Algo OpRisk, consists of three components: Algo Watchdog, Algo OpData, and Algo OpCapital.[33] Algo Watchdog is a bottom-up factor model that uses simulations and Bayesian analysis to predict the sensitivity of operational losses to risk events. Algo OpData provides a flexible framework to store internal data on operational losses. The database is two-dimensional in that each operational risk event (or near miss) is sorted by organizational unit and by risk category. For financial firms, there are nine organizational units (corporate finance, merchant banking, Treasury, sales, market making, retail banking, card services, custody, and corporate agency services)[34] and five risk categories (two categories of employee fraud: collusion and embezzlement and three categories of systems failure: network, software, and hardware). Finally, OpCapital calculates operational risk capital on both an economic and a regulatory basis (following BIS II proposals; see discussion in section 6.3) using an actuarial approach that estimates loss frequency and severity distributions separately.[35]

Another proprietary model called 6 Sigma, developed by General Electric for the measurement of manufacturing firms' operational risk, has been adapted and applied to the operational risk of financial firms by Citigroup and GE Capital. This model primarily utilizes a top-down approach, focusing on variability in outcomes of risk indicator variables, such as the total number of customer complaints, reconciliations, earnings volatility, etc. However, because of the shortcomings of top-down models, 6 Sigma has added a bottom-up component to the model that constructs process maps, fault trees, and causal networks.

Several companies offer automated operational risk scorecard models that assist middle managers in using bottom-up process approaches to create causal networks or fault trees. JP Morgan Chase's Horizon (marketed jointly with Ernst & Young) and Accenture's operational risk management framework focus on key risk indicators identified by the financial institution. These models essentially massage manual data inputs into graphs and charts that assist the manager in visualizing each process's operational risk exposure. Capital requirements (either economic or regulatory) are also computed using the data input into the model. However, if the data inputs are subjective and inaccurate, then the outputs will yield flawed operational risk measures.

The pressure to develop more proprietary models of operational risk measurement has been increased by the BIS II consideration of an operational risk component in international bank capital requirements (see section 6.3). Moreover, in June 2005, the US is scheduled to move to a T + 1 settlement standard, such that all securities transactions will be cleared by one day after the trade. The Securities Industry Association conducted a survey and found that only 61 percent of equity transactions at US asset management firms and 87 percent of equity transactions at US brokerage houses comply with the straight-through-processing standards required to meet the T + 1 requirement. The compliance levels in the fixed income markets were considerably lower: only 34 percent of asset managers and 63 percent of brokerage houses in the US were capable of straight-through-processing (see Bravard and David, 2001). Compliance with T + 1 standards will require an estimated investment of US$8 billion with an annual cost saving of approximately US$2.7 billion. Failure to meet the standard would therefore put firms at a considerable competitive disadvantage. Thus, the opportunity for operational losses, as well as gains through better control of operational risk, will expand considerably.

5.3 HEDGING OPERATIONAL RISK

Catastrophic losses, particularly resulting from LFHS operational risk events, can mean the end of the life of a firm. The greater the degree of financial leverage (or conversely, the lower its capital), the smaller the level of operational losses that the firm can withstand before it becomes insolvent. Thus, many highly levered firms utilize external institutions, markets, and/or internal insurance techniques to better manage their operational risk exposures. Such risk management can take the form of the purchase of insurance, the use of self-insurance, or hedging using derivatives.

5.3.1   Insurance

Insurance contracts can be purchased to transfer some of the firm's operational risk to an insurance company. The insurance company can profitably sell these policies and absorb firm-specific risk because of its ability to diversify the firm's idiosyncratic risk across the policies sold to many other companies.

The most common forms of insurance contract sold to financial firms are: fidelity insurance, electronic computer crime insurance, professional indemnity, directors' and officers' insurance, legal expense insurance, and stockbrokers' indemnity. Fidelity insurance covers the firm against dishonest or fraudulent acts committed by employees. Electronic computer crime insurance covers both intentional and unintentional errors involving computer operations, communications, and transmissions. Professional indemnity insurance covers liabilities to third parties for claims arising out of employee negligence. Directors' and officers' insurance covers any legal expenses associated with lawsuits involving the discharge of directors' and officers' fiduciary responsibilities to the firm's stakeholders. Stockbrokers' indemnity insurance protects against stockbrokers' losses resulting from the regular course of operations – such as the loss of securities and/or cash, forgery by employees, and any legal liability arising out of permissible transactions.

All insurance contracts suffer from the problem of moral hazard; that is, the mere presence of an insurance policy may induce the insured to engage in risky behavior because the insured does not have to bear the financial consequences of that risky behavior. For example, the existence of directors' insurance limiting the directors' personal liability may cause directors to invest less effort in monitoring the firm's activities, thereby undermining their responsibility in controlling the firm's risk taking and questionable activities. Thus, insurance contracts are not written to fully cover all operational losses. There is a deductible, or co-insurance feature which gives the firm some incentive to control its own risk taking activities because it bears some of the costs of operational failures. The impact of insurance, therefore, is to protect the firm from catastrophic losses that would cause the firm to become insolvent, not to protect the firm from all operational risk.

To better align the interests of the insured and the insurer, losses are borne by both parties in the case of an operational risk event. Figure 5.10 shows how operational losses are typically distributed. Small losses fall entirely under the size of the deductible and are thus completely absorbed by the firm (together with the cost of the insurance premium).[36] Once the deductible is met, any further operational losses

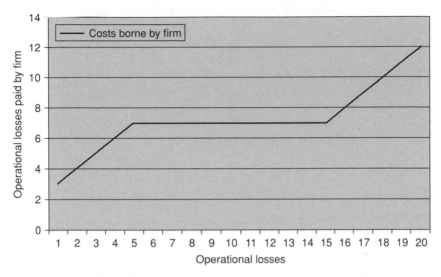

Figure 5.10 The typical payout structure on an operational risk insurance policy

are covered by the policy up until the policy limit is met. The firm is entirely responsible for operational losses beyond the policy limit. The higher (lower) the deductible and the lower (higher) the policy limit, the lower (higher) the cost of the insurance premium and the lower (higher) the insurance coverage area on the policy. Thus, the firm can choose its desired level of risk reduction by varying the deductible and policy limit of each operational risk insurance policy.

Despite their role as outsiders to the inner workings of insured firms, insurance companies have a comparative advantage in absorbing risks. Insurance companies diversify risks by holding large portfolios of policies. Moreover, insurance companies have access to actuarial information and data obtained from past loss experience to better assess operational risk exposure. This expertise can also be used to advise their clients about internal risk management procedures to prevent operational losses. Finally, insurance companies spread risk among themselves using the wholesale reinsurance market.[37]

The primary disadvantage of insurance as a risk management tool is the limitation of policy coverage. Hoffman (1998) estimates that insurance policies cover only 10–30 percent of possible operational losses. Large potential losses may be uninsurable. Moreover, there may be ambiguity in the degree of coverage that results in delays in settling claims, with potentially disastrous impacts on firm solvency.[38] Large claims may threaten the solvency of the insurance companies themselves, as evidenced by the problems suffered after Hurricane Andrew in 1992 (which resulted in insured losses of US$19.6 billion) and the terrorist attacks on the World Trade Center on September 11, 2001. Although estimates of losses to the insurance industry resulting from the September 11 attacks range from US$30 billion to US$70 billion, it is clear that this will be the most expensive catastrophic loss event ever recorded in the history of the insurance industry. Insurance premium costs have gone up and policy coverage narrowed in the wake of the terrorist attacks. Moreover, US property–liability insurers responded to large losses (such as Hurricane Andrew and the Northridge earthquake) by significantly increasing their capital from US$0.88 in equity per dollar of incurred losses in 1991 to US$1.56 in 1997. Thus, Cummins, Doherty, and Lo (2002) find that 92.8 percent of the US property–liability insurance industry could cover a catastrophe of US$100 billion. However, Niehaus (2002) contends that a major disaster would seriously disrupt the insurance industry, particularly since many property/casualty insurers lost money in 2002.

Even without considering the cost of major catastrophes, insurance coverage is expensive. The Surety Association of America estimates that less than 65 percent of all bank insurance policy premiums have been paid out in the form of settlements (see Hoffman, 1998, and Marshall, 2001). Thus, the firm's overall insurance program must be carefully monitored to target the areas in which the firm is most exposed to operational risk so as to economize on insurance premium payments. The firm may obtain economies of scope in its operational risk insurance coverage by using integrated, combined or basket policies. These policies are similar in that they aggregate several sources of risk under a single contract. For example, Swiss Re's Financial Institutions Operational Risk Insurance product provides immediate payout in the event of a wide variety of operational risk incidents. To price such a comprehensive policy, the insurance company often sets very high deductibles, often as high as US$100 million. In exchange for this, the firm receives a wide range of insurance coverage at a relatively low premium cost.

5.3.2 Self-insurance

The firm can reduce the cost of insurance coverage by self-insuring. Indeed, the presence of a deductible and a policy limit amounts to a form of self-insurance. The most common form of self-insurance is the capital provision held as a cushion against operational losses. Regulatory capital requirements set minimum levels of equity capital using some measure of the firm's operational risk exposure (see discussion in section 6.3 for the BIS proposals on operational risk capital requirements).[39] However, capital requirements may be an exceedingly costly form of self-insurance to protect the firm against operational risk losses because equity capital is the most expensive source of funds available to the financial institution. Indeed, Leyden (2002) suggests that internal market risk models that economize on capital requirements have a return on investment of up to 50 percent.

Alternatively, the firm could set aside a portfolio of liquid assets, such as marketable securities, as a cushion against operational losses. Moreover, the firm could obtain a line of credit that precommits external financing to be available in the event of losses. Thus, the firm allocates some of its debt capacity to covering losses resulting from operational risk events. Finally, some firms self-insure through a wholly owned insurance subsidiary, often incorporated in an offshore location such as Bermuda or the Cayman Islands, known as a captive insurer.[40] This allows the firm to obtain the preferential tax treatment accorded to insurance companies. That is, the insurance company can deduct the discounted value of incurred losses, whereas the firm would only be able to deduct the actual losses that were paid out during the year. Suppose that the firm experiences a catastrophic operational risk event that results in a loss of reputation that will take an estimated three years to recover. Under current US tax law, the firm can reduce its tax liabilities (thereby regaining some of the operational losses through tax savings) only by the amount of out-of-pocket expenses actually incurred during the tax year. Operational losses realized in subsequent tax years are deductible in those years, assuming that the firm survives until then. In contrast, a captive insurer can deduct the present value of all future operational losses covered by the policy immediately in the current tax year. Thus, the formation of a captive insurer allows the firm to co-insure with the relevant tax authorities.

Risk prevention and control can be viewed as a form of self-insurance. The firm invests resources to construct risk mitigation techniques in the form of risk identification, monitoring, reporting requirements, external validation, and incentives to promote activities that control operational risk. Of course, these techniques must themselves be credible since operational risk problems may be pervasive and may even infect the risk monitoring and management apparatus.

Self-insurance tends to be less costly than external insurance when the firm has control over its risk exposure. Thus, routine, predictable losses that can be controlled using internal management and monitoring techniques are most often self-insured. If the risk is unique to a particular firm, and thus cannot be diversified by an insurance company, then it is more efficient for the firm to self-insure. The very largest catastrophic operational risks, most subject to moral hazard considerations, are often uninsurable and thus the firm has no choice but to self-insure in these cases. Thus, the costs of external and self-insurance must be compared for each source of operational risk exposure to determine the optimal insurance program. Doerig (2000) presents a hierarchy of insurance strategies such that catastrophic losses (exceeding US$100 million) should be insured using captive insurance companies and external insurance if possible. Significant losses (US$51 to US$100 million) should be covered using a combination of insurance, self-insurance, and captive insurance. Small operational losses (US$11 million to US$50 million) can be self-insured or externally insured. The smallest HFLS operational losses (less than US$10 million) can be fully self-insured. Doerig (2000) cites a 1998 McKinsey study that estimates that 20 percent of all operational risk is self-insured (including captive insurance), with the expectation that it will double to 40 percent in the near future.

5.3.3   Hedging using derivatives

Derivatives can be viewed as a form of insurance that is available directly through financial markets rather than through specialized firms called insurance companies. Swaps, forwards, and options can all be designed to transfer operational risk as well as other sources of risk (e.g., interest rate, exchange rate, and credit risk exposures). In recent years, there has been an explosive growth in the use of derivatives. For example, as of December 2000, the total (on-balance-sheet) assets for all US banks was US$5 trillion and for Euro area banks over US$13 trillion. The value of non-government debt and bond markets worldwide was almost US$12 trillion. In contrast, global derivatives markets exceeded US$84 trillion in notional value (see Rule, 2001). BIS data show that the market for interest rate derivatives totalled $65 trillion (in terms of notional principal), foreign exchange rate derivatives exceeded $16 trillion, and equities almost $2 trillion.[41] The young and still growing credit derivatives market has been estimated at US$1 trillion as of June 2001.[42] By comparison to these other derivatives markets, the market for operational risk derivatives is still in its infancy.

5.3.3.1 Catastrophe options

In 1992, the Chicago Board of Trade (CBOT) introduced catastrophe futures contracts that were based on an index of underwriting losses experienced by a large pool of property insurance policies written by 22 insurers. Futures contracts were written on both national and regional indices. Because the contracts were based on an industry index, moral hazard concerns associated with the actions of any particular insurer were reduced and more complete shifting of aggregate risk became possible (see Niehaus and Mann, 1992). However, the CBOT futures contracts contained significant amounts of basis risk for insurers who bought them to hedge their catastrophe risk because the payoffs were not tied to any particular insurer's losses. Thus, the CBOT replaced the futures contract with an options contract in 1994.

Options can be written on any observable future outcome – whether it is a catastrophic loss of a company's reputation, the outcome of a lawsuit, an earthquake, or simply the weather. Catastrophe options trade the risk of many diverse events. Catastrophe ("cat") options, introduced in 1994 on the Chicago Board of Trade (CBOT), are linked to the Property and Claims Services Office (PCS) national index of catastrophic loss claims that dates back to 1949. To limit credit risk exposure, the CBOT cat option trades like a catastrophe call spread, combining a long call position with a short call at a higher exercise price.[43] If the settlement value of the PCS index falls within the range of the exercise prices of the call options, then the holder receives a positive payoff. The payoff structure on the cat option mirrors that of the catastrophe insurance policy shown in figure 5.10.

Niehaus (2002) claims that the trading volume in cat options is still (six years after their introduction) surprisingly small, given their potential usefulness to insurers concerned about hedging their exposure to catastrophic risk.[44] Cat options are valuable to investors other than insurance companies because they show no correlation with the S&P500 equity index, making them highly valuable as a diversification tool for investors. Cruz (1999) cites a study by Guy Carpenter & Co. that finds that if 5 percent cat risk is added to a portfolio comprised of 60 percent equities and 40 percent bonds, (say, by allocating a portion of the bond portfolio to cat bonds; see section 5.3.3.2), then the return on the portfolio would increase by 1.25 percent and the standard deviation would decrease by 0.25 percent, thereby increasing return while also decreasing the risk of the portfolio.

In recent years, the market for a particular cat option, weather derivatives, has been steadily growing. Cao and Wei (2000) state that about US$1 trillion of the US$7 trillion US economy is affected by the weather. However, the market's growth has been hampered by the absence of a widely accepted pricing model.[45] Note that this market is characterized by wide bid/ask spreads despite the presence of detailed amounts of daily temperature data. Clearly, the pricing/data problems are much more daunting for other operational risk options.

The most common weather derivatives are daily heating degree day (HDD) and cooling degree day (CDD) options written on a cumulative excess of temperatures over a one month or a predetermined seasonal period of time. That is, the intrinsic value of the HDD/CDD weather options is:

$$\text{daily HDD} = \max\ (65°F - \text{daily average temperature},\ 0),$$

$$\text{daily CDD} = \max\ (\text{daily average temperature} - 65°F,\ 0).$$

The daily average temperature is computed over the chosen time period (e.g., a month or a season) for each weather option. Cao and Wei (2000) find that the estimate of daily temperature patterns is subject to autocorrelation (lagged over three days) and is a function of a long range weather forecast. Because a closed form solution is not available, they use several simulation approaches. One approach, similar to VaR calculations, estimates the average value of the HDD/CDD contract as if it were written every year over the period for which data are available. The temperature pattern distribution is then obtained by equally weighting each year's outcome. This method, referred to as the "burn rate" method, equally weights extreme outcomes without considering their reduced likelihood of occurrence, thereby increasing the simulated variability in temperature patterns and overstating the option's value. Cao and Wei (2000) suggest using long-range US National Weather Service forecasts (even if the forecast only predicts seasonal levels, rather than daily temperatures) to shape the simulated distribution. Unfortunately, the US National Weather Service does not forecast other operational risk factors.

5.3.3.2   Cat bonds

Sometimes options are embedded into debt financing in order to provide operational risk hedging through the issuance of structured debt. For example, in 1997, the US Automobile Association (USAA) issued US$477 million of bonds that stipulated that all interest and principal payments would cease in the event of a hurricane in the Gulf of Mexico or along the eastern seaboard of the US. That would allow the USAA to use the debt payments to service any claims that would arise from hurricane damage. This was the first of a series of catastrophe-linked or "cat" bonds. Since its inception, the market has grown to an annual volume of approximately US$1 billion.[46] Most cat bonds put both interest and principal at risk and thus, 96 percent of the bonds issued between April 2000 and March 2001 were rated below investment grade (see Schochlin, 2002). Early issues (81 percent of those issued before March 1998) had maturities under 12 months, but currently 11 percent of new issues (between April 2000 and March 2001) have maturities over 60 months, with approximately one-third having maturities under 12 months and another third having maturities between 24 to 36 months.

There are three types of cat bonds: indemnified notes, indexed notes and parametric notes. The cash flows (compensation payments) on indemnified notes are triggered by particular events within the firm's activities. In contrast, payments on indexed notes are triggered by industry-wide losses as measured by a specified index, such as the PCS. In the case of parametric notes, the cash flows are determined by the magnitude of a given risk event according to some predetermined formula; that is, the compensation payment may be some multiple of the reading on the Richter scale for a cat bond linked to earthquakes.

Indemnified notes are subject to moral hazard and information asymmetry problems because they require analysis of the firm's internal operations to assess the catastrophe risk exposure. Indexed and parametric notes, on the other hand, are more transparent and less subject to moral hazard risk taking by individual firms. Thus, although indemnified notes offer the firm more complete operational risk hedging, the trend in the market has been away from indemnified notes. From April 1998 to March 1999, 99 percent of the cat bonds that were issued were in the form of indemnified notes. During April 1998 to March 1999, the fraction of indemnified notes dropped to 55 percent and further to 35 percent during April 2000 to March 2001 (see Schochlin, 2002).

The earliest cat bonds were typically linked to a single risk. However, currently more than 65 percent of all new issues link pay-offs to a portfolio of catastrophes. During April 2000 to March 2001, 11 percent of all newly issued cat bonds had sublimits that limited the maximum compensation payment per type of risk or per single catas-trophe within the portfolio. Despite this limitation, the introduction of cat bonds allows access to a capital market that has the liquidity to absorb operational risk that is beyond the capacity of traditional insurance and self-insurance vehicles. Since cat bonds are privately placed Rule 144A instruments, most investors were either mutual funds/investment advisors or proprietary/hedge funds, accounting for 50 percent of the market in terms of dollar commitments at the time of primary distribution (see Schochlin, 2002). The remainder of the investors consisted of reinsurers/financial intermediaries (21 percent), banks (8 percent), non-life insurers (4 percent) and life insurers (17 percent of the new issues market).

Cat bonds would be impractical if the cost of the catastrophic risk hedge embedded in the bond was prohibitively expensive. Cruz (1999) shows that this is not the case. For a pure discount bond[47] with a yield of 5 percent, the added annual cost for approximately $26.8 million worth of operational loss insurance (at the 1 percent VaR level) would be 1 percent, for a total borrowing cost of 6 percent per annum. Cruz (1999) compares that cost to an insurance policy issued to protect a large investment bank against fraud (limited to a single trading desk for losses up to $300 million) that had a premium of 10 percent.[48] As an illustration of the order of magnitude on cat bond pricing, consider a five year zero coupon, plain vanilla default risk free bond with a $100 par value yielding 5 percent p.a. The price would be calculated as: $100/1.05^5 = \$78.35$. However, if the bond were a cat bond, then the price would be calculated as: $(100(1 - \alpha))/1.05^5$ where α denotes the probability of occurrence of an operational loss event's occurrence.[49] Alternatively, the cat bond could be priced as: $100/(1 + 0.05 + ORS)^5$ where ORS is 1 percent p.a. (the operational risk spread estimated by Cruz, 1999). Substituting $ORS = 0.01$ into the pricing for-mula, the price of the cat bond would be $74.73. This corresponds to an α of only 4.6 percent over the five-year life of the cat bond.

The cost of the cat bond may be reduced because of the bonds' attrac-tiveness to investors interested in improving portfolio efficiency who are attracted to the bond's diversification properties resulting from the low (zero) correlation between market risk and catastrophic risk.[50] Thus, cat bonds may provide a low cost method for firms to manage their operational risk exposure. Furthermore, not only does the cat bond provide operational loss insurance at a significantly lower cost, but the firm does not have to wait for the insurance company to pay off on the policy in the event of a triggering event, since the proceeds from the bond issue are already held by the firm.[51] Similarly, a new product, equity based securitization (or "insuritization"), entails the issuance of a contingent claim on equity markets such that equity is raised if a large operational loss is realized.[52]

5.3.4   Limitations to operational risk hedging

Operational risk management presents extremely difficult risk control challenges when compared to the management of other sources of risk exposure, such as market risk, liquidity risk, and credit risk. The internal nature of the exposure makes both measurement and management difficult. Young (1999) states that "open socio-technical systems have an infinite number of ways of failing. . . . The complexity of human behavior prevents errors from being pre-specified and reduced to a simple numerical representation" (p. 10). Operational risk is embedded in a firm and cannot be easily separated out. Thus, even if a hedge performs as designed, the firm will be negatively impacted in terms of damage to reputation or disruption of business as a result of an LFHS operational risk event.

Assessing operational risk can be highly subjective. For example, a key sponsor of operational risk reports, books, and conferences, as well as an operational risk measurement product was the accounting firm Arthur Andersen. However, when it came to assessing its own operational risk exposure, key partners in the accounting firm made critical errors in judgment that compromised the entire firm's reputation. Thus, the culture of a firm and the incentive structure in place yields unanticipated cross correlations in risk taking across different business units of the firm. One unit's operational problems can bring down other, even unrelated units, thereby requiring complex operational risk analysis undertaking an all encompassing approach to the firm, rather than a decentralized approach that breaks risk down into measurable pieces.

The data problems discussed in chapter 4 in reference to credit risk measurement are even more difficult to overcome when it comes to operational risk measurement models. Data are usually unavailable, and when available are highly subjective and non-uniform in both form and function. Since each firm is individual and since operational risk is so dependent on individual firm cultural characteristics, data from one firm are not easily applicable to other firms. Moreover, simply extrapolating from the past is unlikely to provide useful predictions of the future. Most firms are allotted only one catastrophic risk event in their lifetime. The observation that a catastrophic operational risk event has not yet occurred is no indication that it will not occur in the future. All of these challenges highlight the considerable work remaining before we can understand and effectively hedge this important source of risk exposure.

5.4   SUMMARY

Operational risk is particularly difficult to measure given its nature as the residual risk remaining after consideration of market and credit risk exposures. In this chapter, top-down techniques are contrasted with bottom-up models of operational risk. Top-down techniques measure the overall operational risk exposure using a macrolevel risk indicator such as earnings volatility, cost volatility, the number of customer complaints, etc. Top-down techniques tend to be easy to implement, but they are unable to diagnose weaknesses in the firm's risk control mechanisms and tend to be backward looking. More forward looking bottom-up techniques map each process individually, concentrating on potential operational errors at each stage of the process. This enables the firm to diagnose potential weaknesses, but requires large amounts of data that are typically unavailable within the firm. Industry-wide data are used to supplement internal data, although there are problems of consistency and relevance. Operational risk hedging can be accomplished through external insurance, self-insurance (using economic or regulatory capital or through risk mitigation and control within the firm), and derivatives such as catastrophe options and catastrophe bonds. However, the development of our understanding of operational risk measurement and management is far behind that of credit risk and market risk measurement and management techniques.

APPENDIX 5.1   COPULA FUNCTIONS

Contrary to the old nursery rhyme, "all the King's horses and all the King's men" could have put Humpty Dumpty together again if they had been familiar with copula functions.[53] If marginal probability distributions can be derived from a joint probability distribution, can the process be reversed? That is, if one knows the marginal probability distributions, can they be rejoined to formulate the joint probability distribution? Copula functions have been used in actuarial work for life insurance companies and for reliability studies to recreate the joint distribution from the marginal distributions. However, the resulting joint probability distribution is not unique and the process requires several important assumptions. To reconstitute a joint probability distribution, one must specify the marginal distributions, the correlation structure, and the form of the copula function. We consider each of these inputs in turn.

5.A1   The marginal distributions

Suppose that the time until the occurrence of a specified risk event is denoted T.[54] Then the distribution function of T is $F(t) = \Pr[T \leq t]$ where $t \geq 0$, denoting the probability that the risk event occurs within t years (or periods).[55] Conversely, the survival function is $S(t) = 1 - F(t) = \Pr[T \geq t]$, where $t \geq 0$, denoting that $S(t)$ is the probability that the risk event has not occurred as of time t. The conditional event probability is defined to be $_t q_x = \Pr[T - x \leq t/t > x]$ where $T \geq x$ is the probability that an event will occur within t years (or periods) conditional on the firm's survival without a risk event until time x. The probability density function can be obtained by differentiating the cumulative probability distribution such that

$$f(t) = F'(t) = -S'(t) = \lim_{\Delta \to 0} \frac{\Pr\ [t \leq T < t + \Delta]}{\Delta}. \qquad (5.A1)$$

The hazard rate function, denoted $h(x)$, can be obtained as follows:

$$h(x) = \frac{f(x)}{1 - F(x)}, \qquad (5.A2)$$

and is interpreted as the conditional probability density function of T at exact age x given survival to that time. Thus, the conditional event probability can be restated as:

$$_t q_x = 1 - e^{-\int_0^t h(s+x)\,ds} \qquad (5.A3)$$

These functions must be specified for each process, security, and firm in the portfolio.

5.A2   The correlation structure

The event correlation can be defined as:

$$\rho_{A,B} = \frac{\text{cov}(T_A T_B)}{\sqrt{\text{var}(A)\text{var}(B)}}. \tag{5.A4}$$

This is a general specification of the survival time correlation and has no limits on the length of time used to calculate correlations. Indeed, the correlation structure can be expected to be time varying, perhaps in relation to macroeconomic conditions (see Allen and Saunders (2002) for a survey of cyclical effects in credit risk correlations). Since the general correlation structure is usually not available in practice, the discrete event correlation is typically calculated over a fixed period of time, such as one year. For example, as shown in section 4.3.2.2, CreditMetrics calculates asset correlations using equity returns.

5.A3   The form of the copula function

Li (2000) describes three copula functions commonly used in biostatistics and actuarial science. They are presented in bivariate form for random variables U and V defined over areas $\{u,v)/0 < u \leq 1, 0 < v \leq 1\}$.

Frank copula

$$C(u,v) = \frac{1}{\alpha} \ln\left[1 + \frac{(e^{\alpha u} - 1)(e^{\alpha v} - 1)}{e^{\alpha} - 1}\right] \quad \text{where } -\infty < \alpha < \infty. \tag{5.A5}$$

Bivariate normal copula

$$C(u,v) = \Phi_2(\Phi^{-1}(u), \Phi^{-1}(v), \rho) \quad \text{where } -1 \leq \rho \leq 1 \tag{5.A6}$$

where Φ_2 is the bivariate normal distribution function with the correlation coefficient ρ and Φ^{-1} is the inverse of a univariate normal distribution function. This is the specification used by CreditMetrics, assuming a one-year asset correlation, in order to obtain the bivariate normal density function. As an illustration of how the density function could be derived using the bivariate normal copula function, substitute the marginal distributions for a one-year risk event probability (say, default for CreditMetrics) random variables T_A and T_B into equation (5.A6) such that:

$$\Pr[T_A < 1,\ T_B < 1] = \Phi_2(\Phi^{-1}(F_A(1)),\ \Phi^{-1}(F_B(1)),\gamma),$$

where F_A and F_B are cumulative distribution functions for T_A and T_B, respectively. If the one-year asset correlation ρ is substituted for γ, equation (4.10) is obtained.

Bivariate mixture copula

A new copula function can be formed using two copula functions. As a simple example, if the two random variables are independent, then the copula function $C(u,v) = uv$. If the two random variables are perfectly correlated, then $C(u,v) = min(u,v)$. The polar cases of uncorrelated and perfectly correlated random variables can be seen as special cases of the more general specification. That is, the general mixing copula function can be obtained by mixing the two random variables using the correlation term as a mixing coefficient ρ such that:

$$C(u,v) = (1 - \rho)uv + \rho\min(u,v) \qquad \text{if } \rho > 0, \qquad (5.A7)$$

$$C(u,v) = (1 + \rho)uv - \rho(u - 1 + v)\theta(u - 1 + v) \quad \text{if } \rho \leq 0, \qquad (5.A8)$$

where $\theta(x) = 1$ if $x \geq 0$ and $\theta(x) = 0$ if $x < 0$

Once the copula function is obtained, Li (2000) demonstrates how it can be used to price credit default swaps and first-to-default contracts. Similar applications to operational risk derivatives are possible.

CHAPTER SIX

APPLYING VaR TO REGULATORY MODELS

The 1988 Basel[1] Capital Accord (BIS I) was revolutionary in that it sought to develop a single capital requirement for credit risk across the major banking countries of the world.[2] A major focus of BIS I was to distinguish the credit risk of sovereign, bank, and mortgage obligations (accorded lower risk weights) from non-bank private sector or commercial loan obligations (accorded the highest risk weight). There was little or no attempt to differentiate the credit risk exposure within the commercial loan classification. All commercial loans implicitly required an 8 percent total capital requirement (Tier 1 plus Tier 2),[3] regardless of the inherent creditworthiness of the borrower, its external credit rating, the collateral offered, or the covenants extended.[4] Since the capital requirement was set too low for high risk/low quality business loans and too high for low risk/high quality loans, the mispricing of commercial lending risk created an incentive for banks to shift portfolios toward those loans that were more underpriced from a regulatory risk capital perspective; for example, banks tended to retain the most credit risky tranches of securitized loan portfolios. (See Jones (2000) for a discussion of these regulatory capital arbitrage activities.) Thus, the 1988 Basel Capital Accord had the unintended consequence of encouraging a long-term deterioration in the overall credit quality of bank portfolios.[5] The proposed goal of the new Basel Capital Accord of 2003 (BIS II) – to be fully implemented, if approved as proposed, in 2006 – is to correct the mispricing inherent in BIS I and incorporate more risk sensitive credit exposure measures into bank capital requirements.[6]

Another shortcoming of BIS I was its neglect of market risk, liquidity risk, and operational risk exposures.[7] To partially rectify this, BIS I was amended in 1996 to incorporate a market risk component into bank capital requirements.[8] Moreover, BIS II proposes to integrate credit risk, market risk, and operational risk into an overall capital requirement so that, if adopted, overall capital adequacy after 2006 will be measured as follows:

Regulatory total capital = Credit risk capital requirement

+ Market risk capital requirement

+ Operational risk capital requirement

where:

1 The credit risk capital requirement depends on the bank's choice of either the standardized or the internal ratings-based (foundation or advanced) Approaches (see discussion in section 6.2).
2 The market risk capital requirement depends on the bank's choice of either the standardized or the internal model approach (e.g., RiskMetrics, historical simulation or Monte Carlo simulation); see discussion in section 6.1.
3 The operational risk capital requirement (as proposed in November 2001) depends on the bank's choice between a basic indicator approach (BIA), a standardized approach, and an advanced

measurement approach (AMA); see discussion in section 6.3.[9] While part of the 8 percent ratio under BIS I was viewed as capital allocated to absorb operational risk, the proposed new operational risk requirement in BIS II aims to separate out operational risk from credit risk and, at least for the basic indicator and standardized approaches, has attempted to calibrate operational risk capital to equal 12 percent of a bank's total regulatory capital requirement.[10]

In this chapter, we discuss how each of these regulatory proposals apply VaR techniques to the design of minimum regulatory capital requirements, with special emphasis on the latest BIS II proposals. Whenever BIS II is adopted, overall regulatory capital levels are targeted (by the BIS) to remain unchanged for the system as a whole, at the current average level of 8 percent of the banks' total risk-based off- and on-balance sheet assets. To the extent that these regulatory models accurately measure bank risk exposure, then regulatory minimums will more closely conform to the bank's economic capital requirements. However, divergence between regulatory and economic capital (i.e., the bank's own privately determined optimal capital level) is costly both on the upside and the downside. That is, if regulatory capital is set too low, then banks do not consider capital requirements to be binding constraints and therefore, minimum capital charges cannot be used by regulators to influence bank portfolio and risk-taking policies. On the other hand, if regulatory capital requirements are set too high, then the cost of providing banking services is increased, thus reducing entry into the industry and encouraging banks to circumvent (or arbitrage) requirements, thereby undermining the supervisory function of bank regulators and imposing welfare losses to bank customers to the extent that such costs are passed on by the bank.[11]

Capital requirements are just the first of three pillars comprising the BIS II proposals. The second pillar consists of a supervisory review process that requires bank regulators to assess the adequacy of bank risk management policies. Several issues, such as interest rate risk included in the banking book and liquidity risk on the banking book, have been relegated to the second pillar (i.e., supervisory oversight) rather than to explicit capital requirements. The third pillar of BIS II is market discipline. The Accord sets out disclosure requirements to increase the transparency of reporting of risk exposures so as to enlist the aid of market participants in supervising bank behavior. Indeed, the adequacy of disclosure requirements is a prerequisite for supervisory approval of bank internal models of risk measurement.

6.1   BIS REGULATORY MODELS OF MARKET RISK

In 1995, the BIS proposed an amendment to BIS I designed to incorporate the market risk on fixed-income securities, foreign exchange,
and equities into international bank capital requirements; see BIS (1993,
1995, 1996). This amendment was adopted in the EU in December
1996 and in the US in January 1998. "The objective in introducing
this significant amendment to the Capital Accord is to provide an explicit
capital cushion for the price risks to which banks are exposed, particularly those arising from their trading activities" (BIS, 1996, p. 1).
The market risk amendment applies to foreign exchange and commodity
price risk throughout the bank, although consideration of interest rate
and equity price risk is limited to the trading book only. Banks can
choose to measure their market risk exposure either using the BIS
standardized framework or using an internal model that is approved
by the bank regulators and subject to a formalized methodology of
backtesting and regulatory audit.

6.1.1   The standardized framework for market risk

The standardized framework sets common parameters to be used by
all banks to determine their capital requirements. However, implementation requires the bank to report detailed data on the composition,
maturity structure, and risk measures (e.g., duration for fixed income
securities) of its portfolio.

6.1.1.1   Measuring interest rate risk

The capital charge for the market risk on fixed-income securities is
comprised of a specific risk charge plus a general market risk charge.
The specific risk charge uses BIS I methodology to calculate the credit
risk of each security. That is, securities are assigned a specific risk weight
ranging from 0 percent (for US Treasury securities) to 8 percent (for
nonqualifying corporate debt such as junk bonds). The specific risk
charge for each individual position is obtained by multiplying the specific
risk weight by the absolute dollar values of all long and short positions in fixed income securities. The portfolio's specific risk charge is
calculated by summing the specific risk charges for each fixed income
security held in the trading book.

The general market risk charge is based on a (modified) duration approach that estimates the price sensitivity of each bond in the portfolio as a result of an interest rate shock expected to occur over a short time horizon (e.g., the standardized model of interest rate risk specifies one year). That is, the general market risk charge is calculated as the bond's modified duration times the expected interest rate shock times the size of the position.[12] However, simply adding the general market risk charges for all long and short positions in the portfolio might underestimate the portfolio's interest rate risk exposure because that assumes that all interest rates of "similar" maturity securities move together in lock step, such that the risk exposure on long positions perfectly offsets the risk exposure on short positions for securities of a "similar" maturity. Since all yields across all instruments of the same maturity do not necessarily move together, then portfolios are exposed to "basis" risk. Thus, the BIS standardized framework imposes a series of additional capital charges for basis risk called vertical and horizontal offsets or disallowance factors. Vertical disallowance factors limit the risk hedging across instruments of similar maturity. For example, a short position in long-term (10–15 year) US Treasury securities can hedge only 95 percent of a long position in long-term junk bonds; that is, the standardized framework imposes a 5 percent vertical offset. In contrast, horizontal offsets limit the implicit hedging within the portfolio across maturities. For example, using three maturity zones (1 month to 12 months; 1 year to 4 years; 4 years to 20 years), a short position in any single maturity zone can only partially offset a long position in another maturity zone, and in extreme cases, no offset is allowed at all.

The total market risk-adjusted capital requirement for fixed income securities held in the trading book is determined by summing the specific risk charge and the general market risk charge (incorporating any disallowance factors).

6.1.1.2   Measuring foreign exchange rate risk

The standardized framework requires the bank to calculate its net exposure in each foreign currency, which is then converted into home currency at the current spot exchange rate. All net long positions across all foreign currencies are summed separately from all net short currency positions. The capital charge is then calculated as 8 percent of the higher of the aggregate long positions or the aggregate short positions. For example, if a US bank had a net long currency exposure of

US$750 million to the Euro, a net long currency exposure of US$525 million to the Canadian dollar, and a short net currency exposure of US$1.5 billion to the Japanese yen, then the aggregate longs would be US$1.275 billion and the aggregate shorts would be US$1.5 billion (since the aggregate short $1.5 billion position exceeds the aggregate long $1.275 billion position). The BIS standardized capital charge for foreign exchange rate risk would therefore be 8 percent of US$1.5 billion = US$120 million.[13]

6.1.1.3   Measuring equity price risk

In calculating the capital charge for the market risk of equity price fluctuations, the BIS standardized framework estimates both systematic (market) and unsystematic (diversifiable) risk exposures of the bank's stock portfolio. To obtain a capital charge for unsystematic risk, an x factor of 4 percent is applied to the gross position in each stock (i.e., the aggregated absolute value of both long and short equity positions). Thus, if the bank holds a gross position in Microsoft of $150 million, the unsystematic risk charge would be 4% × $150 million = $6 million. In addition, there is a charge for systematic risk known as the y factor, set to be 8 percent. If the Microsoft position consisted of $100 million long and $50 million short (for a $150 million gross position), then the bank's net position in Microsoft would be long $50 million. Applying the y factor yields a systematic risk charge of 8% × $50 million = $4 million. The total capital charge for equity price risk is the sum of the x factor and the y factor risks, which in this example is $10 million for the Microsoft stock portfolio. This process would be repeated for each individual stock in the portfolio.

6.1.2   Internal models of market risk

The standardized framework for market risk is a simplified model of the true nature of the market risk faced by banks. In the market risk amendment to BIS I, some banks are allowed, with central bank approval, to choose to use their own internal models to calculate their capital requirements for market risk exposure. That is, a market VaR model (such as described in chapters 1–3) can be used to calculate the bank's daily earnings at risk (DEAR) for adverse changes in interest rates, exchange rates, and equity returns. However, certain conditions are imposed on the bank's internal model to assure that the risk estimates are adequate for the purposes of setting minimum capital requirements. First, the stipulated VaR model is set at the 99th percentile, thereby increasing the estimate of the DEAR (as compared to the 95th percentile under RiskMetrics for example). Moreover, the minimum holding period is set to be two weeks (10 business days), thereby requiring the bank to multiply the DEAR estimate by $\sqrt{10}$ (utilizing the square root rule described in section 1.1.2).[14]

The internal models framework of the BIS capital regulations set the minimum capital requirement to be the *larger* of: (i) the previous day's VaR (i.e., DEAR $\times \sqrt{10}$); or (ii) the average daily VaR over the previous 60 days times a multiplicative factor of 3 (i.e., average DEAR $\times \sqrt{10} \times 3$). The use of a multiplicative factor increases the capital charge over the economic capital requirements obtained directly from the VaR model. The size of the multiplicative factor is also used as a backtesting device to discipline banks that systematically underestimate their capital requirements under the so-called "traffic light" system. Specifically, if the bank's internal model underestimates market risk less than four days out of the past 250 days, then the bank is given a green light and the multiplicative factor is set at 3. If the bank's internal model underestimates market risk between 4 and 9 days out of the last 250 days, then the bank receives a yellow light and the multiplicative factor is raised above 3 (set at various increments above 3, but less than 4).[15] In the event that the model underestimates market risk on 10 days or more out of the last 250 days, it is given a red light and the multiplicative factor is raised to 4. The resulting increase in the bank's cost of capital could be high enough to put the bank out of the trading business.[16] Thus, the regulations offer banks the incentive to improve the accuracy of their internal model estimates of market risk.

6.2   BIS REGULATORY MODELS OF CREDIT RISK

BIS II proposals on credit risk follow a three-step (potentially evolutionary) approach. Banks can choose among (or for less sophisticated banks are expected to evolve from) the basic (i) Standardized Model to the (ii) Internal Ratings-Based (IRB) Model Foundation Approach to the (iii) Internal Ratings-Based (IRB) Advanced Model. The Standardized Approach is based on external credit ratings assigned by independent ratings agencies (such as Moody's, Standard & Poor's and Fitch IBCA or accredited local credit rating agencies for non-US countries). Both Internal Ratings approaches require the bank to formulate and use its own internal credit risk rating system. The risk weight assigned to each commercial obligation is based on the ratings assignment, so that higher (lower) rated, high (low) credit quality obligations have lower (higher) risk weights and therefore lower (higher) capital requirements, thereby eliminating the incentives to engage in risk shifting and regulatory arbitrage. They differ according to the number of variables a bank is allowed to input into its internal calculations for regulatory capital.

6.2.1 The Standardized Model for credit risk

The Standardized Model follows a similar methodology as BIS I, but makes it more risk sensitive by dividing the commercial obligor designation into finer gradations of risk classifications (risk buckets), with risk weights that are a function of external credit ratings.[17] Under the current post 1992-system (BIS I), all commercial loans are viewed as having the same credit risk (and thus the same risk weight). Essentially, the book value of each loan is multiplied by a risk weight of 100 percent and then by 8 percent in order to generate the Tier 1 plus Tier 2 minimum capital requirement of 8 percent of risk-adjusted assets, the so-called "8 percent rule." Table 6.1 compares the risk weights for corporate obligations under the proposed new (November 2001) Standardized Model to the old BIS I risk weights. Under BIS II, the bank's assets are classified into each of five risk

Table 6.1 Total capital requirements on corporate obligations under the standardized model of BIS II

External credit rating	AAA to AA– (%)	A+ to A– (%)	BBB+ to BB– (%)	Below BB– (%)	Unrated (%)
Risk weight under BIS II	20	50	100	150	100
Capital requirement under BIS II	1.6	4	8	12	8
Risk weight under BIS I	100	100	100	100	100
Capital requirement under BIS I	8	8	8	8	8

Source: Bank for International Settlements (2001a).

buckets as shown in table 6.1 according to the credit rating assigned the obligor by independent rating agencies. In order to obtain the minimum capital requirement for credit risk purposes, all credit exposures (known as exposure at default, EAD)[18] in each risk weight bucket are summed up, weighted by the appropriate risk weight from table 6.1, and then multiplied by the overall total capital requirement of 8 percent.

The Standardized Approach takes into account credit risk mitigation techniques used by the bank by adjusting the transaction's EAD to reflect collateral, credit derivatives or guarantees, and offsetting on-balance sheet netting. However, any collateral value is reduced by a haircut to adjust for the volatility of the instrument's market value. Moreover, a floor capital level assures that the credit quality of the borrower will always impact capital requirements.[19]

The risk weights for claims on sovereigns and their central banks are shown in table 6.2. The new weights allow for differentiation of credit risk within the classification of OECD nations. Under BIS I, all

Table 6.2 Total capital requirements on sovereigns under the standardized model of BIS II

External credit rating	AAA to AA– or ECA Rating 1 (%)	A+ to A– or ECA Rating 2 (%)	BBB+ to BBB– or ECA Rating 3 (%)	BB+ to B– or ECA Rating 4 to 6 (%)	Below B– or ECA Rating 7 (%)
Risk weight under BIS II	0	20	50	100	150
Capital requirement under BIS II	0	1.6	4	8	12

Notes: ECA denotes Export Credit Agencies. To qualify, the ECA must publish its risk scores and use the OECD methodology. If there are two different assessments by ECAs, then the higher risk weight is used. Sovereigns also have an unrated category with a 100 percent risk weight (not shown). Under BIS I, the risk weight for OECD government obligations is 0 percent. OECD interbank deposits and guaranteed claims, as well as some non-OECD bank and government deposits and securities carry a 20 percent risk weight under BIS I. All other claims on non-OECD governments and banks carry a 100 percent risk weight under BIS I (see Saunders, 2003).
Source: Bank for International Settlements (2001a).

OECD nations carried preferential risk weights of 0 percent on their government obligations, while non-OECD countries carried a 100 percent risk weight. BIS II levies a risk weight that depends on the sovereign's external rating, not on its political affiliation.[20] However, claims on the BIS, the IMF, the European Central Bank, and the European Community all carry a 0 percent risk weight.

6.2.2   The Internal Ratings-Based Models for credit risk

Under the Internal Ratings-Based (IRB) approaches each bank is required to establish an internal ratings model to classify the credit risk exposure of each activity, e.g., commercial lending, consumer lending, etc. – whether on or off the balance sheet. For the Foundation IRB Approach, the required outputs obtained from the internal ratings model are estimates of one year[21] probability of default (PD) and exposure at default (EAD) for each transaction. In addition to these estimates, independent estimates of both the loss given default (LGD) and maturity (M)[22] are required to implement the Advanced IRB Approach. The bank computes risk weights for each individual exposure (e.g., a corporate loan) by incorporating its estimates of PD, EAD, LGD, and M obtained from its internal ratings model and its own internal data systems.[23] The model also assumes that the average default correlation among individual borrowers is between 10 and 20 percent with the correlation a decreasing function of PD; see BIS (November 5, 2001e).[24]

Expected losses upon default can be calculated as PD × LGD, where PD is the probability of default and LGD is the loss given default. However, this considers only one possible credit event – default – and ignores the possibility of losses resulting from credit rating downgrades. That is, deterioration in credit quality caused by increases in PD or LGD will cause the value of the loan to be written down (or sold for less) – in a mark-to-market sense – even prior to default, thereby resulting in portfolio losses (if the loan's value is marked to market). Thus, credit risk measurement models can be differentiated on the basis of whether the definition of a "credit event" includes only default (the default mode or DM models) or whether it also includes non-default credit quality deterioration (the mark-to-market or MTM models). The mark-to-market approach considers the impact of credit downgrades and upgrades on market value, whereas the default mode is only concerned about the economic value of an obligation in the event of default. The IRB capital requirements are calibrated to include mark-to-market losses (e.g., similar to CreditMetrics, as discussed in chapter 4). There are five elements to any IRB approach.

1   A classification of the obligation by credit risk exposure – the internal ratings model.
2   Risk components – PD and EAD for the Foundation model and PD, EAD, LGD, and M for the Advanced model.
3   A risk weight function that uses the risk components to calculate the risk weights.
4   A set of minimum requirements of eligibility to apply the IRB approach – i.e., demonstration that the bank maintains the necessary information systems to accurately implement the IRB approach.
5   Supervisory review of compliance with the minimum requirements.

6.2.2.1   The Foundation IRB Approach

Under the Foundation IRB Approach, the bank is allowed to use its own estimate of probability of default (PD) over a one-year time horizon, as well as each loan's exposure at default (EAD). However, there is a lower bound on PD that is equal to 3 basis points, so as to create a non-zero floor on the credit risk weights (and hence capital required to be held against any individual loan). The average PD for each internal risk grade is used to calculate the risk weight for each internal rating. The PD may be based on historical experience or even potentially on a credit scoring model (see chapter 4 for discussions of traditional credit scoring models as well as newer, more financial theory-based models of credit risk measurement). The EAD for on-balance-sheet transactions is equal to the nominal (book) amount of the exposure outstanding. Credit mitigation factors (e.g., collateral, credit derivatives or guarantees, on-balance-sheet netting) are incorporated following the rules of the IRB Approach by adjusting the EAD for the collateral amount, less a haircut determined by supervisory advice under Pillar II. The EAD for off-balance-sheet activities is computed using the BIS I approach of translating off-balance sheet items into on-balance-sheet equivalents mostly using the BIS I conversion factors (see section 6.2.3). The Foundation IRB Approach sets a benchmark for M, maturity (or weighted average life of the loan) at 3 years. Moreover, the Foundation Approach assumes that the loss given default for each unsecured loan is set at LGD = 50 percent for senior claims and LGD = 75 percent for subordinated claims on corporate obligations.[25]

However, in November 2001, the Basel Committee on Banking Supervision presented potential modifications that would reduce the LGD on secured loans to 45 percent if fully secured by physical, non-real estate collateral and 40 percent if fully secured by receivables.

Under the January 2001 proposal, the Foundation Approach formula for the risk weight on corporate[26] obligations (loans) is:[27]

$$RW = (LGD/50) \times BRW \quad OR \quad 12.50 \times LGD,$$

$$\text{whichever is smaller;} \tag{6.1}$$

where the benchmark risk weight (BRW) is calculated for each risk classification using the following formula:

$$BRW = 976.5 \times N(1.118 \times G(PD) + 1.288)$$

$$\times (1 + 0.0470 \times (1 - PD)/PD^{0.44}) \tag{6.2}$$

The term $N(y)$ denotes the cumulative distribution function for a standard normal random variable (i.e., the probability that a normal random variable with mean zero and variance of one is less than or equal to y) and the term $G(z)$ denotes the inverse cumulative distribution function for a standard normal random variable (i.e., the value y such that $N(y) = z$). The BRW formula is calibrated so that a three-year corporate loan with a PD equal to 0.7 percent and an LGD equal to 50 percent will have a capital requirement of 8 percent, calibrated to an assumed loss coverage target of 99.5 percent (i.e., losses to exceed the capital allocation occur only 0.5 percent of the time, or 5 years in 1,000).[28]

Consultation between the Basel Committee on Banking Supervision and the public fueled concerns about the calibration of the Foundation Approach as presented in equations (6.1) and (6.2). This concern was motivated by the results published in November 2001 of a Quantitative Impact Study (QIS2) that examined the impact of the BIS II proposals on the capital requirements of 138 large and small banks from 25 countries. Banks that would have adopted the IRB Foundation Approach would have seen an unintended 14 percent increase in their capital requirements. Potential modifications were released on November 5, 2001 to lower the risk weights and make the risk weighting function less steep for the IRB Foundation Approach only. Moreover, the potential modifications (if incorporated into the final BIS II proposals in 2003) would make the correlation coefficient a function of the PD, such that the correlation coefficient

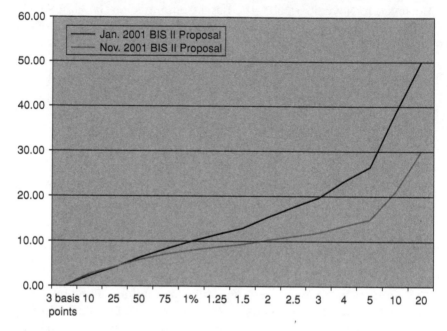

Figure 6.1 Proposed IRB risk weights for corporate exposures
Source: Bank for International Settlements (2001e).

between assets decreases as the PD increases. Finally, the confidence level built into the risk weighting function would be increased from 99.5 percent to 99.9 percent.

Figure 6.1 contrasts the IRB risk weights under the November 2001 proposals to the January 2001 proposals. The November 2001 potential modifications to equations (6.1) and (6.2) corporate loan risk weight curves for the Foundations IRB Approach are as follows:

$$BRW = 12.5 \times LGD \times M \times N[(1 - R)^{-0.5} \times G(PD)$$
$$+ (R/(1 - R))^{0.5} \times G(0.999)], \tag{6.3}$$

where

$$M = 1 + 0.047 \times ((1 - PD)/PD^{0.44}), \tag{6.4}$$

$$R = 0.10 \times [(1 - \exp^{-50PD})/(1 - \exp^{-50})]$$
$$+ 0.20 \times [1 - (1 - \exp^{-50PD})/(1 - \exp^{-50}], \tag{6.5}$$

and

$$RW = (X/50) \times BRW, \tag{6.6}$$

where $X = 75$ for a subordinated loan, $X = 50$ for an unsecured loan, $X = 45$ for a loan fully secured by physical, non-real estate collateral, and $X = 40$ for a loan fully secured by receivables. In equations (6.3) through (6.6), exp stands for the natural exponential function, $N(.)$ stands for the standard normal cumulative distribution function and $G(.)$ stands for the inverse standard normal cumulative distribution function.

Equation (6.4) denotes the maturity factor M. This is reportedly unchanged from the BIS II proposals shown in equation (6.2) in that it is still benchmarked to a fixed three-year weighted average life of the loan.[29] The correlation coefficient R is computed in equation (6.5). The correlation ranges from 0.20 for the lowest PD value to 0.10 for the highest PD value. This inverse relationship appears to be somewhat counterintuitive in that, empirically, asset correlations tend to increase during systemic crises when PDs also tend to increase, thereby implying a direct positive (rather than inverse) relationship between correlation and PD.[30]

Using the potential modifications of November 2001, the benchmark risk weight BRW is calculated using equations (6.3) through (6.5). The actual risk weight RW is then calculated in equation (6.6) where $RW = (X/50) \times BRW$ and $X =$ the stipulated fixed LGD for each type of loan. Risk-weighted assets RWA are then computed by multiplying the risk weight RW times the exposure at default EAD. Finally, the minimum capital requirement is computed by multiplying the risk-weighted assets RWA times 8 percent; that is, the minimum capital requirement on the individual loan $= RW \times EAD \times 8\%$. Under the advanced approach, banks with sufficiently "rich" data on LGDs are to be allowed to input their own estimates of LGD along with own estimates of maturity.

Consider, as an example, a senior unsecured $100 million three-year loan with a PD of 10 percent that would have a 262 percent benchmark risk weight under the November 2001 modifications, computed using equations (6.3) through (6.5). Since the unsubordinated loan in our example is unsecured, using equation (6.6) the $RW = (50/50) \times BRW = 2.62$. Thus, the loan's minimum capital requirement would be $100 million $\times 0.08 \times 2.62 = \$21$ million. In contrast, the same loan's minimum capital requirement under the January 2001 proposals would have been $38.6 million. Moreover, under BIS I the capital requirement would have been $100 million $\times 8\% = \$8$ million.

6.2.2.2   The Advanced IRB Approach

Sophisticated banks are encouraged to move from the Foundation IRB to the Advanced IRB Approach. A primary source for this incentive, as noted above, is permission to use the bank's *actual* LGD experience in place of the fixed assumption of a 40, 45, 50, or 75 percent LGD. Evidence suggests that historical LGD for bank loans is significantly lower than 50 percent[31] and therefore, the shift to the Advanced IRB Approach is expected to reduce bank capital requirements by 2–3 percent. However, the quid pro quo for permission to use actual LGD is compliance with an additional set of minimum requirements attesting to the efficacy of the bank's information systems in maintaining data on LGD.

Another adjustment to the Foundation Approach's BRW is the incorporation of a maturity adjustment reflecting the transaction's effective maturity, defined as the greater of either one year or nominal maturity, which is the weighted average life $(= \Sigma_t t P_t / \Sigma_t P_t$ where P_t is the minimum amount of principal contractually payable at time t) for all instruments with a pre-determined, minimum amortization schedule. The maturity is capped at seven years in order to avoid overstating the impact of maturity on credit risk exposure.

The Advanced IRB Approach allows the bank to use its own credit risk mitigation estimates to adjust PD, LGD, and EAD for collateral, credit derivatives, guarantees, and on-balance sheet netting. The risk weights for the mark-to-market Advanced IRB Approach are calculated as follows:

$$RW = (LGD/50) \times BRW(PD) \times [1 + b(PD) \times (M - 3)] \quad (6.7)$$

where $b(PD) = [0.0235 \times (1 - PD)]/[PD^{0.44} + 0.0470 \times (1 - PD)]$

$$(6.8)$$

and BRW is as defined in equation (6.2) in the Foundation IRB Approach.

The effect of the $[1 + b(PD) \times M(-3)]$ term in equation (6.7) is to adjust the risk of loans for its maturity.[32] For longer maturity instruments, the maturity adjustments increase for low PD rated borrowers (i.e., higher rated borrowers). The intuition is that maturity matters most for low PD borrowers since they can move only in one direction (downwards) and the longer the maturity of the loan, the more likely this is to occur. For high PD (low quality) borrowers who are near default, the maturity adjustment will not matter as much since they may be close to default regardless of the length of the maturity of the loan.[33]

The Advanced IRB Approach entails the estimation of parameters requiring long histories of data that are unavailable to most banks (see the Basel Committee on Banking Supervision (BIS, April 1999) for a survey of current credit risk modeling practices at 20 large international banks located in 10 countries). Given the costs of developing these models and databases, there is the possibility of dichotomizing the banking industry into "haves and have-nots." For example, some anecdotal estimates suggest that no more than 25 US banks will be able to use either of the IRB approaches. Moreover, capital requirements are highly sensitive to the accuracy of certain parameter values; in particular, estimates of LGD and the granularity of PDs are important (see Carey, 2000; Gordy, 2000). Since credit losses are affected by economic conditions, the model parameters should also be adjusted to reflect expected levels of economic activity; for a discussion of cyclical effects see Allen and Saunders (2002). Thus, the data requirements are so substantial that full implementation of the Advanced IRB Approach lies far in the future even for the most sophisticated banks.

6.2.3   BIS regulatory models of off-balance sheet credit risk

Since off-balance sheet (OBS) assets can expose the bank to credit risk, both BIS I and II regulatory models adjust capital requirements to reflect the banks' OBS activity. Some adjustments are as simple as offering a separate risk weighting schedule (such as shown in tables 6.1 and 6.2) based on external credit ratings for OBS items such as asset-backed securities; see the discussion of BIS II Standardized Approach in chapter 14 of Saunders and Allen (2002).

Other adjustments are considerably more complex. For example, BIS I levies a capital charge on the credit risk exposure of an interest rate or exchange rate swap based on: (i) the credit equivalent amounts that are calculated for each contract; and (ii) the appropriate risk weight. Specifically, the notional or face values of all non-exchange-traded swap, forward, and other derivative contracts are first converted into credit equivalent amounts (i.e., "as if" they are on-balance sheet credit instruments). The credit equivalent amount itself is divided into a *potential exposure* element and a *current exposure* element:

Table 6.3 Credit conversion factors for interest rate and foreign exchange contracts in calculating potential exposure (as a percentage of nominal contract value)

Interest rate remaining maturity	(1) Exchange rate Contracts (%)	(2) Contracts (%)
1 One year or less	0.0	1.0
2 One to five years	0.5	5.0
3 Over five years	1.5	7.5

Source: Federal Reserve Board of Governors press release (August 1995), Section IL

Credit equivalent amount of OBS asset

= Potential exposure + Current exposure   (6.9)

The potential exposure component reflects the credit risk if the counterparty to the contract defaults in the future. The probability of such an occurrence is modeled as depending on the future volatility of interest rates/exchange rates. BIS I specifies a set of conversion factors that varied by type of contract (e.g., interest rate or foreign exchange) and by maturity bucket (see table 6.3). The potential exposure conversion factors in table 6.3 are larger for foreign exchange contracts than for interest rate contracts. Also, note the larger potential exposure credit risk for longer-term contracts of both types.

In addition to calculating the potential exposure of an OBS market instrument, a bank must calculate its current exposure to the instrument: the cost of replacing a contract if a counterparty defaults today. The bank calculates this replacement cost or current exposure by replacing the rate or price that was initially in the contract with the current rate or price for a similar contract, and then recalculates all the current and future cash flows to give a current present value measure of the replacement cost of the contract.[34]

After the current and potential exposure amounts are summed to produce the credit equivalent amount of each contract, this dollar number is multiplied by a risk weight to produce the final risk-adjusted asset amount for OBS market contracts. In general, the appropriate risk weight under BIS I is 0.5, or 50 percent. BIS II proposals remove the 50 percent ceiling on risk weights for over-the-counter derivative transactions. If the derivative is unconditionally cancelable or automatically cancels upon deterioration in the borrower's creditworthiness, then the risk weight is set at 0 percent. In contrast, a risk weight of 100 percent is applied to transactions secured by bank collateral or to transactions in which the bank provides third party performance guarantees. The 50 (20) percent risk weight is retained for commitments with an original maturity over (less than) one year.

The growth in the market for credit derivatives[35] has led the BIS to consider special regulatory capital requirements for these instruments. Despite their apparent value as credit risk management tools, credit derivatives have not been well treated under the BIS I capital requirements. According to Wall and Shrikhande (1998), the present US approach is to treat credit derivatives as a loan guarantee, provided the payoff from the credit derivative is sufficiently highly correlated with the loan. If the counterparty is neither a bank nor a government entity, the risk weight is 100 percent; no risk reduction is recognized. If the counterparty is a bank, the risk weight on the loan for the buyer of the guarantee is 20 percent; however, for the bank that issues the guarantee to the counterparty, the risk weight of the guarantee is 100 percent (i.e., it is as if the counterparty has been extended a loan). Thus, in aggregate, the combined-risk-based capital requirements of the two banks could increase as a result of using the derivative. (Under certain conditions, however, this capital burden may be reduced.)

BIS II proposes a harmonization of treatment of credit derivatives under the two approaches – Standardized and IRB Approaches. For buyers of credit protection that use the Standardized Approach, the risk weight for banking book exposures protected using credit derivatives is calculated as follows:*

$$r^* = [w \times r] + [(1 - w)g], \tag{6.10}$$

where r^* = the effective risk weight of the protected position;
r = the risk weight of the underlying obligor (the borrower);
w = the residual risk factor, set at 0.15 for credit derivatives;[36]
g = the risk weight of the protection provider.

For example, if the credit protection was obtained from an AAA rated insurance company (with a 20 percent risk weight under the Standardized Approach) for the bank's underlying credit exposure to a B rated corporate borrower (150 percent risk weight), the effective

* This treatment of derivatives has been dropped from the April 2003 proposals.

risk weight on the credit derivative is 39.5% = (0.15 × 150%) + (0.85 × 20%). If instead of using the Standardized Approach, the bank buying credit protection used the IRB Approach, the risk weights r and g in equation (6.10) would be replaced by the probabilities of default obtained using the bank's credit risk measurement model.

These risk-adjusted capital requirements are for credit derivatives protecting loans on the banking book. BIS II also proposes specific risk capital charges against trading book positions hedged by credit derivatives. If the reference asset, maturity, and currency of the credit derivative exactly matches those of the underlying hedged position, then BIS II allows an 80 percent specific risk offset to avoid risk double-counting. If maturities or currencies are mismatched, but the reference assets are identical, only the higher of the specific risk capital charges will be levied against the entire hedged position.

6.2.4   Assessment of the BIS regulatory models of credit risk

BIS II is a potential improvement over BIS I in its sophistication in measuring credit risk. Moreover, it moves regulatory capital in the direction of economic capital. However, it is far from an integrated portfolio management approach to credit risk measurement. Focus on individual ratings classifications (whether external or internal) prevents an aggregated view of credit risk across all transactions, and regulatory concerns about systemic risk prevent full consideration of cross-asset correlations that might reduce capital requirements further.[37] Thus, capital requirements are likely to be higher than economically necessary when considering actual portfolio correlations.[38] Moreover, incompatible approaches to assessing the capital adequacy of insurance companies and other non-banking firms may obscure their impact on financial system instability.[39] In the US, the insurance industry and Government Sponsored Enterprises (such as Fannie Mae and Freddie Mac), and the Financial Services Authority in the UK all use a variety of models – ranging from minimum ratios, stress test survivorship requirements, to dynamic risk-of-ruin scenario analysis – that include both the asset and liability sides of the balance sheet in order to measure capital requirements.

The proposed risk buckets of the Standardized Approach of BIS II show insufficient risk sensitivity, as discussed in Altman and Saunders (2001a, 2001b) and the Institute of International Finance (2000), especially in the lowest rated bucket for corporates (rated below BB−) which would require a risk weight 3 times greater than proposed under BIS II to cover unexpected losses (based on empirical evidence on corporate bond loss data).[40] By contrast, the risk weight in the first two corporate loan buckets may be too high. Thus, capital regulation arbitrage incentives will not be completely eliminated by the BIS II credit risk weights.

The Unrated risk bucket (of 100 percent) of the Standardized Approach has also been criticized (see Altman and Saunders, 2001a, 2001b). More than 70 percent of corporate exposures were unrated in the 138 banks that participated in a BIS survey (the Quantitative Impact Study QIS2). Since the majority of obligations held by the world's banks are not rated (see Ferri et al., 2001), for example, it is estimated that less than 1,000 European companies are rated,[41] the retention of an unrated risk bucket is a major lapse that threatens to undermine the risk sensitivity of BIS II.[42] Specifically, actual default data on non-rated loans puts them closer to the 150 percent bucket risk weight than the specified 100 percent risk weight. In addition, low quality borrowers that anticipate receiving an external credit rating below BB– have an incentive to eschew independent rating agencies altogether, choosing to reduce their costs of borrowing by remaining unrated, while reducing the availability of credit information available to the market.[43]

On a more fundamental basis, concern has been expressed about tying capital requirements to external ratings produced by rating agencies. Ratings are opinions about the overall credit quality of an obligor, not issue-specific audits.[44] There is a certain amount of heterogeneity within each rating class, since a single letter grade is used to represent a multi-dimensional concept that includes default probability, loss severity, and transition risk. Moreover, since ratings agencies try to avoid discrete jumps in ratings classifications, the rating may be a lagging, not a leading indicator of credit quality (see Reisen and von Maltzan (1999) and Reinhart (2001) for discussions of lags in sovereign credit ratings, Kealhofer (2000) and Altman and Saunders (2001a) for lags in publicly traded corporate ratings, and Bongini, Laeven, and Majnoni (2001) for lags in credit ratings of banks). As ratings change over time, the transaction may be shifted from one risk bucket to another, thereby injecting excessive volatility into capital requirements (see Linnell, 2001) and may lead to an increase in systemic risk since, with increased downgrades in a recession, banks may find their capital requirements peaking at the worst time (i.e., in the middle of a recession when earnings are relatively weak). Indeed, there is evidence (see Ferri et al., 2001; Monfort and Mulder, 2000; Altman and Saunders, 2001b) that ratings agencies behave procyclically since ratings are downgraded in a financial crisis, thereby increasing capital requirements at just the point in the business cycle that stimulation is required (see Reisen, 2000; Allen and Saunders, 2002). Thus, pegging capital requirements to external ratings may exacerbate systemic risk concerns. Concern about systemic risk may lead to regulatory attempts to influence ratings agencies, thereby undermining their independence and credibility.[45]

Although an important advantage of external ratings is their validation by the market, the credit rating industry is not very competitive. There are only a handful of well-regarded rating agencies. This leads to the risk of rating shopping.[46] Since the obligors are free to choose their rating agency, moral hazard may lead rating agencies to shade their ratings upward in a bid to obtain business. Moreover, since there is no single, universally accepted standard for credit ratings, they may not be comparable across rating agencies and across countries (see discussions in White, 2001; Cantor, 2001; Griep and De Stefano, 2001). This is likely to distort capital requirements more in less developed countries (LDCs), because of greater volatility in LDC sovereign ratings, less transparent financial reporting in those countries, and the greater impact of the sovereign rating as a de facto ceiling for the private sector in LDCs.[47]

Moreover, banks are considered "delegated monitors" (see Diamond, 1984) who have a comparative advantage in assessing and monitoring the credit risks of their borrowers. Indeed, this function is viewed as making banks "special." This appears to be inconsistent with the concept underlying the Standardized Model, which essentially attributes this bank monitoring function to external rating agencies for the purposes of setting capital requirements. Adoption of this approach may well reduce bank incentives to invest time and effort in monitoring, thereby reducing the availability of information and further undermining the value of the banking franchise.

Even the Advanced IRB Approach contains some properties that may distort bank incentives to manage their credit risk exposure. For example, Allen (2002a) finds that the maturity adjustment in the Advanced IRB Approach (see equation 6.7) creates perverse incentives when dealing with loans with maturities greater than three years such that the loan adjustment factor *decreases* the loan's risk weight as the loan quality (credit rating) declines. Moreover, the Advanced IRB Approach penalizes increases in LGD more than increases in PD.

The IRB Approaches of BIS II are based on a prespecified threshold insolvency level; that is, capital levels are set so that the estimated probability of insolvency of each bank is lower than a threshold level such as 99.9 percent (or 0.1 percent probability of failure per year, or 1 bank insolvency every 1,000 years).[48] However, there are two potential shortcomings to this approach from the regulator's point of view. First, without considering the relationship between individual banks' insolvency probabilities, BIS II cannot specify an aggregate, system-wide insolvency risk threshold (see Acharya, 2001). Second, there is no information about the magnitude of loss given bank insolvency. The deposit insurer, for example, may be concerned about the cost to the deposit insurance fund in the event that the bank's capital is exhausted. (See Gordy (2000) for a discussion of the estimation of the "expected tail loss.") BIS II addresses neither of these concerns. However, there is evidence (see Jackson, Perraudin, and Saporta, 2001) that banks hold capital in excess of the regulatory minimum in response to market pressure; for example, in order to participate in the swap market, the bank's credit quality must be higher than would be induced by complying with either BIS I or II.[49] Thus, regulatory capital requirements may be considered lower bounds that do not obviate the need for more precise credit risk measurement.

6.3 BIS REGULATORY MODELS OF OPERATIONAL RISK

As banks become more proficient at measuring their market risk and credit risk exposures, they become more dependent on systems that might expose them to operational risk. Thus, banks may be trading relatively transparent market and credit risk for even more opaque operational risk exposure. BIS (2001c) defines operational risk to be "the risk of loss resulting from inadequate or failed internal processes, people and systems or from external events." Explicitly excluded from this definition are systemic risk, strategic and reputational risks, as well as all indirect losses or opportunity costs, which may be open-ended and huge in size compared to direct losses.

In the BIS II proposals, banks can choose among three methods for calculating operational risk capital charges: (i) the Basic Indicator Approach (BIA); (ii) the Standardized Approach; and (iii) the Advanced Measurement Approach (AMA) which itself has three possible models. Banks are encouraged to evolve to the more sophisticated AMA operational risk measurement models.

Table 6.4 Analysis of QIS data: basic indicator approach based on 12 percent of minimum regulatory capital

	Median	Mean	Weighted average	Standard deviation	Weighted average standard deviation	Minimum	25th percentile	75th percentile	Maximum	No. of banks
All banks	0.193	0.221	0.183	0.132	0.117	0.020	0.138	0.244	0.678	126
Large banks	0.170	0.219	0.179	0.133	0.118	0.056	0.140	0.224	0.547	53
Small banks	0.203	0.222	0.220	0.132	0.108	0.020	0.137	0.247	0.678	73

Source: Bank for International Settlements (2001c), p. 27.

6.3.1   The Basic Indicator Approach

Banks using the Basic Indicator Approach (BIA) are required to hold capital for operational risk set equal to a fixed percentage (denoted α) of a single indicator. The proposed indicator is gross income,[50] such that

$$K_{BIA} = \alpha\pi, \tag{6.11}$$

where K_{BIA} is the operational risk capital charge under the BIA, α is the fixed percentage, and π is the indicator variable, set to be gross income; defined as net interest income plus net fees and commissions plus net trading income plus gross other income excluding operational risk losses and extraordinary items.

The Basel Committee is still gathering data in order to set the fixed percentage α so as to yield a capital requirement that averages 12 percent of the current minimum regulatory capital. The 12 percent target was set to conform to data obtained in a Quantitative Impact Study (QIS) conducted by BIS (2001c) that related operational risk economic capital from unexpected operational losses to overall economic capital for a sample of 41 banks.[51] The mean (median) ratio of operational risk capital to overall economic capital was 14.9 percent (15.0 percent). However, as a proportion of minimum regulatory capital, the mean (median) ratio of operational risk capital was 15.3 percent (12.8 percent). The figure of 12 percent was chosen because "there is a desire to calibrate regulatory capital to a somewhat less stringent prudential standard than internal economic capital" (BIS, 2001c, p. 26).

Once the overall 12 percent target was set, the QIS collected data on the relationship between the target operational risk capital charges (i.e., 12 percent of the regulatory capital minimums) and gross income in order to set the value of α.[52] These data were collected from 140 banks in 24 countries. The sample consisted of 57 large, internationally active banks and 83 smaller institutions. Table 6.4 shows the September 2001 results of the QIS designed to calibrate the α value. Means are in the 0.22 range, although BIS (2001c) states that it is unlikely that α will be set equal to the simple mean. The proposals conclude that "an α in the range of 17 to 20 percent would produce regulatory capital figures approximately consistent with an overall capital standard of 12 percent of minimum regulatory capital" (BIS, 2001c, p. 28).

The design of the BIA illustrates the "top-down" approach in that the BIS II proposals are calibrated to yield an overall target capital requirement. This is to be contrasted with a "bottom-up" approach that would have related capital charges to actual loss experiences. It is the intent of the Basel Committee on Banking Supervision to benchmark all three operational risk model parameters using actual loss data so as to avoid double counting and to further validate the models' specifications using the "bottom-up" approach.

6.3.2   The Standardized Approach

The BIA is designed to be implemented by even the least sophisticated banks. Moving to the Standardized Approach requires the bank to collect data about gross income by line of business.[53] The model specifies eight lines of business: Corporate finance, Trading and sales, Retail banking, Commercial banking, Payment and settlement, Agency services and custody, Asset management, and Retail brokerage. For each business line, the capital requirement is calculated as a fixed percentage, denoted β, of the gross income in that business line. The total capital charge is then determined by summing the regulatory capital requirements across all eight business lines as follows:

$$K_{SA} = \sum_{i=1}^{8} \beta_{L,i} \pi_i, \qquad (6.12)$$

where K_{SA} is the total operational risk capital requirement under the Standardized Approach, π_i is the gross income for business line $i = 1$, ..., 8, and $\beta_{L,i}$ is the fixed percentage assigned to business line $i = 1$, ..., 8. The value of $\beta_{L,i}$ is to be determined using the industry data presented in table 6.5 (obtained from the QIS) for bank j operating in business line i according to the following formula:

$$\beta_{j,i} = \frac{0.12 * MRC_j^* OpRiskShare_{j,i}}{\pi_{j,i}}, \qquad (6.13)$$

where MRC_j is the minimum regulatory capital for bank j, $OpRiskShare_{j,i}$ is the share of bank j's operational risk economic capital allocated to business line i, and $\pi_{j,i}$ is the volume of gross income in business line i for bank j. Using the estimates of $\beta_{j,i}$ for banks in the industry, the parameter $\beta_{L,i}$ to be used in equation (6.15) is then determined using an industry "average." All banks will use the same measure of $\beta_{L,i}$ in equation (6.15) to calculate their operational risk measure regardless of their individual measures of $\beta_{j,i}$. Table 6.5 shows that the median $\beta_{L,i}$ for i = Retail Brokerage is the lowest (0.113), whereas the median $\beta_{L,i}$ for i = Payment and Settlement (0.208) is the highest across all eight lines of business. However, that ranking differs when comparing the means or the weighted averages across the eight business lines. For both the means and the weighted averages, the Retail Banking $\beta_{L,i}$ is the lowest (a mean of 0.127 and a weighted average $\beta_{L,i}$ of 0.110) and the $\beta_{L,i}$ for Trading and Sales is the highest (a mean of 0.241 and a weighted average of 0.202). The wide dispersion in $\beta_{j,i}$ shown in table 6.5 within each business line raises questions regarding the calibration of the Standardized Approach model. Statistical tests for equality of the means and medians across business lines do not reject the hypothesis that the $\beta_{j,i}$ estimates are the same across all i business lines.[54] Thus, it is not clear whether the $\beta_{L,i}$ estimates are driven by meaningful differences in operational risk across business lines or simply the result of differences in operational efficiency across banks, data definition, measurement error problems, or small sample bias. If there is no significant difference in $\beta_{L,i}$ estimates across different lines, then the Standardized Approach reverts to the Basic Indicator Approach.

6.3.3   The Advanced Measurement Approach

The most risk sensitive of the three regulatory operational risk capital models is the Advanced Measurement Approach (AMA) that permits banks to use their own internal operational risk measurement system to set minimum capital requirements, subject to the qualitative and quantitative standards set by regulators. The AMA is structured to resemble the Internal Models approach for market risk capital charges (see section 6.1.2). To be eligible, the bank must be able to map internal loss data into specified business lines and event types. External industry data may be required for certain event types and to supplement the bank's loss experience database.

There are three BIS II AMA operationally risk model approaches: (i) the internal measurement approach; (ii) the loss distribution approach; and (iii) the scorecard approach. The BIS II AMA proposals intentionally do not specify one particular operational risk measurement model so as to encourage development across all three major areas of operational risk modeling. However, there are several quantitative standards proposed in BIS II. The first is the setting of a floor

Table 6.5 Analysis of QIS data: the standardized approach based on 12 percent of minimum regulatory capital

Lines of business	Median	Mean	Weighted average	Standard deviation	Weighted average standard deviation	Minimum	25th percentile	75th percentile	Maximum	No. of banks
Corporate finance	0.131	0.236	0.120	0.249	0.089	0.035	0.063	0.361	0.905	19
Trading and sales	0.171	0.241	0.202	0.183	0.129	0.023	0.123	0.391	0.775	26
Retail banking	0.125	0.127	0.110	0.127	0.066	0.008	0.087	0.168	0.342	24
Commercial banking	0.132	0.169	0.152	0.116	0.096	0.048	0.094	0.211	0.507	27
Payment and settlement	0.208	0.203	0.185	0.128	0.068	0.003	0.100	0.248	0.447	15
Agency services and custody	0.174	0.232	0.183	0.218	0.154	0.056	0.098	0.217	0.901	14
Retail brokerage	0.113	0.149	0.161	0.073	0.066	0.050	0.097	0.199	0.283	15
Asset management	0.133	0.185	0.152	0.167	0.141	0.033	0.079	0.210	0.659	22

Source: Bank for International Settlements (2001c), p. 29.

level constraining capital requirements under AMA to be no lower than 75 percent of the capital requirement under the Standardized Approach.[55] The BIS II proposals also specify a one-year holding period and a 99.9 percent confidence level to delineate the tail of the operational risk loss distribution. The bank must maintain a comprehensive database identifying and quantifying operational risk loss data by each of the eight business lines specified in the Standardized Approach and by event in accordance with the BIS II proposal's definitions and covering a historical observation period of at least five years.[56] The BIS II proposals specify the following seven operational risk events: internal fraud; external fraud; employment practices and workplace safety; clients, products and business practices; damage of physical assets; business disruption and system failures; execution, and delivery and process management. Table 6.6 offers a definition of each of these operational risk events.

6.3.3.1 The internal measurement approach

The internal measurement approach (IMA) assumes a stable relationship between expected losses and unexpected losses, thereby permitting the bank to extrapolate unexpected losses from a linear (or nonlinear) function of expected losses. Since expected losses (EL) equal the exposure indicator, π, times PE (the probability that an operational risk event occurs over a given time horizon, usually assumed to be one year) times LGE (the average loss given that an event has occurred), then the IMA capital charge can be calculated as follows:

$$K_{IMA} = \sum_i \sum_j \gamma_{ij} \mathrm{EL}_{ij} = \sum_i \sum_j \gamma_{ij} \pi_{ij} \mathrm{PE}_{ij} \mathrm{LGE}_{ij}, \qquad (6.14)$$

where K_{IMA} is the overall operational risk capital charge using the IMA for all eight business lines i and for all credit events j (such as listed in table 6.6); $\pi_{j,i}$ is the bank's exposure indicator, e.g., the volume of gross income in business line i exposed to operational event type j; EL_{ij} is the expected losses for business line i from event j, defined to be equal to $\pi_{j,i} \times \mathrm{PE}_{ij} \times \mathrm{LGE}_{ij}$; and γ_{ij} is the transformation factor relating expected losses to unexpected losses in the tail of the operational loss distribution. The value of γ_{ij} is to be verified by bank supervisors. This value is assumed to be fixed, except for special cases when operational losses are viewed to be significantly above or below industry norms. In these cases, an additional multiplication factor (the RPI) is

Table 6.6 Loss event type classification: the advanced measurement approach

Event type category	Definition	Activity examples
Internal fraud	Losses due to acts of a type intended to defraud, misappropriate property or circumvent regulations, the law or company policy, excluding diversity/discrimination events, which involves at least one internal party.	Unreported transactions (intentional); Unauthorized transactions; Mismarking of positions (intentional); credit fraud; worthless deposits; theft; extortion; embezzlement; misappropriation of assets; forgery; check kiting; smuggling; impersonation; tax evasion (willful); bribes; insider trading
External fraud	Losses due to acts of a type intended to defraud, misappropriate property or circumvent the law, by a third party.	Theft/robbery; forgery; check kiting; theft of information (with monetary loss); hacking damage.
Employment practices and workplace safety	Losses arising from acts inconsistent with employment, health or safety laws or agreements, from payment of personal injury claims, or from diversity/discrimination events.	Compensation, benefit, termination issues; organized labor activity; general liability; employee health and safety rules events; workers compensation; all discrimination types.

Category	Definition	Examples
Clients, products, and business practices	Losses arising from an unintentional or negligent failure to meet a professional obligation to specific clients (including fiduciary and suitability requirements), or from the nature or design of a product.	Fiduciary breaches; disclosure issues; breach of privacy; aggressive sales; account churning; misuse of confidential information; lender liability; antitrust; improper trade and market practices; market manipulation; insider trading (on firm's account); unlicensed activity; money laundering; product defects; model errors; failure to investigate client per guidelines; exceeding client exposure limits; performance disputes for advisory activities.
Damage to physical assets	Losses arising from loss or damage to physical assets from natural disaster or other events.	Natural disaster losses; human losses from external sources (terrorism, vandalism).
Business disruption and system failures	Losses arising from disruption of business or system failures.	Hardware; software; telecommunications; utility outage/disruptions.
Execution, delivery and process management	Losses from failed transaction processing or process management, from relations with trade counterparties and vendors.	Miscommunication; data entry, maintenance or loading error; missed deadline; system problem; accounting error; delivery failure; collateral management failure; reference data maintenance; failed mandatory reporting; inaccurate external report; client disclaimers missing; legal documents missing; unapproved access given to accounts; incorrect client records; negligent loss of client assets; non-client counterparty misperformance; outsourcing vendor disputes.

Source: Bank for International Settlements (2001c), pp. 21–3.

used to multiply the right-hand-side of equation (6.14). If the bank is viewed as having more (less) operational risk than average for the bank's peer group, the RPI is set greater than (less than) one. However, the precise calibration of the RPI has yet to be determined by regulators.

6.3.3.2   The loss distribution approach

The loss distribution approach (LDA) estimates unexpected losses directly using a VaR approach, rather than backing out unexpected losses using expected losses as in the IMA. Thus, the LDA does not suffer from the shortcoming of the IMA that the relationship between expected losses and the tail of the loss distribution (unexpected losses) is assumed to be fixed regardless of the composition of operational losses. The LDA directly estimates the operational loss distribution assuming specific distributional assumptions (e.g., a Poisson distribution for the number of loss events and the lognormal distribution for LGE, the severity of losses given that the event has occurred). Using these assumptions, different operational loss distributions can be obtained for each risk event. The operational risk charge for each event is then obtained by choosing the 99.9 percent VaR from each event's operational loss distribution. If all operational risk events are assumed to be perfectly correlated, the overall operational risk capital requirement using LDA is obtained by summing the VaR for all possible risk events. In contrast, if operational risk events are not perfectly correlated, an overall operational loss distribution can be calculated for all operational risk events. Then the overall operational risk charge using LDA is the 99.9 percent VaR obtained from this overall operational loss distribution. However, as of yet, there is no industry consensus regarding the shape and properties of this loss distribution.

6.3.3.3   The scorecard approach

Both the IMA and the LDA rely heavily on past operational loss experience to determine operational risk capital charges. However, these methodologies omit any consideration of improvements in risk control or adoption of improved operational risk management techniques that may alter future operational loss distributions. The scorecard approach incorporates a forward-looking, predictive component to operational risk capital charges (see discussion in section 5.2.1.1). The bank determines an initial level of operational risk capital for each business line i and then modifies these amounts over time on the basis of scorecards that assess the underlying risk profile and risk control environment for each business line *i*. The scorecards use proxies for operational risk events and severities. The initial operational risk charge may be set using historical loss data, but changes to the capital charges over time may deviate from past experience. However, the scorecards must be periodically validated using historical data on operational losses both within the bank and in the industry as a whole.

Whichever methodology is chosen, the AMA is the only operational risk measurement model that permits banks to utilize correlations and other risk-mitigating factors, such as insurance, in their operational risk estimates, provided that the methodology is transparent to bank regulators. However, there may be limitations on the permissible level of insurance risk mitigation due to concerns about such factors as delays in insurance payment or legal challenges of contractual terms. The BIS II proposals have not fully resolved many of the issues surrounding insurance as a mitigating factor reducing operational risk exposure. BIS II proposals specify that all methodologies must be scalable to reflect possible scale changes from mergers or divestitures. Moreover, scenario analysis should be performed regularly as part of the process of contingency planning for rare, but potentially catastrophic, operational risk events.

In addition to the quantitative requirements, the BIS II proposes qualitative requirements attesting to the bank's capability in designing and supporting a rigorous, conceptually sound model of operational risk based on accurate and objective data. The bank must have an independent operational risk management function that measures risk at the firm level. The board of directors and senior management must be involved in the process. The internal model of operational risk must be closely integrated into the day-to-day risk management processes of the bank and must be reviewed and validated on a regular basis. The model and the data should be transparent so as to be verifiable by bank supervisors.

6.4 SUMMARY

In this chapter, we describe international regulations that set minimum capital requirements for banks. Current capital requirements are risk-based with separate capital charges for market risk, credit risk, and operational risk. Although operational risk minimum capital requirements are still only proposals, credit risk and market risk regulations have been in place since 1992. The regulations follow an evolutionary approach, permitting smaller, less sophisticated banks to use standardized, somewhat crude models that have few data requirements and are easy to estimate. As the bank's risk measurement apparatus becomes more sophisticated, the bank can progress to advanced models that make capital requirements more sensitive to risk exposures. Since this often allows banks to reduce their capital charges, this regulatory structure provides an incentive for banks to invest in improvements in their risk measurement technology.

CHAPTER SEVEN

VaR: OUTSTANDING RESEARCH

Value at Risk modeling is still in its infancy. Many of the models analyzed in this book are still in their first generation of development. Some of the "older" models are in their second stage of development. There remains much work to be done, however, to improve the accuracy and relevance of these models. Our suggestions for future research involve three major areas: (i) data availability; (ii) model integration; and (iii) dynamic modeling.[1]

7.1   DATA AVAILABILITY

VaR outputs are only as good as their data inputs. Data problems plague all areas of risk measurement. Despite the apparent abundance of market data to estimate market risk, there are still problems in estimating correlations and extrapolating into the future using historic market return data.[2] Off-balance sheet activities are particular areas of data insufficiency. For example, many countries do not require their banks to reveal any information about off-balance sheet activities, such as loan commitments, options, forwards, and swaps. Even data on US banks' off-balance sheet activities, which must be disclosed in the call reports for banks (e.g., Schedule L for bank loan commitments), are limited in their usefulness as inputs into a VaR model. For example, call report data on options is divided into options bought and sold, without any distinction as to whether the options are puts or calls. Bank loan commitment data in Schedule L are overly aggregated and do not furnish data on borrower industry, credit rating, borrower concentration, etc.[3]

These problems are exacerbated in the credit risk measurement arena. The databases required in order to generate estimates of default probabilities, loss rates, exposures and correlations are just being developed internally within banking firms. Collaboration across banks is difficult to achieve given concerns about customer confidentiality and revelation of competitive trade secrets. However, operational risk databases cannot even be contemplated without imposing some intra-industry data pooling. That is because catastrophic operational risk events are "one-off" events that typically end the life of the firm. If such low frequency, high severity events are to be included in operational risk VaR models, then data must be pooled across both surviving and failed firms.

Data are generally drawn from accounting and financial statements. However, these data are of limited usefulness as inputs into a VaR model if they reflect GAAP rules that permit book valuation, as opposed to market valuation. In the wake of FASB 115 and 133, there has been an increase in market valuation in the financial statements of financial intermediaries. However, we are far from full mark-to-market accounting. Until financial statements achieve greater transparency, data inputs into VaR models will be biased by accounting regulations that obscure true market values.

7.2 MODEL INTEGRATION

In this book we have covered the VaR treatment of market risk as distinct from credit risk and operational risk. Of course, this is a pedagogical nicety. All sources of risk are integrated and VaR models should (where possible) include correlations among market, credit and operational risk. For example, market fluctuations can create operational losses and credit risk may drive market fluctuations. Indeed, the regulatory approach, which is essentially additive is fundamentally at odds with VaR, which is a subadditive measure (see Szego, 2002). Thus, rather than separate market risk, credit risk, and operational risk elements for bank capital requirements, an integrated approach would measure overall risk incorporating all sources of volatility (see Jaschke (2001) for a critique of VaR as a regulatory tool).

7.3   DYNAMIC MODELING

All the models described in this book are essentially static. They describe the risk profile of the firm or financial institution at a single point in time, assuming that all parameter values are fixed at some historic average. In reality, risk is a dynamic concept. Firms adapt their risk profiles as market and business conditions change. We are only beginning to think about how we can incorporate dynamic effects into VaR models.

One way to recognize dynamic effects is to incorporate macro-economic and cyclical effects into the model. Thus, parameter estimates would be conditional on macroeconomic or systematic factors that differentiate between *ex post* realizations of risk (e.g., bad luck in recessions and good luck in booms) and *ex ante* risk shifting. Allen and Saunders (2002) survey the literature and find great gaps in our knowledge as to how these factors affect risk measures. For example, there is very little consensus in the literature about the fundamental relationship between credit quality and default probability and recovery rates. Indeed since we are only beginning to investigate the correlations between these variables, there is clearly much more work to be done in this area.

Another way to model dynamic factors is to incorporate systemic risk effects driven by correlations across firms. Acharya (2001) has examined the (unintended) systemic effects associated with capital requirements as banks simultaneously respond to regulations. Thus, actions that might mitigate risk on an individual firm level, may exacerbate risk when all banks are simultaneously attempting the same policy. VaR models are focused on individual firms and individual portfolios. We have not yet applied the methodology to incorporate possible feedback effects from cross-firm systemic forces.

NOTES

Chapter 1   Introduction to Value at Risk (VaR)

1   Modern portfolio theory is based on Markowitz's insight that diversification can reduce, but not generally eliminate risk, thereby necessitating a risk–reward guide to portfolio selection. To estimate the efficient investment frontier in a mean-variance world requires data on expected returns, standard deviations of returns and correlations between returns for every possible pair of financial securities. On the occasion of the fiftieth anniversary of the publication of the seminal Markowitz's (1952) paper, Rubinstein (2002) offers an interesting discussion of the development of modern portfolio theory by Markowitz and others.

2   For example, Sharpe's (1963) paper was followed by Mossin (1968).

3   Dissatisfaction with the β measure began as early as Douglas (1969), with mounting doubts leading to Roll's (1977) paper. The practitioner world closely followed the academic debate with articles such as Wallace's (1980) "Is Beta Dead?" Beta's death knell was sounded by Fama and French's (1992) paper that found that after controlling for firm size and the market to book ratio, the firm's β had no statistically significant power to explain returns on the firm's equity.

4   In their introduction Mina and Xiao (2001) stress that RiskMetrics is not strictly a VaR model, although it can be used to estimate a VaR model. RiskMetrics' critical role in the dissemination of VaR among financial market practitioners stems in large part from the availability of real time data on financial market fluctuations provided freely in the public domain. Recognizing that value added, RiskMetrics has currently formed a separate data service, DataMetrics which covers almost 100,000 data series.

5   The market risk amendment to the Basel capital requirements was adopted in November 1996 in Europe and in January 1998 in the US.

6   RAROC (risk-adjusted return on capital) models are risk-sensitive measures of economic performance that can be used to allocate risk capital within the firm. See chapter 13 of Saunders and Allen (2002).

7   The Gramm–Leach–Bliley Act of 1999 permitted the creation of finan-
    cial service holding companies that could include commercial banking,
    investment banking and insurance subsidiaries under a single corporate
    umbrella, thereby effectively repealing the Glass Steagall Act.

8   The initial Basel capital requirements implemented in 1992 were
    amended in 1996 to include a market risk capital charge. See discussion
    in chapter 7.

9   Insurance regulators in the US adopted their own risk–based capital require-
    ments for life and property-casualty insurers in the mid- to late 1990s.

10 In August 1994, the Derivatives Policy Group (DPG) voluntarily adopted
    the scenario approach as the methodology to be used by securities firms
    (not subject to commercial bank capital requirements) to compute core
    risk factors and capital at risk. See chapter 9 in Allen (1997).

11 Since VaR is only concerned with losses, the probabilities shown in table
    1.1 represent one-tailed cutoff points.

12 We discuss the derivation of, and exceptions to, the "square root rule"
    in section 1.1.4.

13 Although RiskMetrics does not explicitly assume value non-negativity,
    the model is based on logarithmic returns, such that $\log(P_1/P_0) \approx P_1/P_0 - 1$
    for price changes from time $t = 0$ to $t = 1$. This approximation is good for
    small price changes only. Thus, RiskMetrics does not perform well for large
    discrete changes (e.g., that might reduce the asset value to zero).

14 Of course, the *ex ante* expectation is not necessarily realized *ex post*.

15 That is, daily volatilities are independent and uncorrelated.

16 Most parameter inputs extrapolate from historical data to estimate future
    values. However, if options prices are available, implied volatility can also
    be used to directly estimate future volatility levels.

17 See section 2.1.3 for a detailed discussion and references of this issue.

18 The disadvantages of using absolute level changes can be illustrated in
    an entirely different context – the circuit breakers at the NYSE that
    were initiated as a result of the crash of October 1987. The idea was that
    once the market moves by "too much," shutting down the market for a
    while is a positive measure in order to prevent market meltdown. The
    length of the shutdown may vary from suspending trading for a few hours
    or for the rest of the trading day, depending on various parameters. When
    first introduced, circuit breakers were stated in absolute terms – for ex-
    ample, if the Dow Jones moves by 300 points or more, then the market
    should close down for two hours. This is presumably just enough time
    for traders to take a lithium pill and go back to trading more reasonably.
    When initiated, this 300 point circuit breaker represented a move of approx-
    imately 10 percent in the Dow (which was, at the time, at a level of just
    over 3,000). In the late 1990s, with the Dow getting closer to a level of
    10,000, circuit breakers were repeatedly tripped because the levels of the
    circuit breakers were not updated and the lower threshold level of

approximately 3 percent of the level of the Dow made them more likely to be activated. The circuit breaker system has since been updated to be consistent with return calculation methods. The levels at which the breakers go into effect are updated quarterly as a function of the beginning-of-quarter level of the Dow so as to avoid the problem of defining cutoffs calculated in absolute change terms.

19   The variance of the two period rate of return is simply $2\sigma^2$ because the intertemporal covariance is zero.

20   In a spread trade or a relative value position we buy a certain asset and short a related (and highly correlated asset) so as to bet on a relative rise in the long asset or a fall in the short asset, or both, without taking any market direction position. We could, for example, bet on a rise in the value of GM relative to Ford without taking market risk by going long GM and short Ford (or vice versa, of course). This trade would be market neutral only under the assumption that both assets have the same market beta, i.e., the same market sensitivity. The foreign currency spread trade example in the text could be easily implemented by shorting GBP/Euro futures in LIFFE.

21   The asset weights necessary for the percentage VaR method are undefined for a zero investment strategy such as the spread trade in our example. However, the dollar VaR method is completely general.

22   Of course, all formulas can be generalized to the N-asset case.

23   Note that the negative correlation could have been accounted for equally well by specifying a correlation of -0.80 between the positions rather than a positive correlation between the risk factors and an opposite exposure due to the short position in the Euro.

24   This is the case with a delta neutral portfolio of derivatives – for example, if we purchase puts and calls in equal amounts and with equal sensitivity to the underlying, then their correlation is precisely minus one. In that case as the price of the underlying security rises, the calls gain precisely what the puts lose. As will be discussed in chapter 3, this is true only locally because movements in the value of the underlying asset create a wedge between the market sensitivities of the two options. Furthermore, the delta neutral hedge portfolio may suffer from slippage if the volatility of the underying asset is not constant.

Chapter 2   Quantifying Volatility in VaR Models

1   To be precise, this is a fixed maturity yield series that is calculated from combining the yields of two T-Bills with a maturity just longer than – and just shorter than – eighty-nine days. Since the US Treasury issues 3-month bills at auction on a weekly basis, this series can be easily derived.

2 A detailed discussion of the technical aspects of tails is beyond the scope of this book. The interested reader can find multiple additional references in the academic arena, such as Fama (1963), Fama (1965), and Blattberg and Gonedes (1974). More recent studies include Koedijk, Huisman, and Pownall (1998).

3 See for instance, Allen and Saunders (1992) and Spindt and Hoffmeister (1988).

4 The interested reader may find more on predictability of asset returns in Fama and French (1988) and Campbell, Lo, and McKinlay (1997). For critique of the predictability result relevant references see Richardson (1993) and Boudoukh and Richardson (1993).

5 This is a popular model in recent econometric literature, invoked in order to better understand seemingly unstable time series. This is also a particularly useful example for our purposes. See James Hamilton (1990, 1995).

6 The interested reader can read more about this econometric model in Hamilton (1990, 1995).

7 In this particular case we use RiskMetrics™ volatility with a smoothing parameter $\lambda = 0.94$. Details on this method will appear in section 2.2.4 of this chapter.

8 Again, in this case, we use a RiskMetrics approach to volatility estimation.

9 See, for example, the STDEV(. . .) function in Excel.

10 The interested reader can learn more from RiskMetrics's Technical Document (1995) and other supplemental notes and technical comments that can be found on www.riskmetrics.com. Engle and Mezrich (1995), Hendricks (1996), Boudoukh, Richardson, and Whitelaw (1997), and Jorion (2001a, 2001b) also include a technical discussion of some of these issues.

11 See Engle (1982) and Bollerslev (1986) for a detailed presentation of the original GARCH models. For a discussion of volatility estimation in the context of risk management, see Boudoukh, Richardson, and Whitelaw (1997).

12 The kernel function $K(.)$ has to obey some mild regularity conditions to insure asymptotic convergence. A common kernel is the normal kernel

$$K(x) = (2/\pi)^{-m/2} exp\{-0.5x'x\}$$

where m is the number of conditioning variables. The reader will recognize this as a multivariate normal density. This is chosen for convenience, and only relates to the efficiency of the density estimate; it is not a distributional assumption per se. For more details see Scott (1992) and Boudoukh, Richardson, and Whitelaw (1997).

13 In practice, many risk managers have almost "unconciously" applied MDE by using data periods that seem to best match current economic conditions, usually in the context of an HS approach.

14 For a detailed discussion of MDE see Scott (1992), and for application in financial risk management see Boudoukh, Richardson, and Whitelaw (1997).

15 Another issue is what price to plug into the option pricing model to derive the implied volatility; i.e., should the bid or offer or midpoint price be used? In many cases, the bid–offer price spread can be quite large and the implied volatilities differ considerably according to which price is used.

16 Given the implied volatilities of, for example, the USD/GBP, GBP/Euro, and Euro/USD, one could obtain the USD/GBP and USD/Euro implied volatility as well as the implied correlation between the two. For details see Campa and Chang (1997).

17 For comparison of various methods for volatility estimation including implied volatility and "horse racing" methods against one another see French, Schwert, and Stambaugh (1987), Christiansen and Prabhala (1998) and Jorion (1995). For opposing views regarding the informativeness of implied volatility see Day and Lewis (1992) and Lamoureux and Lastrapes (1993).

18 For formal models of non-contemporaneous data and nonsynchronous trading and their effect on covariances see Fisher (1966), Cohen, Maier, Schwartz, and Whitcomb (1986), Scholes and Williams (1977), Lo and MacKinlay (1990), and Boudoukh, Richardson, and Whitelaw (1994).

19 Note that we did not define a metric for "poor" versus "good" performance. Quantifying the error is important. Defining normative values with respect to the performance of the estimator is subjective and clearly context-dependent. For example, we may not mind being somewhat off on a specific asset's volatility as long as there is no pervasive bias in our overall estimation that may tilt the results. This issue is related to model risk which is outside the scope of our dicussion here.

Chapter 3   Putting VaR to Work

1 This may be due to omitted risk factors or irrational mispricing. We discuss the former in the last sections of this chapter, but not the latter explanation for deviations from theoretical derivatives prices.

2 The delta defines the change in the value of the derivative for any given change in the underlying factor price.

3 Assuming 256 trading days in a year we divide the annual volatility by the square root of the number of trading days: $20\%/\sqrt{(256)} = 1.25\%$.

4 This example is taken from Boudoukh, Richardson, Stanton, and Whitelaw (1997).

5 The Cholesky decomposition involves finding two matrices A and its transpose A' such that their product is the matrix Σ. Intuitively, the A' matrix

contains historical information about the returns and correlations among assets.

6   On contagion and the rationality–irrationality debate, see Kodres and Pritsker (2002) and Rigobon and Forbes (2002).

7   See King and Wadhwani (1990), Yuan (2000), Kyle and Xiong (2001) and Kodres and Pritsker (2002).

8   However, diversification can involve monitoring costs and problems compared to a more concentrated portfolio. See Acharya, Hasan, and Saunders (2003).

9   Bank regulators limit loan concentrations to individual borrowers to a maximum of 15% of the bank's capital.

10 The interested reader can find more quantitative information on these topics in Jorion (2001a) and Mina and Xiao (2001), the RiskMetrics technical document. On pricing using Monte Carlo Simulation, see also Boyle, Broadie, and Glasserman (1997). On contagion and the rationality–irrationality debate, see Kodres and Pritsker (2002). On correlation breakdown in the context of global equity markets, see Longin and Solnik (2001).

11 This section draws heavily on Boudoukh, Richardson, and Whitelaw (1995).

12 The interested reader may refer to Tuckman (2002) for a detailed discussion of this as well as many other relevant topics in the fixed income area.

13 Duration is a linear (first order) approximation of the exact price–yield relationship.

Chapter 4   Extending the VaR Approach to Non-tradable Loans

1   A type 1 error misclassifies a bad loan as good. A type 2 error misclassifies a good loan as bad.

2   The maximal fully connected two-layer network with 10 input variables and 12 hidden units has a maximum of $1 + 12(10 + 2) = 145$ number of weights. All possible combinations of these weights within the two layers (treating the ordering of the connections as unique) is: $2^{145} = 4.46 \times 10^{43}$.

3   Most ratings are reviewed at least once a year to update their accuracy.

4   In order to adopt the Internal-Ratings Based Approach in the new Basel Capital Accord, banks must adopt a risk rating system that assesses the borrower's credit risk exposure separately from that of the transaction.

5   A short time horizon may be appropriate in a mark-to-market model, in which downgrades of credit quality are considered, whereas a longer time horizon may be necessary for a default mode that considers only the default event. See Hirtle et al. (2001).

6   However, Mester (1997) reports that only 8% of banks with up to $5 billion in assets used scoring for small business loans. In March 1995, in order to make credit scoring of small business loans available to small banks, Fair, Isaac introduced its Small Business Scoring Service, based on 5 years of data on small business loans collected from 17 banks.

7   For example, Bucay and Rosen (1999) compare historical transition matrices (denoting the probabilities of all possible credit events) obtained using bond ratings data to transition matrices estimated using the structural (KMV) approach.

8   See Aziz (2001) for a more technical comparison of the two approaches to asset valuation.

9   Assuming that shareholders are protected by limited liability, there are no costs of default, and that absolute priority rules are strictly observed, then the shareholders' payoff in the default region is zero.

10   Delianedis and Geske (1998) consider a more complex structure of liabilities.

11   Using put–call parity, Merton (1974) values risky debt as a put option on the firm's assets giving the shareholders the right, not the obligation, to sell the firm's assets to the bondholders at the value of the debt outstanding. The default region then corresponds to the region in which the shareholders exercise the put option.

12   See Finger et al. (2002) for the technical document. The CreditGrades website, www.creditgrades.com, provides real-time default probabilities (expressed as credit spreads) for all publicly traded firms.

13   Moreover, CreditGrades uses a shifted lognormal distribution to model asset values. This results in more realistic estimates of PD, particularly for short maturities.

14   Exceptions are the jump-diffusion models of Zhou (2001a) and Collin-Dufresne and Goldstein (2001) who allow leverage ratios to fluctuate over time.

15   This assumes that the default probability is independent of the security's price, something that does not hold for swaps with asymmetric counterparty credit risk, for example. Duffie and Singleton (1999) specify that one should use a "pure" default-free rate r that reflects repo specials and other effects. The US Treasury short rate, typically used as the empirical proxy for r, may be above or below the pure default-free rate.

16   To illustrate the double subscript notation, the yield on a B rated two-year maturity zero coupon bond to be received one year from now would be denoted $_1y_2$. This bond would mature three years from today – one year until it is delivered on the forward contract and then two years until maturity from then. Spot rates are for transactions with immediate delivery; the first subscript of a spot rate is always zero.

17   Although most intensity-based models assume that LGD is fixed, Unal, Madan, and Guntay (2001) find that LGD varies intertemporally and cross-sectionally.

18 Duffie and Singleton (1999) show that PD and LGD cannot be separately identified in defaultable bond prices because risky debt is priced on the credit spread, PD × LGD.

19 Using equation (4.10) to calculate the PD over a five-year time horizon, we obtain a PD of 0.005 for the A rated firm and 0.2212 for the B rated firm.

20 The intensity of the sum of independent Poisson processes is just the sum of the individual processes' intensities; therefore, the portfolio's total intensity is: 1,000*0.001 + 100*0.05 = 6 defaults per year.

21 Indeed, with constant intensity, the two terms are synonymous.

22 In 2000, there was a total of $17.7 trillion in domestic (traded and untraded) debt outstanding; see Basak and Shapiro (2001).

23 As of 1998, about $350 billion of bonds traded each day in the US as compared to $50 billion of stocks that are exchanged (see Bohn, 1999).

24 Of course, for mark-to-market models, the entire matrix of credit transition probabilities must be computed in addition to the default probability for default mode models.

25 However, Bucay and Rosen (1999) estimate the CreditMetrics model using both ratings agency migration matrices and credit migration matrices obtained from KMV EDFs.

26 Kreinin and Sidelnikova (2001) describe algorithms for constructing transition matrices.

27 This example is based on the one used in Gupton, Finger, and Bhatia (1997).

28 If the +/− modifiers ("notches") are utilized, there are 22 different rating categories, see Bahar and Nagpal (2000).

29 Technically, from a valuation perspective the credit-event occurs (by assumption) at the very end of the first year. Currently, CreditMetrics is expanding to allow the credit event "window" to be as short as 3 months or as long as 5 years.

30 The assumption that interest rates are deterministic is particularly unsatisfying for credit derivatives because fluctuations in risk-free rates may cause the counterparty to default as the derivative moves in- or out-of-the-money. Thus, the portfolio VaR, as well as VaR for credit derivatives, (see, for example, CIBC's CreditVaR II) assume a stochastic interest rate process that allows the entire risk free term structure to shift over time. See Crouhy, Galai, and Mark (2000).

31 In this simplified example, we annualize semi-annual rates corresponding to coupon payment dates on US Treasury securities.

32 CreditMetrics assumes that recovery values are stochastic with a beta distribution.

33 In this section, we calculate the VaR assuming the normal distribution; see the discussion in chapter 2 on RiskMetrics. The calculation of VaR using the actual distribution is illustrated by example in Appendix 4.1.

34 If the actual distribution is used rather than assuming that the loan's value is normally distributed, the 1% VaR in this example is $14.8 million (see Appendix 4.1).

35 Note that expected losses of $460,000 are incorporated into the $6.97 million unexpected losses for regulatory capital purposes. As shown in figure 4.3, loan loss reserves to cover expected losses (here $460,000) are added to the economic capital requirement ($6.97 million in this example) to obtain total regulatory capital of $7.43 million ($6.97 million plus $0.46 million).

36 Although it is worth noting, as was discussed in chapter 2, that portfolio distributions tend to become more "normal" as the size and diversity of the portfolio increases. This also tends to be true for loans and loan portfolios.

37 Implicitly, correlations for borrowers reflect correlations among systematic risk factors that impact their returns.

38 CreditMetrics also calculates a Monte Carlo-based VaR for the loan portfolio for non-normal loan distributions.

39 We consider only one industry index for each firm in this example, but clearly there may be more than one industry index that drives equity returns for each company.

40 The general form of equation (4.16) for IM industry indices for company M and IN industry indices for company N is: $\rho(M,N) = \Sigma_{IM} \Sigma_{IN} B_{M,IM} B_{N,IN} \rho(IM,IN)$ where $B_{M,IM} B_{N,IN}$ are the systematic industry sensitivity coefficients for firms M and N obtained from estimating equations (4.14) and (4.15) using equity returns for firms M and N.

41 A probability of 1 (100%) represents the entire area under the standardized normal distribution.

42 At the time of evaluation, each firm's asset value is assumed to be equal to its mean value. Therefore, the VaR measures are calculated as unexpected deviations from the mean portfolio value.

43 This equation is derived in Appendix 6.1 using a bivariate normal copula function.

44 The 99 percent Credit VaR using the actual loan distribution is $9.23 million. See Appendix 4.1.

45 The portfolio model of CreditMetrics can be adjusted to allow for stochastic interest rates. Moreover, a cyclicality index reflecting interest rate fluctuations can be incorporated into the model. See Allen and Saunders (2002).

46 However, unconditional credit migration matrices and non-stochastic yield curves (similar to those used in CreditMetrics) are fundamental inputs into the MtF model. Nevertheless, Algorithmics permits scenario-driven shifts in these static migration probabilities and yield curves.

47 The primary disadvantage of the scenario-based MtF is its computational complexity. The cost of implementing the model is directly related to the number of simulations that must be performed in order to estimate the portfolio's loss distribution. To reduce that cost, MtF separates the scenario analysis stage from the exposure analysis stage. Therefore, MtF loss estimates (denoted MtF Cubes) are calculated for each instrument

independent of the actual counterparty exposures. Individual exposure loss distributions are then computed by combining the MtF Cubes across all scenarios using conditional obligor default/migration probabilities (assuming exposures are not scenario-dependent). Aggregation across the assets in the portfolio is simplified because once conditioned on a particular scenario, obligor credit events are independent.

48   Finger (2000a) proposes an extension of CreditMetrics that would incorporate the correlation between market risk factors and credit exposure size. This is particularly relevant for the measurement of counterparty credit risk on derivatives instruments because the derivative can move in or out of the money as market factors fluctuate. In June 1999, the Counterparty Risk Management Policy Group called for the development of stress tests to estimate "wrong-way credit exposure" such as experienced by US banks during the Asian currency crises; i.e., credit exposure to Asian counterparties increased just as the foreign currency declines caused FX losses on derivatives positions.

49   Fraser (2000) finds that a doubling of the spread between BAA rated bonds over US Treasury securities from 150 basis points to 300 basis points increases the 99 percent VaR measure from 1.77 percent to 3.25 percent for a Eurobond portfolio.

50   Although the default boundary is not observable, it can be computed from the (unconditional) default probability term structure observed for BB rated firms.

51   Default is assumed to be an absorbing state, so figure 4.5 shows that the curve representing the firm's asset value in Scenario 1 coincides with the default boundary for all periods after year 3.

Chapter 5   Extending the VaR Approach to Operational Returns

1   Instefjord, Jackson, and Perraudin (1998) examine four case studies of dealer fraud: Nick Leeson's deceptive trading at Barings Bank, Toshihide Iguchi's unauthorized positions in US Treasury bonds extending more than 10 years at Daiwa Bank New York, Morgan Grenfell's illegal position in Guinness, and the Drexel Burnham junk bond scandal. They find that the incentives to engage in fraudulent behavior must be changed within a firm by instituting better control systems throughout the firm and by penalizing (rewarding) managers for ignoring (identifying) inappropriate behavior on the part of their subordinates. Simply punishing those immediately involved in the fraud may perversely lessen the incentives to control operational risk, not increase them.

2   This result is from research undertaken by Operational Risk Inc. Smithson (2000) cites a PricewaterhouseCoopers study that showed that

financial institutions lost more than US$7 billion in 1998 and that the largest financial institutions expect to lose as much as US$100 million per year because of operational problems. Cooper (1999) estimates US$12 billion in banking losses from operational risk over the last five years prior to his study.

3   Marshall (2001) reports the results of a PricewaterhouseCoopers/British Bankers Association survey in which 70 percent of UK banks considered their operational risks (including risks to reputation) to be as important as their market and credit risk exposures. Moreover, Crouhy, Galai, and Mark (2001) report that 24 percent of the British banks participating in the survey had experienced operational losses exceeding £1 million during the three years before the survey was conducted.

4   The sheer number of possible processes and procedures may appear daunting, but Marshall (2001) notes the Pareto Principle that states that most risks are found in a small number of processes. The challenge, therefore, is to identify those critical processes.

5   Bottom-up models will be described in depth in section 5.2, whereas top-down models are covered in section 5.1.3.

6   Several industry initiatives are under way to construct this data consortium; e.g., the Multinational Operational Risk Exchange (MORE) project of the Global Association of Risk Professionals and the Risk Management Association managed by NetRisk and the British Bankers Association Global Operational Loss Database (GOLD). A proprietary database is OpData (see section 5.2.3).

7   In 1993, Bankers Trust became the first major financial institution to systematically gather data on operational losses, combining both internal and external, industry-wide data sources. Five operational risk exposure classes were defined: relationship risks, people/human capital risks, technology and processing risks, physical risks, and other external risks (see Hoffman, 1998).

8   Bootstrapping enhances the statistical properties of small samples by repeatedly drawing from the sample with replacement. Thus, the bootstrap sample may have more observations than in the original sample database. The jackknife method examines the impact of outliers by re-estimating the model using a sample of size $n - 1$, where n is the original sample size, obtained by consecutively dropping each observation in turn from the sample. For application of these methods to the pricing of cat bonds, see Cruz (1999). For a general treatment, see Efron and Tibshirani (1993).

9   For a description of each of these statistical distributions, see Marshall (2001), chapter 7.

10   This brief survey of operational risk measurement models draws from Marshall (2001).

11   Some of the same statistical techniques (e.g., regression analysis) are used in bottom-up models, but the focus is different. See section 5.2 for a description of bottom-up models.

12 These discrete shifts in equity returns can be incorporated using dummy variables to control for such events and their impact on "normal" residual returns.

13 This can be done using a scaling process to adjust for mergers or changes in assets or staff levels. Alternatively, a time series model can be used to adjust expenses for secular change.

14 This approach is similar to the Algorithmics Mark-to-Future model of credit risk measurement (see chapter 4, section 4.4).

15 Risk indicators can be identified on a hybrid level – both top-down for the entire firm and bottom-up for an individual business unit or operational process. The use of hybrid risk indicators allows comparisons across different busines units and processes, as well as across the entire firm. See Taylor and Hoffman (1999).

16 Acronyms such as KRI, KPI and KCI are often used to represent the key risk indicators, the key performance indicators, and the key control indicators, respectively, chosen by management to track operational risk.

17 Marshall (2001) includes factor models as bottom-up models when the risk indicators are disaggregated and applied to specific activities individually. In this section, we concentrate on the process and actuarial approaches.

18 This section draws heavily on coverage from Marshall (2001).

19 However, Bayesian belief networks link the probabilities of each event's occurrence to each node on the event tree. Indeed, probabilities of certain events can be estimated by analyzing the interdependencies across events in the entire process map.

20 The probabilities are assigned to indicate the extent to which the dependent factor causes the fault in the tree; i.e., there is a 40 percent chance that late settlement will be caused by late confirmation, etc.

21 If the failure rate is constant over time, then the time between events equals the event failure rate, i.e., $\lambda(t) = p(t)$. Many processes have a decreasing failure rate during the early (burn-in) period of their life cycle, followed by a period of constant failure rate, followed by a burnout period characterized by an increasing failure rate.

22 However, credit risk measurement models typically make different distributional assumptions for the loss frequency and for loss severity. For example, CreditMetrics assumes lognormally distributed frequencies, but loss severities (LGD) that are drawn from a beta distribution. Other credit risk measurement models, such as CreditRisk +, distinguish between the distribution of default probabilities and loss rates in a manner similar to operational risk measurement models.

23 The data used are illustrative, i.e., derived from models based on real world data. See Laycock (1998).

24 In practice, of course, there would be many more than two interdependent variables.

25   For large samples of identically distributed observations, Block Maxima Models (Generalized Extreme Value, or GEV distributions) are most appropriate for extreme values estimation. However, the Peaks-Over-Threshold (POT) models make more efficient use of limited data on extreme values. Within the POT class of models is the generalized Pareto distribution (GPD). See McNeil (1999) and Neftci (2000). Bali (2001) uses a more general functional form that encompasses both the GPD and the GEV – the Box-Cox-GEV.

26   If $\xi = 0$, then the distribution is exponential and if $\xi < 0$ it is the Pareto type II distribution.

27   The example depicted in figure 5.8 is taken from chapter 6 of Saunders and Allen (2002).

28   The threshold value u = US\$4.93 million is the 95th percentile VaR for normally distributed losses with a standard deviation equal to US\$2.99 million. That is, using the assumption of normally distributed losses, the 95th percentile VaR is $1.65 \times \$2.99$ = US\$4.93 million.

29   These estimates are obtained from McNeil (1999) who estimates the parameters of the GPD using a database of Danish fire insurance claims. The scale and shape parameters may be calculated using maximum likelihood estimation in fitting the (distribution) function to the observations in the extreme tail of the distribution.

30   Some have argued that the use of EVT may result in unrealistically large capital requirements (see Cruz, Coleman, and Salkin, 1998).

31   In this section, we focus on full service operational risk proprietary models that include a database management function, operational risk estimation and evaluation of operational capital requirements. Other related proprietary models not described in detail are: Sungard's Panorama which integrates credit VaR and market VaR models with a back office control system (www.risk.sungard.com); Decisioneering Inc's Crystal Ball which is a Monte Carlo simulation software package (www.decisioneering.com); Palisade Corp's @Risk which performs both Monte Carlo simulation and decision tree analysis (www.palisade.com); Relex Software which provides reliability modeling geared toward manufacturing firms (www.faulttree.com); Austega's scenario analysis consulting program (www.austega.com), and Symix Systems' event simulation software (www.pritsker.com).

32   Proprietary operational risk models are still quite new, as evidenced by the fact that the two major products were introduced into the market in 2001. Given the undeveloped nature of their methodologies, the quality of data inputs tends to be most critical in determining model accuracy. OpVantage currently offers the largest external database and thus is characterized as the "leading model" in this section.

33   In June 2001, Algorithmics, Arthur Andersen and Halifax created a strategic alliance to acquire Operational Risk Inc's ORCA product and incorporate it into Algo OpData.

34 These organizational units do *not* coincide with the business units specified in BIS II proposals (see discussion in chapter 6). Thus, the Algo OpData database must be reformulated for regulatory purposes.

35 Operational risk event frequency can be modeled using the Poisson, binomial, non-parametric and Bernoulli distributions. Loss severity takes on a normal, lognormal, student t, or non-parametric distribution.

36 These insurance policies are called "excess-of-loss" policies because they cover losses over a certain threshold deductible amount.

37 However, many reinsurers have experienced credit problems (e.g., Swiss Re) resulting from credit risk exposure emanating from the large amounts of CDO/CBOs and credit derivatives bought in past years. In November 2002, the US Congress passed legislation that provides a government backstop to insurer catastrophic losses due to terrorism, thereby limiting their downside risk exposure, such that the federal government is responsible for 90 percent of losses arising from terrorist incidents that exceed $10 billion in the year 2003, up to $15 billion in 2005 (with an annual cap of $100 billion). Federal aid is available only after a certain insurance industry payout is reached; set equal to 7 percent of each company's commercial property and casualty premiums in 2003, rising to 15 percent in 2005.

38 Hoffman (1998) states that very few insurance claims are actually paid within the same quarterly accounting period during which the operational loss was incurred. This lag could create severe liquidity problems that threaten even insured firms.

39 Alternatively, a RAROC approach could be used to assign economic capital to cover the operational risk of each process. See Saunders and Allen (2002), ch. 13.

40 Doerig (2000) reports that there are 5,000 captive insurers worldwide.

41 Comprehensive global data on the size of OTC derivatives markets do not exist, so Rule (2001) estimates the size of the market using OCC data showing that US commercial banks held $352 billion notional credit derivatives outstanding on March 31, 2001 pro-rated for US banks' share using a British Bankers Association survey showing that the global market totalled $514 billion in 1999.

42 However, since all derivatives are subject to counterparty credit risk, their pricing requires evaluation of each counterparty's credit quality. See Nandi (1998) for a discussion of how asymmetric credit quality affects the pricing of interest rate swaps.

43 Cat call spreads were also introduced by the CBOT in 1993. The cat call spread hedges the risk of unexpectedly high losses incurred by property-casualty insurers as a result of natural disasters such as hurricanes and earthquakes. The option is based on the insurer's loss ratio, defined to be losses incurred divided by premium income. If the loss ratio is between 50 to 80 percent, then the cat call spread is in the money and the insurance company receives a positive payoff. The payoff is capped at a maximum

value for all loss ratios over 80 percent. However, if upon expiration the insurer's loss ratio is less than 50 percent, then the option expires worthless and the insurance company bears the loss of the option premium.

44 Harrington and Niehaus (1999) and Cummins, Lolande, and Phillips (2000) find that state specific cat options would be effective hedges for insurance companies, particularly those with Florida exposure.

45 Cao and Wei (2000) propose an algorithm for pricing weather options.

46 However, the growth of the market has been impeded by the lowering of prices in the reinsurance market. Schochlin (2002) predicts that the market for cat bonds will grow considerably as a result of reinsurance rationing and premium increases in the wake of September 11, 2001.

47 Most cats are sold as discount bonds.

48 Cruz (1999) uses extreme value theory to analyze operational losses in the event of a catastrophically bad year that is approximately seven times worse than the worst recorded year in the firm's database.

49 Unambiguously defining the operational loss event is not trivial. For example, several insurers successfully defended themselves against lawsuits in the wake of September 11 brought by businesses in major airports in the US on the grounds that business interruption insurance claims need not be paid, since the airport terminals were technically open, although all air traffic was shut down.

50 Hoyt and McCullough (1999) find no significant relationship between quarterly catastrophe losses and both the S&P500 and fixed-income securities (US Treasury bills and corporate bonds). However, man-made catastrophic risk (such as the September 11 terrorist attacks and the accounting scandals at WorldCom and other firms) may not have zero correlation with the market.

51 Cat bonds are typically structured using a wholly owned risk transfer company or a special purpose vehicle to take the risk and issue the bond linked to the operational events at the issuing firm.

52 These instruments have been named the CatEPut because the firm exercises a put option on its own stock in the event of a catastrophic risk event.

53 This section is adapted from Li (2000).

54 The risk event could be default for default-mode credit risk measurement models or an operational risk event for operational risk measurement models.

55 A starting time period must be specified, usually assumed to be the present, denoted $t = 0$.

Chapter 6   Applying VaR to Regulatory Models

1 The Basel Committee consists of senior supervisory representatives from Belgium, Canada, France, Germany, Italy, Japan, Luxemburg, the

Netherlands, Sweden, Switzerland, the UK, and the US. It usually meets at the Bank for International Settlements in Basel, where its permanent Secretariat is located.

2 More than 100 countries have adopted BIS I.

3 Tier 1 consists of the last, residual claims on the bank's assets, such as common stock and perpetual preferred stock. Tier 2 capital is slightly more senior than Tier 1, e.g., preferred stock and subordinated debt.

4 An indication of BIS I's mispricing of credit risk for commercial loans is obtained from Flood (2001) who examines the actual loan loss experience for US banks and thrifts from 1984 to 1999. He finds that in 1984 (1996) 10 percent (almost 3 percent) of the institutions had loan losses that exceeded the 8 percent Basel capital requirement. Moreover, Falkenheim and Powell (2001) find that the BIS I capital requirements for Argentine banks were set too low to protect against the banks' credit risk exposures. See ISDA (1998) for an early discussion of the need to reform BIS I.

5 However, Jones (2000) and Mingo (2000) argue that regulatory arbitrage may not be all bad because it set the forces of innovation into motion that will ultimately correct the mispricing errors inherent in the regulations.

6 The original timeline has been pushed back two years. The final draft of the proposals is scheduled for the end of 2002, followed by a comment period, with possible implementation in 2006.

7 McKinsey estimates that operational risk represents 20 percent, market risk comprises 20 percent, and credit risk 60 percent of the overall risk of a typical commercial bank or investment bank. See Hammes and Shapiro (2001), p. 106.

8 The market risk amendment had an adjustment for "market liquidity" not banking book liquidity risk, such as bank runs, etc. Consideration of both liquidity risk and interest rate risk for the banking book has been left to pillar 2 (supervisory oversight) of the capital requirements.

9 The BIA levies a single operational risk capital charge for the entire bank, the standardized approach divides the bank into eight lines of business, each with its own operational risk charge, and the AMA uses the bank's own internal models of operational risk measurement to assess a capital requirement. See BIS (2001c) and section 6.3.

10 For banks adopting the AMA, the operational risk capital requirement could be lowered to 9 percent of total regulatory capital, especially if the bank introduces credit risk mitigation techniques.

11 Ayuso, Perez, and Saurina (2002) use data on Spanish banks to show the existence of considerable capital buffers averaging 40 percent over minimum capital requirements.

12 Short maturity instruments are assumed to have larger interest rate shocks than longer maturity instruments, thereby allowing the risk weight to vary across the yield curve. Modified duration is calculated as

the duration of an instrument with a prespecified (by the BIS) coupon maturing at the midpoint of a "maturity band," divided by one plus a prespecified interest rate. The BIS specifies 13 different maturity bands.

13 The capital charge is calculated as: max (aggregate long position, aggregate short position) × 0.08. In this case, max($1.275 billion, $1.5 billion) × 0.08 = $120 million.

14 That is, even if an adverse price event occurs tomorrow, the bank cannot be assumed to be able to sell off the entire position tomorrow (even if prices are low). Rather it is assumed to be locked into that portfolio (and thus suffer price risk) for 10 days. Clearly, such an assumption is too long for some securities, such as US Treasury securities, and may well be too short for other securities, such as emerging market sovereign debt instruments.

15 Hendricks and Hirtle (1997) report a penalty function that is driven by statistical tests on model accuracy. Five underestimates of market risk out of the past 250 days result in a 3.4 multiplicative factor; 6 underestimates yield a factor of 3.5; 7 underestimates result in a factor of 3.65; 8 underestimates yield 3.75; and 9 underestimates set the factor at 3.85.

16 White and Rai (1999) show that many banks may prefer to use the standardized framework so as to avoid the penalties associated with inaccurate forecasting under internal models.

17 Similar fine tuning is applied to interbank and sovereign credits. See Saunders and Allen (2002), ch. 3.

18 The EAD for on-balance-sheet items is the nominal outstanding amount, whereas EAD for off-balance-sheet items is determined using most of the same credit conversion factors from BIS I, with the exception of loan commitments maturing in less than one year that now have a 20% conversion factor rather than the 0% under BIS I.

19 For example, the sovereign risk weight acts as a floor on the risk weight of any bank's interbank loans. That is, a bank that is headquartered in a given country cannot have a lower risk weight than the sovereign government of that country. See Saunders and Allen (2002) for a discussion of standardized risk weights for banks under BIS II proposals.

20 Korea and Mexico (both OECD members) will move under the proposals from a zero risk weight to a positive risk weight corresponding to their credit ratings. Powell (2001) uses the Standardized Approach to estimate that capital requirements for banks lending to Korea (Mexico) will increase by $3.4 billion ($5 billion) resulting in an estimated increase in bond spreads of 74.8 basis points for Korea and 104.5 basis point for Mexico. If the Internal Ratings-Based Approach is used, the impact is even greater.

21 The use of a one-year time horizon assumes that banks can fully recapitalize any credit losses within a year. Carey (2001b) argues that a two- to three-year time horizon is more realistic.

22   Maturity is the Weighted Average Life of the loan, i.e., the percentage of principal repayments in each year times the year(s) in which these payments are received. For example, a two-year loan of $200 million repaying $100 million principal in year 1 and $100 million principal in year 2 has a Weighted Average Life (WAL) = $[1 \times (100/200)] + [2 \times (100/200)] = 1.5$ years.

23   The format of the IRB approaches is to use PD, LGD and M to determine the loan's risk weight and then to multiply that risk weight times the EAD times 8 percent in order to determine the loan's capital requirement.

24   According to Carey (2001b), the January 2001 IRB proposal is calibrated to a 4.75 percent Tier 1 capital ratio with a Tier 2 subordinated debt multiplier of 1.3 and a PD error multiplier of 1.2. This results in a target capital ratio minimum of $4.75 \times 1.3 \times 1.2 = 7.4$ percent. Since the BIS I 8 percent ratio incorporates a safety factor for operational risk, it makes sense that the pure credit risk IRB minimum capital requirement would be calibrated to a number less than 8 percent.

25   The Foundation Approach assumes a constant LGD although Altman and Brady (2001) find that LGD is directly related to PD.

26   We present the BIS II proposals for risk weights for corporate obligations only. For a description of the retail risk weights, see Allen et al. (forthcoming) and Bank for International Settlements (2003).

27   PD is expressed in decimal format in all formulas.

28   Historical insolvency for AA (A) rated bonds corresponds to a 99.97 percent (99.5 percent) target loss percentile. Jackson, Perraudin, and Saporta (2001) use CreditMetrics to show that BIS I provides a 99.9 percent solvency rate (equivalent to a BBB rating) for a high quality bank portfolio and 99 percent (BB rating) for a lower quality bank portfolio.

29   In contrast to the Advanced IRB Approach, the Foundation IRB Approach does not input the loan's actual maturity into the risk weight calculation.

30   Das, Freed, Gang, and Kapadia (2001) and Lopez (2002) find an inverse relationship between PD and average asset correlations, although this specification is not supported by many other studies (e.g., Crouhy, Galai, and Mark, 2001; Zhou, 2001b; Barnhill and Maxwell, 2002). Lopez (2002) also finds that correlations are found to be directly related to firm size, a factor omitted from the BIS II specification of default correlations (see Allen and Saunders, 2002).

31   Carty (1998) finds the mean LGD for senior unsecured (secured) bank loans is 21 percent (13 percent). Carey (1998) finds mean LGD of 36 percent for a portfolio of private placements. Asarnow and Edwards (1995) find a 35 percent LGD for commercial loans. Gupton (2000) finds a 30.5 percent (47.9 percent) LGD for senior secured (unsecured) syndicated bank loans. Gupton, Gates, and Carty (2000) obtain similar estimates for expected LGD, but find substantial variance around the mean.

32   This may incorporate a mark-to-market adjustment. However, the mark-to-market adjustment in BIS II does not incorporate the transition risk (deterioration in credit quality) and spread risk (change in the market price of credit risk) components of a fully mark-to-market model. There is also an alternative specification of b(PD) adjustment based on the default mode assumption.

33   That is, for loans with maturities longer than 3 years, the increase in the capital requirement relative to the BRW decreases as the loan quality deteriorates. This could increase the relative cost of long-term bank credit for low risk borrowers (see Allen, 2002a).

34   If NPV > 0, then the replacement value equals current exposure. However, if NPV < 0, then current exposure is set to zero because a bank cannot be allowed to gain by defaulting, on an out-of-the money contract.

35   Estimates in June 2001 put the market at approximately US$1 trillion in notional value worldwide.

36   The residual risk factor w reflects the possibility of default on the credit derivative itself. ISDA has criticized the proposal to set $w = 0.15$ as both unnecessary and excessive. In November 2001, the Basel Committee on Banking Supervision released potential modifications to the BIS II proposals that could eliminate the w factor from minimum capital requirements; residual risk would instead be subject to regulatory oversight under Pillar II of the BIS II proposals.

37   Hoggarth, Reis, and Saporta (2001) show that cumulative output losses during systemic crises average 15–20 percent of annual GDP.

38   That is, the IRB frameworks are calibrated to an asset correlation of 0.20, which is higher than actual correlations that averaged 9–10 percent for Eurobonds; see Jackson, Perraudin, and Saporta (2001). The November 2001 potential modifications to BIS II proposals incorporate a correlation coefficient that is inversely related to the PD. However, Freixas, Parigi, and Rochet (2000) show that systemic crises may occur even if all banks are solvent.

39   Most reinsurers are either weakly regulated or non-regulated with respect to capital requirements. In 2002, many of the largest reinsurers in the world suffered huge losses.

40   Similarly, Powell (2001) finds insufficient convexity in the Standardized Approach for sovereign debt.

41   For less developed countries, the proportion of companies with external credit ratings is much lower than for developed countries. Powell (2001) reports that only 150 corporates in Argentina are rated, although the central bank's credit bureau lists 25,000 corporate borrowers. Ferri, Liu, and Majnoni (2001) surmise that borrowers in less developed countries are likely to suffer a substantial increase in borrowing costs relative to those in developed countries upon adoption of BIS II.

42 Linnell (2001) and Altman and Saunders (2001b) suggest that, at the very least, the unrated classification risk weight should be 150 percent. There is evidence that the failure ratio on non-rated loans is similar to the failure ratio in the lowest (150%) rated bucket; see Altman and Saunders (2001b).

43 To mitigate this problem, Griep and De Stefano (2001) suggest that more unsolicited ratings be used. German bank associations plan to pool credit data so as to address the problem of unrated small and medium sized businesses. Because of the importance of this market sector to the German economy, Chancellor Schroder has threatened to veto the BIS II proposal. (See *The Economist*, November 10, 2001.) Allen (2002b) surveys the special problems of credit risk measurement for middle market firms.

44 Moody's, in its ratings of about 1,000 banks worldwide, uses a complex interaction of seven fundamental factors: (1) operating environment (competitive, regulatory, institutional support); (2) ownership and governance; (3) franchise value; (4) recurring earning power; (5) risk profile (credit, market, liquidity risks, and asset-liability management, agency, reputation, operational, etc.) and risk management; (6) economic capital analysis; (7) management priorities and strategies. See Cunningham (1999) and Theodore (1999).

45 Moreover, the usefulness of external ratings for regulatory purposes is questionable since the rating incorporates the likelihood that the firm will be bailed out by the government in the event of financial distress. Only Fitch IBCA and Moody's provide standalone creditworthiness ratings, but these cannot be used to calculate the PD; see Jackson, Perraudin, and Saporta (2001).

46 Jewell and Livingston (1999) find that the Fitch ratings are slightly higher on average than ratings from S&P and Moody's. Fitch is the only rating agency that explicitly charges for a rating.

47 Moreover, contagious regional financial crises in confidence may lead to excessive downgradings of sovereign ratings, see Cantor and Packer (1996), Ferri, Liu, and Majnoni (2001), and Kaminsky and Schmukler (2001).

48 Jackson, Perraudin, and Saporta (2001) show that BIS II is calibrated to achieve a confidence level of 99.96 percent (i.e., an insolvency rate of 0.4 percent), whereas banks choose a solvency standard of 99.9 percent in response to market pressures. This conforms to observations that banks tend to hold capital in excess of regulatory requirements.

49 Jackson, Perraudin, and Saporta (2001) find that a decrease in the bank's credit rating from A+ to A would reduce swap liabilities by approximately £2.3 billion.

50 Other proposed indicator variables are fee income, operating costs, total assets adjusted for off-balance sheet exposures, and total funds under

management. However, Shih, Samad-Khan, and Medapa (2000) find that the severity of operational losses is not related to the size of the firm as measured by revenue, assets or the number of employees.

51   In surveying banks, the QIS did not explicitly define economic capital, but relied on the banks' own definitions. Operational risk was defined as in the BIS II proposals and therefore banks were asked to exclude strategic and business risk from their estimates of operational risk capital.

52   If at a later date the 12 percent target ratio is changed to say X, then the α values in table 6.4 can be adjusted by simply multiplying the existing value by $X/12$.

53   Out of the 140 banks participating in the QIS, only about 100 were able to provide data on gross income broken down by business line and only 29 banks were able to provide data on both operational risk economic capital and gross income by business line.

54   The p-value of the test on the means is 0.178 and the test of the hypothesis that the medians are equal has a p-value of 0.062, considered to be statistically insignificant at conventional confidence levels. Statistical testing is complicated by the small number of observations in the data set.

55   BIS II states its intention to revisit this floor level with the aim of lowering or even eliminating it as the accuracy of operational risk measurement models improves over time.

56   Upon adoption of the BIS II proposals, this requirement will be reduced to three years during an initial transition period only.

Chapter 7   VaR: Outstanding Research

1   This list of future research topics is not meant to be exhaustive. Other suggestions for future research include development of conditional VaR and expected shortfall. See the July 2002 special issue of the *Journal of Banking and Finance*, and Berkowitz and O'Brien (2002) for alternatives to the VaR approach.

2   Lopez and Walter (2000) examine the performance of VaR models using a portfolio of currency exposures and find that the covariance matrix forecasts are important determinants of model accuracy. They find that exponentially-weighted moving averages perform best in their tests, but find that distributional assumptions can also add error to the analysis.

3   Unlike in some other countries, such as Italy, banks in the US are not required to disclose the industrial concentrations of their credit portfolios, making it extremely difficult to use the call reports in order to evaluate loan portfolio concentrations and diversification.

REFERENCES

Acharya, V. V. (2001) "A Theory of Systemic Risk and Design of Prudential Bank Regulation." New York University, dissertation thesis, January 2001.

Acharya, V. V., Hasan, I., and Saunders, A. (2003) "The Effects of Focus and Diversification on Bank Risk and Return: Evidence from Individual Bank Loan Portfolios," presented at the AFA, Washington DC, January 2003.

Allen, L. (1997) *Capital Markets and Institutions: A Global View*, New York: John Wiley.

Allen, L. (2002a) "Comments on Credit Ratings and the BIS Reform Agenda." In *Ratings, Rating Agencies, and the Global Financial System*, ed. R. Levich, Amsterdam: Kluwer.

Allen, L. (2002b) "Credit Risk Modeling of Middle Markets," presented at the Wharton Conference on Credit Risk Modeling and Decisioning, May 29–30.

Allen, L., Delong, G., and Saunders, A. (forthcoming) "Issues in the Credit Risk Modeling of Retail Markets," *Journal of Banking and Finance*.

Allen, L. and Saunders, A. (1992) "Bank Window Dressing: Theory and Evidence," *Journal of Banking and Finance*, 10, 585–623.

Allen, L. and Saunders, A. (2002) "Cyclical Effects in Credit Risk Ratings and Default Risk." In *Credit Ratings: Methodologies, Rationale and Default Risk*, ed. Michael Ong. London: Risk Books.

Altman, E. I. (1968) "Financial Ratios, Discriminant Analysis and the Prediction of Corporate Bankruptcy," *Journal of Finance*, September, 589–609.

Altman, E. and Lavallee, M. (1981) "Business Failure Classification in Canada," *Journal of Business Administration*, Summer.

Altman, E. and Narayanan, P. (1997) "An International Survey of Business Failure Classification Models," *Financial Markets, Institutions and Instruments*, 6(2).

Altman, E. I., with Brady, B. (2001) "Explaining Aggregate Recovery Rates on Corporate Bond Defaults," Salomon Center Working Paper, November.

Altman, E. I. and Saunders, A. (2001a) "An Analysis and Critique of the BIS Proposal on Capital Adequacy and Ratings," *Journal of Banking and Finance*, January, 25–46.

Altman, E. I. and Saunders, A. (2001b) "Credit Ratings and the BIS Reform Agenda." Paper presented at the Bank of England Conference on Banks and Systemic Risk, London, May 23–25.

Altman, E., Baidya, T., and Ribeiro-Dias, L. M. (1979) "Assessing Potential Financial Problems of Firms in Brazil," *Journal of International Business Studies*, Fall.

Altman, E., Kim, D. W., and Eom, Y. H. (1995) "Failure Prediction: Evidence from Korea," *Journal of International Financial Management and Accounting*, 6(3), 230–49.

Altman, E., Marco, G., and Varetto, F. (1994) "Corporate Distress Diagnosis: Comparison Using Linear Discriminant Analysis and Neural Networks (the Italian Experience)," *Journal of Banking and Finance*, 18(3), 505–29.

Asarnow, E. and Edwards, D. (1995) "Measuring Loss on Defaulted Bank Loans: A 24-Year Study," *The Journal of Commercial Lending*, March, 11–23.

Ayuso, J., Perez, D., and Saurina, J. (2002) "Are Capital Buffers Procyclical?" Banco de Espana working paper, April.

Aziz, A. (2001) "Fundamental Theorem of Asset Pricing for Credit-Risky Securities," in *Credit Risk: Enterprise Credit Risk Using Mark-to-Future*, Toronto: Algorithmics Publications, September, 119–42.

Baetge, J., Huss, M., and Niehaus, H. (1988) "The Use of Statistical Analysis to Identify the Financial Strength of Corporations in Germany," *Studies in Banking and Finance*, 7, 183–96.

Bahar, R. and Nagpal, K. (2000) "Modeling the Dynamics," *Credit*, March.

Bali, T. (2001) "The Generalized Extreme Value Distribution: Implications for the Value at Risk," February, Baruch College Working Paper.

Bank for International Settlements (1993) "The Supervisory Treatment of Market Risks," Basle, April.

Bank for International Settlements (1995) "Proposal to Issue a Supplement to the Basel Accord to Cover Market Risks," Basle, April.

Bank for International Settlements (1996) *Standardized Model for Market Risk*, Basle, Switzerland: Bank for International Settlements.

Bank for International Settlements (1999a) "Credit Risk Modeling: Current Practices and Applications," Basel Committee on Banking Supervision, Document no. 49, April.

Bank for International Settlements (1999b) "Sound Practices for Loan Accounting and Disclosure," Basel Committee on Banking Supervision, Document no. 55, July.

Bank for International Settlements (2000) "Range of Practice in Banks' Internal Ratings Systems," Basel Committee on Banking Supervision, Document no. 66, January.

Bank for International Settlements (2001a) "The New Basel Capital Accord," January.

Bank for International Settlements (2001b) "Long-term Rating Scales Comparison," April 30.

Bank for International Settlements (2001c) "Working Paper on the Regulatory Treatment of Operational Risk," September.

Bank for International Settlements (2001d) "Results of the Second Quantitative Study," November 5.

Bank for International Settlements (2001e) "Potential Modifications to the Committee's Proposals," November 5.

Bank for International Settlements (2003) "The New Basel Capital Accord," Consultation document, April.

Barnhill, T. M., Jr., and Maxwell, W. F. (2001) "Modeling Correlated Interest Rate, Spread Risk, and Credit Risk for Fixed Income Portfolios," *Journal of Banking and Finance*, 26(2–3) (February 2002).

Basak, S. and Shapiro, A. (2001) "A Model of Credit Risk, Optimal Policies, and Asset Prices," NYU Working Paper, June.

Berkowitz, J. and O'Brien, J. (2002) "How Accurate are Value-at-Risk Models at Commercial Banks?" *Journal of Finance*, LVII(3), 1093–111.

Bhatia, U. (1988) "Predicting Corporate Sickness in India," *Studies in Banking and Finance*, 7, 57–71.

Bilderbeek, J. (1979) "An Empirical Study of the Predictive Ability of Financial Ratios in the Netherlands," *Zeitschrift fur Betriebswirtschaft*, May, no. 5.

Blattberg, R. C. and Gonedes, N. J. (1974) "A Comparison of the Stable and Student Distributions as Statistical Models for Stock Prices," *Journal of Business*, 47, 244–80.

Bohn, J. R. (1999) "Characterizing Credit Spreads," KMV Corporation, mimeo, June.

Bollerslev, T. (1986) "Generalized Autoregressive Conditional Heteroskedasticity," *Journal of Econometrics*, 31, 307–27.

Bongini, P., Laeven, L., and Majnoni, G. (2001) "How Good is the Market at Assessing Bank Fragility: A Horse Race Between Different Indicators," World Bank, Working Paper, January.

Boudoukh, J. and Richardson, M. (1993) "The Statistics of Long-Horizon Regressions Revisited," *Mathematical Finance*, 4/2, 103–19, special issue.

Boudoukh, J., Richardson, M., and Whitelaw, R. (1994) "A Tale of Three Schools: A Reexamination of Autocorrelation Patterns in Stock Returns," *Review of Financial Studies*, 7/3, 539–73.

Boudoukh, J., Richardson, M., and Whitelaw, R. (1995) "Expect the Worst – Rethinking the Value at Risk Concept using Worst Case Scenario Analysis and its Implications for Risk Management," *Risk*, 8(9), 100–1.

Boudoukh, J., Richardson, M., and Whitelaw, R. (1997) "Investigation of a Class of Volatility Estimators," *Journal of Derivatives*, 4(3), 63–71.

Boudoukh, J., Richardson, M., Stanton, R., and Whitelaw, R. (1997) "Pricing Mortgage-Backed Securities in a Multifactor Interest Rate Environment: A Multivariate Density Estimation Approach," *Review of Financial Studies*, 10(2), 405–46.

Boyle, P., Broadie, M., and Glasserman, P. (1997) "Monte Carlo Methods for Security Pricing," *Journal of Economic Dynamics and Control*, 21, 1267–321.

Bravard, J. L. and David, G. (2001) "White Paper: Future-Proofing the Back Office and Processing Utilities in the Financial Services Industry," EDS website www.eds.com, December.

Bucay, N. and Rosen, D. (1999) "Credit Risk of an International Bond Portfolio: A Case Study," *Algo Research Quarterly*, 2(1), 9–29.

Campa, J. and Chang, K. (1997) "The Forecasting Ability of Correlations Implied in Foreign Exchange Options," NBER Working Paper no. 5974.

Campbell, J., Lo, A., and MacKinlay, C. (1997) *The Econometrics of Financial Markets*, Princeton, NJ: Princeton University Press.

Cantor, R. (2001) "Moody's Investors Service Response to the Consultative Paper Issued by the Basel Committee on Bank Supervision: 'A New Capital Adequacy Approach'," *Journal of Banking and Finance*, January, 171–86.

Cantor, R. and Packer, F. (1996) "Determinants and Impacts of Sovereign Credit Ratings," *Economic Policy Review*, Federal Reserve Bank of New York, October, 37–53.

Cao, M. and Wei, J. (2000) "Pricing the Weather," *Risk*, May, 67–70.

Carey, M. (1998) "Credit Risk in Private Debt Portfolios," *Journal of Finance*, August, 1363–87.

Carey, M. (2000) "Dimensions of Credit Risk and their Relationship to Economic Capital Requirements," NBER, Working Paper 7629, March.

Carey, M. (2001a) "Consistency of Internal versus External Credit Ratings and Insurance and Bank Regulatory Capital Requirements," Federal Reserve Board, Working Paper, February.

Carey, M. (2001b) "A Policymaker's Guide to Choosing Absolute Bank Capital Requirements," Federal Reserve Board Working Paper, June 3, presented at the Bank of England Conference on Banks and Systemic Risk, May 23–25.

Carey, M. and Hrycay, M. (2001) "Parameterizing Credit Risk Models with Rating Data," *Journal of Banking and Finance*, 25(1), 197–270.

Carty, L. V. (1998) "Bankrupt Bank Loan Recoveries," Moody's Investors Service, *Rating Methodology*, June.

Cavallo, M. and Majnoni, G. (2001) "Do Banks Provision for Bad Loans in Good Times? Empirical Evidence and Policy Implications," World Bank, Working Paper 2691, June.

Ceske, R. and Hernandez, J. (1999) "Where Theory Meets Practice," Operational Risk Special Report, *Risk*, November, 17–20.

Christensen, B. J. and Prabhala, N. R. (1998) "The Relation Between Implied and Realized Volatility," *Journal of Financial Economics*, 50, 125–50.

Cohen, K., Maier, S., Schwartz, R., and Whitcomb, D. (1986) *The Microstructure of Securities Markets*, Englewood Cliffs, NJ: Prentice-Hall.

Collin-Dufresne, P. and Goldstein, R. S. (2001) "Do Credit Spreads Reflect Stationary Leverage Ratios?" *Journal of Finance*, October, LVI(5), 1929–57.

Cooper, L. (1999) "Reputation is All," Operational Risk Special Report, *Risk* November, 1.

Crouhy, M., Galai, D., and Mark, R. (2000) "A Comparative Analysis of Current Credit Risk Models," *Journal of Banking and Finance*, January, 57–117.

Crouhy, M., Galai, D., and Mark, R. (2001a) "Prototype Risk Rating System," *Journal of Banking and Finance*, January, 47–95.

Crouhy, M., Galai, D., and Mark, R. (2001b) *Risk Management*, New York: McGraw-Hill.

Cruz, M. (1999) "Taking Risk to Market," Operational Risk Special Report, *Risk*, November, 21–4.

Cruz, M., Coleman, R., and Salkin, G. (1998) "Modeling and Measuring Operational Risk," *The Journal of Risk*, 1(1), Fall, 63–72.

Cummins, J. D., Lolande, D., and Phillips, R. (2000) "The Basis Risk of Catastrophic-Loss Index Securities," Working Paper University of Pennsylvania.

Cummins, J. D., Doherty, N., and Lo, A. (2002) "Can Insurers Pay for the 'Big one?' Measuring the Capacity of the Insurance Market to Respond to Catastrophic Losses," *Journal of Banking and Finance*, 26, 557–83.

Cunningham, A. (1999) "Bank Credit Risk in Emerging Markets," Moody's Investors Service, *Rating Methodology*, July.

Das, S. and Tufano, P. (1996) "Pricing Credit-Sensitive Debt when Interest Rates, Credit Ratings, and Credit Spreads are Stochastic," *Journal of Financial Engineering*, June, 161–98.

Das, S. R., Freed, L., Geng, G., and Kapadia, N. (2001) "Correlated Default Risk," September 14, Working Paper, Santa Clara University.

Day, T. and Lewis, C. (1992) "Stock Market Volatility and the Information Content of Stock Index Options," *Journal of Econometrics*, 52, 267–87.

Delianedis, G. and Geske, R. (1998) "Credit Risk and Risk-Neutral Default Probabilities: Information about Rating Migrations and Defaults," paper presented at the Bank of England Conference on Credit Risk Modeling and Regulatory Implications, London, September 21–2.

Dembo, R. S., Aziz, A. R., Rosen, D., and Zerbs, M. (2000) "Mark-to-Future: a Framework for Measuring Risk and Reward," May, Algorithmics Publications.

Diamond, D. (1984) "Financial Intermediation and Delegated Monitoring," *Review of Economic Studies*, 51, 393–414.

Doerig, H. U. (2000) "Operational Risk in Financial Services: an Old Challenge in a New Environment," Working Paper Institut International D'Etudes Bancaires, London, October.

Douglas, G. W. (1969) "Risk in Equity Markets: an Empirical Appraisal of Market Efficiency," *Yale Economic Essays*, IX (Spring).

Duffie, D. and Singleton, K. J. (1998) "Simulating Correlated Defaults," paper presented at the Bank of England Conference on Credit Risk Modeling and Regulatory Implications, London, September 21–2.

Duffie, D. and Singleton, K. J. (1999) "Modeling Term Structures of Defaultable Bonds," *Review of Financial Studies*, 12, 687–720.

Earl, M. J. and Marais, D. (1982) "Predicting Corporate Failure in the UK Using Discriminant Analysis," *Accounting and Business Research*.

Efron, B. and Tibshirani, R. (1993) *An Introduction to Bootstrap*. New York: Chapman and Hall.

Engle, R. (1982) "Autoregressive Conditional Heteroskedasticity with Estimates of the Variance of UK Inflation," *Econometrica*, 50, 654–708.

Engle, R. and Mezrich, J. (1995) "Grappling with GARCH," *Risk*, September, 112–17.

Falkenheim, M. and Powell, A. (2001) "The Use of Credit Bureau Information in the Estimation of Appropriate Capital and Provisioning Requirements." Central Bank of Argentina, Working Paper.

Fama, E. F. (1963) "Mandelbrot and the Stable Perentian Hypothesis," in *The Random Character of Stock Market Prices*, ed. P. Costner, Cambridge, MA: MIT Press.

Fama, E. F. (1965) "The Behavior of Stock Market Prices," *Journal of Business*, 38, 34–105.

Fama, E. F. and French, K. R. (1988) "Dividend Yields and Expected Stock Returns," *Journal of Financial Economics*, 22, 23–49.

Fama, E. F. and French, K. R. (1992) "The Cross Section of Expected Stock Returns," *Journal of Finance*, 47(June), 427–65.

Fernandez, A. I. (1988) "A Spanish Model for Credit Risk Classification," *Studies in Banking and Finance*, 7, 115–25.

Ferri, G., Liu, L. G., and Majnoni, G. (2001) "The Role of Rating Agency Assessments in Less Developed Countries: Impact of the Proposed Basel Guidelines," *Journal of Banking and Finance*, January, 115–48.

Finger, C. C. (2000a) "Toward a Better Estimation of Wrong-Way Credit Exposure," *RiskMetrics Journal*, Spring, 25–40.

Finger, C. C. (2000b) "A Comparison of Stochastic Default Rate Models," *RiskMetrics Journal*, November, 49–75.

Finger, C. C., Finkelstein, V., Pan, G., Lardy, J. P., Ta, T., and Tierney, J. (2002) "Credit Grades Technical Document," May.

Fisher, L. (1966) "Some New Stock Market Indexes," *Journal of Business*, 39, 191–225.

Flood, M. (2001) "Basel Buckets and Loan Losses: Absolute and Relative Loan Underperformance at Banks and Thrifts." Office of Thrift Supervision, Working Paper, March 9.

Fraser, R. (2000) "Stress Testing Credit Risk Using CreditManager 2.5," *RiskMetrics Journal*, 1, 13–23.

Freixas, X., Parigi, B., and Rochet, J. C. (2000) "Systemic Risk, Interbank Relations, and Liquidity Provision by the Central Bank," *Journal of Money, Credit and Banking*, 32(3), Part II, August.

French, K. R., Schwert, G. W., and Stambaugh, R. F. (1987) "Expected Stock Returns and Volatility," *Journal of Financial Economics*, 19, 3–29.

Gloubos, G. and Grammatikos, T. (1988) "The Success of Bankruptcy Prediction Models in Greece," *Studies in Banking and Finance*, 7, 37–46.

Gordy, M. B. (2000) "A Comparative Anatomy of Credit Risk Models," *Journal of Banking and Finance*, January, 119–49.

Gordy, M. B. (2001) "A Risk-Factor Model Foundation for Ratings-Based Bank Capital Rules," Board of Governors of the Federal Reserve System, Working Paper, February 5.

Griep, C. and De Stefano, M. "Standard & Poor's Official Response to the Basel Committee's Proposal," *Journal of Banking and Finance*, January, 149–70.

Gully, B., Perraudin, W., and Saporta, V. (2001) "Risk and Economic Capital for Combined Banking and Insurance Activities," paper presented at the Bank of England Conference on Banks and Systemic Risk, London, May 23–5.

Gupton, G. M. (2000) "Bank Loan Loss Given Default," Moody's Investors Service, *Special Comment*, November.

Gupton, G. M. Finger, C. C., and Bhatia, M. (1997) "CreditMetrics," RiskMetrics Technical Document, April.

Gupton, G. M., Gates, D., and Carty, L. V. (2000) "Bank-Loan Loss Given Default," Moody's Investors Service, *Global Credit Research* November.

Hamilton, J. (1990) "Analysis of Time Series Subject to Changes in Regime," *Journal of Econometrics*, 45, 39–70.

Hamilton, J. (1995) "Uncovering Financial Market Expectations of Inflation," *Journal of Political Economy*, 93, 1224–41.

Hammes, W. and Shapiro, M. (2001) "The Implications of the New Capital Adequacy Rules for Portfolio Management of Credit Assets," *Journal of Banking and Finance*, January, 97–114.

Hancock, D. and Kwast, M. L. (2001) "Using Subordinated Debt to Monitor Bank Holding Companies: Is it Feasible?" *Journal of Financial Services Research*, 201(2/3)(October/December), 147–87.

Harrington, S. E. and Niehaus, G. (1999) "Basis Risk with PCS Catastrophe Insurance Derivative Contracts," *Journal of Risk and Insurance*, 66, 49–82.

Harris, R. S. and Marston, F. C. (1999) "The Market Risk Premium: Expectational Estimates Using Analysts' Forecasts," Darden Graduate School of Business University of Virginia Working Paper no. 99-08, October.

Hendricks, D. (1996) "Evaluation of Value-at-Risk Models using Historical Data," *Economic Policy Review*, Federal Reserve Bank of New York, 2, 36–69.

Hendricks, D. and Hirtle, B. (1997) "Bank Capital Requirements for Market Risk: the Internal Models Approach," *Economic Policy Review*, Federal Reserve Bank of New York, December, 1–12.

Hill, D. (1975) "A Simple Approach to Inference about the Tail of a Distribution," *Annals of Statistics*, 13, 331–41.

Hirtle, B. J., Levonian, M., Saidenberg, M., Walter, S., and Wright, D. (2001) "Using Credit Risk Models for Regulatory Capital: Issues and Options," *Economic Policy Review*, Federal Reserve Bank of New York, March, 19–36.

Hoffman, D. G. (1998) "New Trends in Operational Risk Measurement and Management," in *Operational Risk and Financial Institutions*, Arthur Andersen Risk Books, 29–42.

Hoggarth, G., Reis, R., and Saporta, V. (2001) "Costs of Banking System Instability: Some Empirical Evidence," paper presented at the Bank of England Conference on Banks and Systemic Risk, London, May 23–5.

Hoyt, R. E. and McCullough, K. A. (1999) "Catastrophe Insurance Options: Are they Zero-Beta Assets?" *Journal of Insurance Issues*, 22(2), 147–63.

Hull, J. and White, A. (1998) "Value at Risk when Daily Changes in Market Variables are Not Normally Distributed," *Journal of Derivatives*, 5, 9–19.

Instefjord, N., Jackson P., and Perraudin, W. (1998) "Securities Fraud and Irregularities," in *Operational Risk and Financial Institutions*, Arthur Andersen Risk Books, 147–58.

Institute of International Finance/International Swap Dealers Association (2000) "Modeling Credit Risk: Joint IIF/ISDA Testing Program" (February).

International Swaps and Derivatives Association (ISDA) (1998) *Credit Risk and Regulatory Capital*. New York/London, March.

Iscoe, I., Kreinin, A., and Rosen, D. (1999) "An Integrated Market and Credit Risk Portfolio Model," *Algo Research Quarterly*, 2(3), September, 21–37.

Izan, H. Y. (1984) "Corporate Distress in Australia," *Journal of Banking and Finance*, 8(2), 303–20.

Jackson, P., Perraudin, W., and Saporta, V. (2001) "Setting Minimum Capital for Internationally Active Banks," paper presented at the Bank of England Conference on Banks and Systemic Risk, London, May 23–5.

Jagannathan, R., McGrattan, E. R., and Scherbina, A. (2000) "The Declining US Equity Premium," *Quarterly Review*, Fall.

Jarrow, R. A. (2001) "Default Parameter Estimation using Market Prices," *Financial Analysts Journal*, September/October, 75–92.

Jarrow, R. A. and Turnbull, S. M. (1995) "Pricing Derivatives on Financial Securities Subject to Credit Risk," *Journal of Finance*, 50, March, 53–85.

Jarrow, R., Lando, D., and Turnbull, S. (1997) "A Markov Model for the Term Structure of Credit Spreads," *Review of Financial Studies*, Summer, 481–523.

Jaschke, S. R. (2001) "Quantile-VaR is the Wrong Measure to Quantify Market Risk for Regulatory Purposes," Working Paper, July.

Jewell, J. and Livingston, M. (1999) "A Comparison of Bond Ratings from Moody's, S&P, and Fitch," *Financial Markets, Institutions, and Instruments*, 8(4).

Jones, D. (2000) "Emerging Problems with the Basel Capital Accord: Regulatory Capital Arbitrage and Related Issues," *Journal of Banking and Finance*, 24, 35–58.

Jorion, P. (1995) "Predicting Volatility in the Foreign Exchange Market," *Journal of Finance*, 50, 507–28.

Jorion, P. (2001a) *Financial Risk Manager Handbook: 2001–2002*. New York: John Wiley and Sons.

Jorion, P. (2001b) *Value at Risk: The New Benchmark for Managing Financial Risk,* 2nd edn, New York: McGraw-Hill.

Kallberg, J. G. and Udell, G. F. (2001) "The Value of Private Sector Credit Information Sharing: the US Case," NYU Working Paper, December 17.

Kaminsky, G. and Schmukler, S. (2001) "Emerging Markets Instability: Do Sovereign Ratings Affect Country Risk and Stock Returns?" World Bank, Working Paper, February 28.

Kealhofer, S. (2000) "The Quantification of Credit Risk," KMV Corporation, January (unpublished).

Kim, K. S. and Scott, J. R. (1991) "Prediction of Corporate Failure: an Artificial Neural Network Approach," Southwest Missouri State University, Working Paper, September.

King, M. and Wadhwani, S. (1990) "Transmission of Volatility between Stock Markets," *Review of Financial Studies,* 3, 5–33.

Kingsley, S., Rolland, A., Tinney, A., and Holmes, P. (1998) "Operational Risk and Financial Institutions: Getting Started," in *Operational Risk and Financial Institutions,* Arthur Andersen Risk Books, 3–28.

Ko, C. J. (1982) "A Delineation of Corporate Appraisal Models and Classification of Bankruptcy Firms in Japan," New York University, thesis.

Kodres, L. and Pritsker, M. (2002) "A Rational Expectation Model of Financial Contagion," *Journal of Finance,* 57, 769–99.

Kocherlakota, N. R. (1996) "The Equity Premium: It's Still a Puzzle," *Journal of Economic Literature,* 34, 42–71.

Koedijk, K., Huisman, R., and Pownall, R. (1998) "VaR-x: Fat Tails in Financial Risk Management," *Journal of Risk,* 1, 47–62.

Kreinin, A. and Sidelnikova, M. (2001) "Regularization Algorithms for Transition Matrices," *Algo Research Quarterly,* 4 (1/2), 25–40.

Kyle, A. and Xiong, W. (2001) "Contagion as a Wealth Effect," *Journal of Finance,* 56, 1401–40.

Lamoureux, G. and Lastrapes, W. (1993) "Forecasting Stock Return Variance: Toward Understanding Stochastic Implied Volatility," *Review of Financial Studies,* 6, 293–326.

Laycock, M. (1998) "Analysis of Mishandling Losses and Processing Errors," in *Operational Risk and Financial Institutions,* Arthur Andersen Risk Books, 131–45.

Leonhardt, D. (2001) "More Falling Behind on Mortgage Payments," *New York Times,* June 12, A1, C5.

Leyden, L. (2002) "Time is on your Side," *The Banker,* Supplement June, 4–5.

Li, D. X. (2000) "On Default Correlation: a Copula Function Approach," The RiskMetrics Group Working Paper no. 99-07, February.

Linnell, I. (2001) "A Critical Review of the New Capital Adequacy Framework Paper Issued by the Basel Committee on Banking Supervision and its Implications for the Rating Agency Industry," *Journal of Banking and Finance,* January, 187–96.

Lo, A. and MacKinlay, C. (1990) "An Econometric Analysis of Non-synchronous Trading," *Journal of Econometrics*, 45, 181–211.

Longin, F. and Solnik, B. (2000) "Extreme Correlation of International Equity Markets," *Journal of Finance*, April LVI2, 649–76.

Longstaff, F. A. and Schwartz, E. F. (1995) "A Simple Approach to Valuing Risky Fixed and Floating Rate Debt," *Journal of Finance*, July, 789–819.

Lopez, J. A. (2002) "The Empirical Relationship Between Average Asset Correlation, Firm Probability of Default and Asset Size," Federal Reserve Bank of San Francisco working paper, April 23.

Lopez, J. A. and Walter, C. A. (2000) "Evaluating Covariance Matrix Forecasts in a Value-at-Risk Framework," Federal Reserve Bank of San Francisco working paper, September.

Madan, D. B. and Unal, H. (1998) "Pricing the Risks of Default," *Review of Derivative Research*, 2, 121–60.

Mandelbrot, B. (1963) "The Variations of Certain Speculative Prices," *Journal of Business*, 36, 394–419.

Marais, D. A. J. (1979) "A Method of Quantifying Companies' Relative Financial Strength," *Working Paper No. 4*. London, Bank of England.

Markowitz, H. (1952) "Portfolio Selection," *Journal of Finance*, 7, 77–91.

Marshall, C. (2001) *Measuring and Managing Operational Risk in Financial Institutions*. Singapore: John Wiley.

McNeil, A. J. (1999) "Extreme Value Theory for Risk Managers," working paper, Department of Mathematics, Swiss Federal Technical University, Zurich, May 17.

McQuown, J. A. and Kealhofer, S. (1997) "A Comment on the Formation of Bank Stock Prices," KMV Corporation, April.

Merton, R. C. (1974) "On the Pricing of Corporate Debt: The Risk Structure of Interest Rates," *Journal of Finance*, June, 449–70.

Mester, L. (1997) "What's the Point of Credit Scoring?" Federal Reserve Bank of Philadelphia Business Review, September/October, 3–16.

Mina, J. and Xiao, J. Y. (2001) *Return to RiskMetrics: The Evolution of a Standard*. New York: RiskMetrics.

Mingo, J. J. (2000) "Policy Implications of the Federal Reserve Study of Credit Risk Models at Major US Banking Institutions," *Journal of Banking and Finance*, January, 15–33.

Monfort, B. and Mulder, C. (2000) "Using Credit Ratings for Capital Requirements on Lending to Emerging Market Economies – Possible Impact of a New Basel Accord," *International Monetary Fund*, Working Paper WP/00/69.

Mossin, J. (1968) "Optimal Multiperiod Portfolio Policies," *Journal of Business*, 41, 215–29.

Nandi, S. (1998) "Valuation Models for Default-Risky Securities: an Overview," Federal Reserve Bank of Atlanta, *Economic Review*, 4th quarter, 22–35.

Neftci, S. N. (2000) "Value at Risk Calculations, Extreme Events, and Tail Estimation," *Journal of Derivatives*, 7(3), 23–38.

Niehaus, G. (2002) "The Allocation of Catastrophe Risk," *Journal of Banking and Finance*, 26, 585–96.

Niehaus, G. and Mann, S. V. (1992) "The Trading of Underwriting Risk: A Comparison of Reinsurance and Insurance Futures Contracts," *Journal of Risk and Insurance*, 59, 601–27.

Ong, M. K. (1998) "On the Quantification of Operational Risk: A Short Polemic," in *Operational Risk and Financial Institutions*, Arthur Andersen Risk Books, 181–4.

Pascale, R. (1988) "A Multivariate Model to Predict Firm Financial Problems: the Case of Uruguay," *Studies in Banking and Finance*, 7, 171–82.

Poddig, T. (1994) "Bankruptcy Prediction: A Comparison with Discriminant Analysis," in *Neural Networks in Capital Markets*, ed. A.P. Refenes. New York: John Wiley, 311–23.

Powell, A. (2001) "A Capital Accord for Emerging Economies?" World Bank working paper, July 11.

Rachlin, C. (1998) "Operational Risk in Retail Banking," in *Operational Risk and Financial Institutions*, Arthur Andersen Risk Books, 113–27.

Reinhart, C. (2001) "Sovereign Credit Ratings Before and After Financial Crises," Department of Economics, University of Maryland, February 21, presented at the Conference on Rating Agencies in the Global Financial System, Stern School of Business New York University, June 1.

Reisen, H. (2000) "Revisions to the Basel Accord and Sovereign Ratings," in R. Hausmann and U. Hiemenz (eds.), *Global Finance from a Latin American Viewpoint*, IDB/OECD Development Centre.

Reisen, H. and von Maltzan, J. (1999) "Boom and Bust and Sovereign Ratings," *International Finance*, 2.2, 273–93.

Richardson, M. (1993) "Temporary Components of Stock Prices: a Skeptic's View," *Journal of Business and Economics Statistics*, April, 199–207.

Rigobon, R. and Forbes, K. (2002) "No Contagion, Only Interdependence: Measuring Stock Market Co-movements," *Journal of Finance*, 57(5), 2223–61.

Roll, R. (1977) "A Critique of the Capital Asset Theory Tests – Part I: On Past and Potential Testability of the Theory," *Journal of Financial Economics*, Vol. 4.

Rubinstein, M. (2002) "Markowitz's 'Portfolio Selection': A Fifty-Year Retrospective," *Journal of Finance*, LVII(3), 1041–5.

Rule, D. (2001) "The Credit Derivatives Market: Its Development and Possible Implications for Financial Stability," *Financial Stability Review*, June 117–40.

Saunders, A. and Allen, L. (2002) *Credit Risk Measurement: New Approaches to Value at Risk and Other Paradigms*, 2nd edn. New York: John Wiley.

Saunders, A. and Cornett, M. M. (2003) *Financial Institutions Management: A Risk Management Approach*, 4th edn. Boston, MA: McGraw-Hill.

Saunders, A., Srinivasan, A., and Walter, I. (2002) "Price Formation in the OTC Corporate Bond Markets: A Field Study of the Inter-Dealer Market," *Journal of Economics and Business*, 54(1) (January/February), 95–114.

Schochlin, A. (2002) "Where's the Cat Going? Some Observations on Catastrophe Bonds," *Journal of Applied Corporate Finance*, 14(4), 100–7.

Scholes, M. and Williams, J. (1977) "Estimating Betas from Nonsynchronous Data," *Journal of Financial Economics*, 5, 309–27.

Scott, D. (1992) *Multivariate Density Estimation: Theory, Practice and Visualization*. New York: John Wiley.

Schwartz, T. (1998) "Estimating the Term Structures of Corporate Debt," *The Review of Derivatives Research*, 2(2/3), 193–230.

Senior, A. (1999) "A Modern Approach to Operational Risk," *Risk Professional*, 1/3, 24–27.

Sharpe, W. F. (1963) "A Simplified Model for Portfolio Analysis," *Management Science*, 9, 277–93.

Shih, J., Samad-Khan, A. and Medapa, P. (2000) "Is the Size of an Operational Loss Related to Firm Size?" *Operational Risk*, January.

Smithson, C. (2000) "Measuring Op Risk," *Risk*, March, 58–61.

Spindt, P. A. and Hoffmeister, J. R. (1988) "The Micromechanics of the FF Market: Implications for the Day-of-the-Week Effects in Funds Rate Variability," *Journal of Financial and Quantitative Analysis*, 23, 401–16.

Suominen, S. I. (1988) "The Prediction of Bankruptcy in Finland," *Studies in Banking and Finance*, 7, 27–36.

Szego, G. (2002) "Measures of Risk," *Journal of Banking and Finance*, 26(7), 7, 1253–72.

Ta, H. P. and Seah, L. H. (1981) "Business Failure Prediction in Singapore," *Studies in Banking and Finance*, 7, 105–13.

Takahashi, K., Kurokawa Y., and Watase, K. (1984) "Corporate Bankruptcy Prediction in Japan," *Journal of Banking and Finance*, 8(2), 229–47.

Taylor, D. and Hoffman, D. (1999) "How to Avoid Signal Failure," Operational Risk Special Report, *Risk*, November, 13–15.

Theodore, S. S. (1999) "Rating Methodology: Bank Credit Risk (An Analytical Framework for Banks in Developed Markets)," Moody's Investors Service, *Rating Methodology*, April.

Treacy, W. F. and Carey, M. (2000) "Credit Risk Rating Systems at Large US Banks," *Journal of Banking and Finance*, January, 167–201.

Tuckman, B. (2002) *Fixed Income Securities*, 2nd edn. New York: John Wiley.

Unal, T. (1988) "An Early Warning Model for Predicting Firm Failure in Turkey," *Studies in Banking and Finance*, 7, 141–70.

Unal, H., Madan, D. and Guntay, L. (2001) "A Simple Approach to Estimate Recovery Rates with APR Violation from Debt Spreads," Wharton Financial Institutions Center, Working Paper no. 7, February.

van Frederikslust, R. A. (1978) *Predictability of Corporate Failure*. Leiden: Martinus Nijhoff Social Science Division.

von Stein, J. H. and Ziegler, W. (1984) "The Prognosis and Surveillance of Risks from Commercial Credit Borrowers," *Journal of Banking and Finance*, 8(2), 249–68.

Warga, A. (1999) Fixed Income Securities Database. University of Houston, College of Business Administration (www.uh.edu/~awarga/lb.html).

Wall, L. D. and Koch, T. W. (2000) "Bank Loan-Loss Accounting: A Review of the Theoretical and Empirical Evidence," *Federal Reserve Bank of Atlanta Economic Review*, 2nd quarter, 1–19.

Wall, L., and Shrikhande, M. M. (1998) "Credit Derivatives," paper presented at the FMA Conference, Chicago, October.

Wallace, A. (1980) "Is Beta Dead?" *Institutional Investor*, 14, 22–30.

Weibel, P. F. (1973) *The Value of Criteria to Judge Credit Worthiness in the Lending of Banks*. Stuttgart.

Wharton Financial Institutions Center and the Payment Cards Center of the Federal Reserve Bank of Philadelphia (2002) *Proceedings of Conference on Credit Risk Modeling and Decisioning*, May 29–30.

White, L. (2001) "The Credit Rating Industry: An Industrial Organization Analysis," presented at the Conference on Rating Agencies in the Global Financial System, Stern School of Business, New York University, June 1.

White, L. (2002) "The Credit Rating Industry: An Industrial Organization Analysis," in ed. R. Levich, *Ratings, Rating Agencies, and the Global Financial System*. Amsterdam: Kluwer.

White, N. W. and Rai, A. (1999) "Market Risk for Foreign Currency Options: Basel's Simplified Model," *Financial Management*, 28(1), 99–109.

Yang, Z. R., Platt, M. B. and Platt, H. D. (1999) "Probabilistic Neural Networks in Bankruptcy Prediction," *Journal of Business Research*, February, 67–74.

Young, B. (1999) "Raising the Standard," Operational Risk Special Report, *Risk*, November, 10–12.

Yuan, K. (2000) "Asymmetric Price Movements and Borrowing Constraints: a REE Model of Crisis, Contagion, and Confusion," Working Paper, MIT.

Zhou, C. (2001a) "The Term Structure of Credit Spreads with Jump Risk," *Journal of Banking and Finance*, 25, 2015–40.

Zhou, C. (2001b) "An Analysis of Default Correlations and Multiple Defaults," *The Review of Financial Studies*, Summer, 555–76.

INDEX